ROMAN SPAIN

Conquest and Assimilation

Leonard A. Curchin

BCA

LONDON · NEW YORK · SYDNEY · TORONTO

This edition published 1991 by
BCA
by arrangement with Routledge

First published 1991
by Routledge
11 New Fetter Lane, London EC4P 4EE

Typeset in 10/12pt. Garamond by
Falcon Typographic Art Ltd., Edinburgh & London
Printed in Great Britain by
TJ Press (Padstow) Ltd., Padstow Cornwall

CN 3615

ROMAN SPAIN

CONTENTS

LIST OF ILLUSTRATIONS

FIGURES

MAPS

ACKNOWLEDGEMENTS

The author and publishers would like to thank the following for permission to reproduce the illustrations in *Roman Spain*: Fig. 0.1, courtesy of Servicio de Publicaciones del CSIC, Madrid; Figs 1.2, 8.1, Royal Ontario Museum, Toronto; Figs 1.3, 3.2, 5.2(a), 5.2(b), 7.3, Museo Arqueológico Nacional, Madrid; Fig. 3.1, Musée du Louvre. Clichés des Musées Nationaux, Paris, © PHOTO R.M.N.; Fig. 5.3, Römisch-Germanisches Museum, Köln. Rheinisches Bildarchiv 33517; Fig. 7.1, Courtesy of B.T. Batsford Ltd; Fig. 7.4, Foto Barrera. Museo Nacional de Arte Romano, Mérida (Badajoz); Fig. 7.5, Museo Arqueológico de Córdoba; courtesy of Junta de Andalucía; Fig. 8.3, Deutsches Archäologisches Institut, Madrid. Photo R. Friedrich; Fig. 9.1, Museo de Navarra, Pamplona.

ABBREVIATIONS OF MODERN WORKS

AE   *L'Année Epigraphique*, Paris, 1888– .

ANRW *Aufstieg und Niedergang der römischen Welt*, Berlin, 1972– .

CIL   *Corpus Inscriptionum Latinarum*, Berlin, 1863– .

HAE   A. Beltrán (ed.), *Hispania Antiqua Epigraphica*, Madrid, 1950– .

ILER   J. Vives (ed.), *Inscripciones latinas de la España romana*, Barcelona, 1971–2.

ILS   H. Dessau (ed.), *Inscriptiones Latinae Selectae*, Berlin, 1882–1916.

JRS   *Journal of Roman Studies*, London, 1911– .

PIR²   *Prosopographia Imperii Romani*, 2nd edn, Berlin, 1933– .

RIT   G. Alföldy (ed.), *Die römischen Inschriften von Tarraco*, Berlin, 1975.

PREFACE

The title of this book requires a word of explanation. By 'Roman Spain' is meant, not the territory of modern Spain in Roman times, but the land which the Romans called Spain (*Hispania*), encompassing present-day Spain and Portugal. I beg the indulgence of my Portuguese colleagues and assure them that, when including in 'Spain' sites and monuments actually located in Portugal, I am referring to *Hispania*, not *España*.

There are two ways to write an historical survey of a given region: a strictly chronological sequence, fitting social, economic and cultural details into their respective periods; and a typological approach, treating society, economy, religion and so on diachronically in separate chapters. For Roman Spain neither approach is wholly practicable, because of the nature of our sources. The literary evidence provides fairly full coverage (apart from occasional lacunas owing to accidents of transmission) of the political and military history of the Republican period, but very little on the Empire. On the other hand, the evidence (mostly epigraphic and archaeological) for economic, cultural and social history dates chiefly to the Early Empire. Fortunately, the completion of the Roman conquest of Spain coincides chronologically with the dividing line between these two major historical periods. Hence there is some historical justification, and not merely the desperation of being 'at the mercy of our sources', for dividing this study into two distinct phases, the conquest of Spain under the Republic, and its assimilation under the Empire.

Parts of the manuscript were kindly read by Drs Jonathan Edmondson, Robert Knapp, Patrick Le Roux, Ramsay MacMullen and Lucinda Neuru, all of whom I thank for their warm encouragement and for taking time from their overloaded schedules to

1

review my drafts. Dr Jennifer Price provided valuable assistance on problems of glass production. None of these scholars is responsible for any errors of fact or opinion which have eluded detection. Finally I must thank my editor, Richard Stoneman, who first proposed this project to me and so patiently awaited its realisation.

INTRODUCTION

Although Spain was an integral part of the Roman Empire, a traveller arriving from Rome or a distant province would be astounded by its many peculiarities. The length of the voyage itself – at least a week from Rome to Cádiz, and almost a month from Alexandria – would emphasise in the traveller's mind the remoteness of Spain, whose coastlines and estuaries are oriented more toward the Atlantic than the Mediterranean. Beyond Gibraltar the placid, azure bays of the Mediterranean gradually yield to the grey-green swells of the outer ocean. Ships rigged with Spanish esparto ropes and laden with Spanish amphoras plied both seas, delivering olive oil and fish sauce to distant ports in provinces like Britain and Judaea.

Inland, the Roman visitor would discover a land of light and contour, marked by an impressive variety of landscapes and colours: the parched, rolling plateaus of torrid Castile, the lush, green valleys of rainy Cantabria, the majestic splendour of the snow-capped Pyrenees, the monotonous, treeless steppes of Extremadura, whose hardy peasants would one day colonise the New World. Oak and pine forests, the haunts of boar, deer, wolves and bears, blanketed much of the Iberian Peninsula in Roman times, but in the regions made arable by cultivators our visitor would see olives, grapes and cereals flourishing in the rich, red soil. He would travel on a network of paved roads such as the Herculean Way which hugged the Mediterranean coast, or the Silver Road leading from Emerita Augusta, westernmost provincial capital of the Roman Empire, to the mining country of Asturias. Along the way he would pass mules and ox-carts, inns and villages, and be guided by helpful road signs such as, 'Traveller, bear right for the public highway'.[1] He would pass farmers tending their crops on terraced hillsides, their primitive huts contrasting sharply with the palatial villas of the wealthy, and

3

shepherds leading their flocks to pasture. He would meet Iberian men with wavy hair sometimes ending in curled tresses, and Celtiberians with shaggy hair and bristling beards, their teeth and skin assiduously cleansed with urine. In some places he would see ladies wearing veils, held before their faces by curved rods attached to a metal neckband; in others, women who depilated the front of their scalp to make it shiny.[2] The men would wear tunics hanging almost to the knee and girt at the waist, and in the winter, breeches and capes. Women wore long, brightly coloured robes, and liked to display their filigree earrings and golden brooches. The people might be speaking Latin, Greek, Iberian, Punic or a Celtic dialect.

In the cities, our visitor would see monuments and amenities common to all Roman towns, yet some peculiarities as well. He could walk in the shade of a portico along streets paved with irregular yet tightly fitted stones, rutted by the wheels of heavy wagons, or stroll through public gardens, watered from wells and perhaps containing rare trees.[3] In the forum, amidst the bustle of the crowd and the cries of noisy hawkers, he could encounter a bewildering variety of specialised craftsmen and merchants, such as sundial makers, lamp-wick manufacturers, pearl sellers and pepper dealers.[4] Shopkeepers would make change in a bewildering combination of Roman and Spanish coins. Statues and public buildings erected by local magistrates adorned the public squares and roadways.

In the course of his travels he would see many spectacular monuments: the famous temple of Hercules at Cádiz, the bridge at Alcántara (highest in the Roman world), the tall aqueduct at Mérida, known to a later age as 'the Miracles' because of the superhuman technology that constructed it. For recreation he could visit the hot baths, often located on the site of mineral springs and open to men and women at different hours, or watch various breeds of Spanish horses compete in the chariot races in a local circus. In some towns he could see a boxing match, or the famous dancing girls from Cádiz, in others a combat between men and beasts in the arena, ancestor of the modern bullfight. At the frequent religious festivals he could sample the notorious 'hundred-plant potion' while listening to women playing flutes, cymbals and the cithaera (forerunner of the Spanish guitar). In Bastetania he could even see the women scandalously holding the men's hands while dancing![5]

When visiting homes, our traveller would warm himself at the

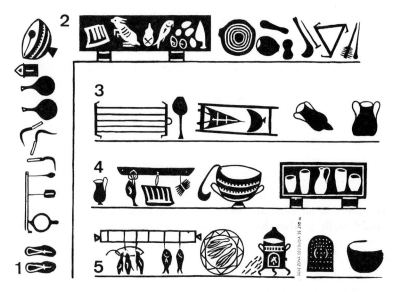

Figure 0.1 Food and kitchen utensils, on a mosaic from Marbella (Málaga); 1st or 2nd century AD. Source: Blázquez (1981). (Courtesy of Servicio de Publicaciones del CSIC).

omnipresent hearth, or walk in luscious gardens watered by flowing fountains. On the brightly painted walls and the mosaic floor panels he might see scenes from the circus or even from Greek mythology, for the mosaicists were often easterners. He could watch the children playing with board games, toy ox-carts or articulated dolls.[6] The kitchen would be well stocked with a variety of meats, poultry, fish and vegetables (Figure 0.1), all cooked in the fruity Baetican olive oil and served in bowls of reddish *terra sigillata,* made in Spain and decorated with boars and rabbits. The delicious, home-cooked cuisine might be washed down with red wine from Catalonia, served in glass cups from southern Spain. In less urbanised areas, the traveller might be invited into a house made of mud brick, or of field stones set between regular blocks, in the African manner. These consisted of only three rooms – a vestibule, a combination living and sleeping area and a pantry – but there was often a wine cellar as well.[7]

How did this beautiful yet rugged land come to be part of the Roman Empire, and how did its proud and diverse inhabitants fit into the unfamiliar mould of Roman life? These are important and obvious questions, yet fraught with difficulty. Many problems and lacunas plague our understanding of the history of the conquest and of the process of cultural assimilation. This book is an attempt to examine, if not to solve, some of these problems and to bring some of the fruits of recent scholarship to the attention of a wider audience.

Part I

CONQUEST

In recent years, students of Roman provincial history have increasingly been moving away from traditional political-military accounts to examine social issues and the acculturation of indigenous peoples under Roman domination. This is a productive trend, to which the present writer subscribes, and indeed a large part of this book is dedicated to the makeup of provincial society and its integration into the Roman world. But the image of rapid and willing romanisation, propagated by writers under the Early Empire and frequently echoed in the modern literature, belies an embarrassing truth. Assimilation of the recalcitrant peoples of Spain became possible only after a bitter struggle of unprecedented length, in which the Romans suffered many defeats and on several occasions achieved success only through treachery. There could hardly be a greater contrast between Gaul, which Caesar conquered in ten years, and Spain, which defied Rome's best generals, including Caesar, for two centuries. Any attempt to write a social history of Spain in the Republican period is ultimately frustrated by the complete absence of Iberian literary sources, the almost total lack of epigraphic evidence, and the Roman writers' concentration on military affairs. Yet even if we had complete sources, the fact would remain that for most of the period from 218 to 16 BC Spain was a war zone, and despite incipient assimilation behind the frontier, the struggle against Rome was a concern that dictated the lives, and often deaths, of many Spaniards. The prolonged military struggle is an inseparable component of the history of Roman Spain, and to this extent the ancient historians were justified in their theme. Yet, consistent with the annalistic historiography of their day, they were more interested in recording what happened than in examining why. While the failure of specific campaigns can be attributed to the

incompetence of individual generals, the overall length of the conquest can be explained by two factors beyond Roman control: the
unyielding nature of the Spanish terrain, which throughout history
has given tremendous advantages to the defender while hindering
the communications and supply lines of the attacker; and the warlike background and tribal ethos of the indigenous peoples, who
combined haughty spirit with guerrilla tactics to keep the invader at
bay for so long. Any account of the conquest of Spain must begin
by considering the land and its pre-Roman inhabitants.

CHRONOLOGY OF THE CONQUEST

8th–4th c. BC	Tartesos flourishing
226 BC	Ebro treaty
218–202 BC	Second Punic War
206 BC	Carthaginians expelled from Spain
197 BC	Spanish provinces created
195 BC	Cato governor of Citerior
179 BC	Gracchus governor of Citerior
155–139 BC	Lusitanian War
153–133 BC	Celtiberian War
138–136(?) BC	Brutus' campaigns in north-west
80–73 BC	Sertorian revolt
49–45 BC	Civil War
26–16 BC	Cantabrian War

1

THE PENINSULA AND ITS INHABITANTS

THE IMPACT OF GEOGRAPHY

Few lands of the ancient world present sharper physical contrasts than the Iberian peninsula. Extremes of elevation, of climate, of vegetation have exercised a profound influence on social and economic development through the ages. The sheer size of the peninsula (581,000 km², or double the area of Italy), the diversity of its topography and the intractibility of its inhabitants have always posed an obstacle to political and cultural unity. Its roughly quadrilateral shape (fancifully likened to an oxhide by ancient Greek geographers) would have been more conducive to internal communications than the tenuous Italian peninsula, were it not for the rugged terrain of the interior and the winter snows which annually block the mountain passes.

'Africa begins at the Pyrenees,' declares an old proverb, whose validity is hardly confined to Spain's notorious summer temperatures. Iberia is not only a peninsula but a virtual subcontinent. The Pyrenees, Spain's only land link to the rest of Europe, serve more as a barrier than a corridor, except at their coastal extremities. On the other hand, the Straits of Gibraltar – known to the Romans as the *fretum Gaditanum* because of their proximity to Cádiz – form a natural bridge with Africa. Attached by land until probably the end of Pliocene times (roughly two million years ago), the straits were easily traversed by Paleolithic man, Carthaginians and Arabs. The narrow crossing – about 14 km at the shortest point, grossly underestimated by Pliny at 5–7 Roman miles – was aptly nicknamed the 'step-across' (*transgressio*).[1] Here stood the Pillars of Hercules –

Calpe (Gibraltar) on the Spanish side, Abila (Ceuta) on the African – one of the most famous landmarks of the ancient world, and revered in superstition as the point beyond which man must not sail.[2] Because of their shallowness, the straits all but sever the warm Mediterranean from the cold Atlantic, forming the practically tideless 'lake' which the Romans called 'our sea'.

The variety of the Spanish landscape is the product of an underlying geographical diversity. The dominant structural feature is the Meseta, an extensive inland plateau covering between one-third and one-half of the peninsula, with an average height of some 600 m. It is bounded on three sides by mountains: the Cantabrian Cordillera to the north, the Iberian range to the north-east and east, the Sierra Morena to the south, the last two being separated by the grassy steppe of Albacete. On the western flank, however, the low mountains of eastern Portugal, pierced by the Douro and Tejo river valleys, pose a slighter obstacle, while to the south-west the declining Meseta gradually blends into the dry and uninviting plateaus of Extremadura. Further south, beyond the Guadalquivir depression, the Baetic Cordillera stretches from Gibraltar to Cape de la Nao on the east coast, and ultimately, submerged, to the Balearic Islands. Though Alpine in structure and containing the peninsula's highest peak (Mulhacén in the Sierra Nevada, at 3,480m), the Baetic Cordillera is punctuated by gaps which render it a less effective barrier than the Pyrenees.

In pointed contrast to the lofty tableland of central Spain is the narrow coastal plain which surrounds it. Whereas the mountains enclosing the Meseta have always been an impediment to penetration, the low Mediterranean coast has throughout history acted as a cultural sponge, successively absorbing and assimilating Iberians, Phoenicians, Greeks, Romans, Goths and Arabs. The eastern shore of Spain in particular offers a flat, easily travelled corridor as far south as Valencia and (after skirting the Baetic massif projecting at Cape de la Nao) Cartagena. The Atlantic seaboard beyond the Gulf of Cadiz was less frequented and relatively unimportant until the fifteenth century. From Ossonoba (Faro) the Roman road turned abruptly inland, meeting the littoral only at the ports of Olisipo (Lisbon, in the estuary of the Tejo) and Cale (Oporto, at the mouth of the Douro) and at Brigantium (La Coruña), site of a renowned lighthouse which survives in modified form.

Today, while the Atlantic coastline of the peninsula offers several good natural harbours, the same can scarcely be claimed for the

Mediterranean side. In antiquity, however, the east coast of Spain was considerably more hospitable to shipping. The Massiliot colony of Emporion (Empúries) on the Gulf of Roses enjoyed a sheltered harbour, which has since become clogged with sand. The Iberian town and Roman colony of Ilici was situated on the Vinalopo river, emptying into the now dessicated *Ilicitanus sinus*; its maritime *entrepôt* was the recently excavated site of Santa Pola, near the entrance to this gulf. The Punic port of Carthago Nova (Cartagena), still an important naval and commercial harbour, was even more capacious in Roman times. The Phoenician settlement at Malaca (Málaga) had a harbour reinforced by sea walls, of which only slight traces have survived the ravages of nature.[3] But not all ancient ports could boast these advantages. Tarraco (Tarragona), capital of Hispania Citerior, was little more than an open beach (Figure 1.1), though important as the terminus of the Republican land route from Italy; Strabo notes that it sits on a bay but has no harbour. Although ships could be beached here, it is perhaps significant that in 210 BC Scipio preferred to disembark at Emporion and continue to Tarraco on foot.[4] The colonies of Valentia (Valencia), Dertosa (Tortosa) and Barcino (Barcelona) were more important for their location at river mouths than for the quality of their harbour facilities; Barcelona had a notoriously poor harbour even in its medieval heyday. On the other hand, Dianium (Denia) and Lucentum (Alicante) had excellent harbours which were still important in Muslim times.

Of the five principal rivers crossing the peninsula, four (the Guadalquivir, Guadiana, Tajo/Tejo and Duero/Douro) flow towards the Atlantic, away from the Roman world. Only the Ebro, the largest in volume of the peninsula's rivers, empties directly into the Mediterranean. All five, while subject to serious flooding on occasion, fulfil a crucial role in transporting the agrarian and mineral products of the interior to the sea. Two of the three Roman provincial capitals were situated on these major rivers: Corduba (Córdoba) on the Guadalquivir, Augusta Emerita (Mérida) on the Guadiana. Other important fluvial ports included Hispalis (Seville) on the Guadalquivir and Caesaraugusta (Zaragoza) on the Ebro. Although the major waterways mostly flowed westward, there were several smaller rivers draining into the Mediterranean, with harbours at their mouths, as well as the important river Ebro which emptied into the Mediterranean at Tortosa, which now lies several kilometers inland as a result of subsequent silting.

The climate of the peninsula is as varied as the topography, and

Figure 1.1 The beach and bay of Tarraco, capital of Hispania Citerior.

determines in large measure its agricultural potential. While modern weather statistics can provide only an approximation of ancient climate, there is little reason to doubt that conditions in Roman times were analogous to today's. Despite modest glacial fluctuations (such as the 'little Ice Age' of the period 1550–1850, which in Spain witnessed several severe floods and the unprecedented freezing of the lower Guadalquivir), the Mediterranean is still in the sub-Atlantic climatic phase which began around 700 BC.[5] Southern Spain (Andalusia) and the east coast enjoy a Mediterranean climate, temperate for the most part, though in the south, summer temperatures sometimes reach 45°C. Average annual rainfall is 500–600 mm in Andalusia, 500–800 in Catalonia; but the south-east coast from Almería to Alicante, facing the Sahara, receives less than 300 mm and has the only subdesert climate in Europe. The central Meseta has a continental climate, bitterly cold in winter (−20° at Teruel), uncomfortably sultry in summer (40°), with 300–600 mm rainfall. The north coast and the northern half of the west coast (beginning around Coimbra) have an Atlantic or oceanic climate marked by relatively cool temperatures but heavy rainfall (in excess of 1,000 mm). This pluviose or humid zone stands in abrupt contrast to the semi-arid conditions prevalent in most of the peninsula.

The soils of the peninsula, while derived from the underlying bedrock, owe their formation largely to the action of wind and water. In the northern Meseta, ancient and modern rivers have carved deep ravines through the limestone crust, exposing the cultivable marls and clays below. Frequent flooding of the numerous tributaries north of the Duero has created the fertile, if dry, alluvial plains of the Tierra del Pan and Tierra de Campos. The southern Meseta is more varied, comprising three distinct zones. On the west is the Extremadura, a plateau system of rugged metamorphic rock laced with quartzite, extending into eastern Portugal. The centre-east region, known as New Castile, is reminiscent of the northern Meseta, with marls capped by eroded limestone. The alluvial valleys of the Tajo and its tributaries slice through both these terrains. The south-eastern zone of the Meseta constitutes the flat, arid plain of La Mancha. The coastal strip of Portugal is composed largely of sandstone, in many places topped by rich alluvium. Andalusia features the rich, black alluvial deposits of the Guadalquivir basin, as well as heavier clays (*tirs*) which in summertime can bake into a hard, impermeable crust. Typical of the east coast, and of the sub-Baetic hills stretching from Cádiz to Alicante, is the famed *terra rossa.* This calcareous red clay (whose colour is due to iron oxides) is highly supportive of grain and fruit farming, but vulnerable to erosion. The east coast is also cut by several alluvial river valleys, of which the most extensive by far is the triangular basin of the Ebro. In contrast to these dry soil types are the brown, siallitic soils of the rainy Cantabrian littoral and the acidic soils of the north-west (Galicia). In the damp Galician lowlands are found peat soils, while on the better-drained plateaus, frequent rainfall has created podsol, leached of lime and other minerals.[6]

In antiquity, much of the peninsula was covered with coniferous and deciduous forest, notably pine and oak. The denudation of these woods in Roman and later times has produced serious erosion, though substantial stands of natural timber still persist in Galicia and on isolated mountain slopes. The evergreen holm-oak, once ubiquitous in Iberia, is particularly well suited to the dry Mediterranean climate. In the highlands are found Pyrenean oak, beech and pine; the last of these also abounds in the sandy soils around Segovia. Deciduous trees like chestnut and oak flourish on the coastal plains, while the famous cork oak is plentiful in south-western Spain and Portugal. The Meseta, now given over largely to scrub, was formerly capable of supporting extensive woodlands. In arid south-eastern Spain, the hinterland of Cartagena, esparto grows in abundance; this hardy grass was woven into stout ropes by the Romans. The Extremadura steppelands provided pasturage suitable for ranching. The two Castiles with their heavy, dry earth served as the granary of Spain, while the rich soils of Andalusia and the east coast were well adapted to olives and grapes. The ancients also noted the existence of wildflowers such as the rose, asparagus plant and *leukoia* (the gillyflower or snowdrop), which continue to be praised in modern Spanish literature. The combination of arable soil and underlying mineral resources made Spain (in Pliny's informed opinion) the richest region of the Roman Empire.[7]

PRE-ROMAN SETTLEMENT

Recent paleontological discoveries at Orce (Granada) and Victoria Cave near Cartagena suggest that human habitation in the Iberian peninsula began at least 1.4 million years ago. The colourful Paleolithic cave paintings of Altamira, rivalling those of Lascaux, the thousands of megalithic dolmens and tholoi, and the elusive Bell Beaker culture of the Chalcolithic age, have assured the peninsula of an important place in European prehistory. Of more immediate interest for our purpose, however, is the question of the origin of the two principal population groups in pre-Roman Spain, the Celts and the Iberians. Since the Celts dwelling beyond the Pillars of Hercules are already mentioned by Herodotus in the fifth century BC, it is reasonably assumed that they had begun to infiltrate the peninsula some time earlier. Apart from frequent references to Celts and Celtiberians in ancient authors, it is clear from toponyms and personal names that Celtic dialects were well established in central and western Spain, and Celtic influence is also apparent in the art of the region.

The identification of the early Celts with the Hallstatt culture of central Europe has long been recognised. The discovery of extensive cemeteries of biconical cinerary urns of Hallstatt B and C types in Catalonia during the Final Bronze age (850–650 BC) has prompted speculation about 'Urnfield invaders' or a 'first Celtic wave'. Significant as these urns (and the cremation rites which they represent) may be, there is no evidence for destruction of indigenous settlements or subjugation of the Bronze age Catalonians, nor is there any sign of the iron technology normally associated with Hallstatt C. Instead of invaders we might better think in terms of a peaceful transfer of information: the concept of incineration, and the design for a suitable container, may gradually have spread from France into north-eastern Spain, perhaps in conjunction with new religious ideas. In the Ebro valley and the northern Meseta we find further urnfields and excised pottery dating to Hallstatt C and D (c. 700–500). This material, in itself, is hardly more convincing as evidence of invasion than the similar finds in Catalonia, unless the greater size of the dispersion area is a factor. But it has also been observed that the brooches of the northern Meseta include Hallstatt-inspired types, whereas those of Catalonia derive from indigenous tradition; and the northern Meseta also has *castros* (hill-forts) which are a common feature of Celtic villages in times of conflict (though it would exceed the evidence to speculate on the threat of uprisings against the new Celtic overlords). The dearth of urnfields and excised ware in the southern Meseta is somewhat discomforting to the theory of Celtic cultural diffusion throughout the interior, but the cemetery at Alpiarça (near Santarém) in west-central Portugal lends material reinforcement to the Greek literary sources and to toponymic evidence (Conimbriga to the north of Alpiarça, Mirobriga to the south, both bearing the Celtic suffix

-*briga* 'hill-fort') of Celtic settlement in the far west.[8] The real problem, however, is the absence of iron technology which invaders from the Hallstatt C–D culture should have possessed. It has been suggested that they did not bring sufficient competent ironsmiths with them, and had to settle for native bronze metalwares.[9] Neither this theory, nor the possibility that suitable iron ore could not be found (though it does exist in the northern Meseta) is entirely satisfying.

The fifth century at last witnesses the widespread use of iron – in weapons, for instance, though brooches and some other items are still made from bronze – thus initiating what is commonly called the Second Iron age. Although this period does not represent a new wave of peoples, it is marked by an increasing tendency towards fortified hill settlements, suggestive of hostility among rival Celtic tribes. Apart from the hill-forts themselves – consisting of one or more concentric circuit walls of tightly packed field stone, often with one or more ditches – most of our evidence comes from the cremation burials. In the initial phase of this period we find hand-made pottery with combed and stamped decoration, but beginning in the fourth century the technique of wheel-turned pottery is introduced, apparently acquired from the Celts' neighbours on the Mediterranean coast. On the basis of different types of swords and pottery, archaeologists have hypothesised a 'Duero culture' in the north and 'Tagus culture' in the south. However, these two groups were far from isolated: both acquire the technology of wheel-made pottery in the fourth century, and weapons from both 'cultures' overlap in the cemeteries of La Osera and Las Cogotas in Avila province.[10] Another feature which links both cultures in the western Meseta (primarily in Avila and Salamanca provinces) is the *verracos*, sculpted stone bulls and boars whose purpose is debated. In the eastern Meseta, the Celtic inhabitants came into contact with the Iberians, and the resulting assimilation produced what was known to the Romans as the Celtiberian culture. This cultural contact between the two groups was probably first established in the upper valley of the Jalón river, a tributary of the Ebro, whence it was diffused westward and southward. The Celtiberian label is often used indiscriminately by classical authors to refer to the inhabitants of the Spanish interior or even to Spaniards generally: Livy, for instance, unhelpfully defines Celtiberia as located between the Atlantic and the Mediterranean![11] Strictly speaking, the 'Celtiberi' are found only in the upper Ebro valley and the eastern Meseta (especially Soria,

Figure 1.2 Silver denarius of Bolskan, 2nd century BC, showing a mounted lancer. Diameter 18.4 mm. (Royal Ontario Museum, Toronto.)

Guadalajara and Cuenca provinces), where the Celtic and Iberian cultures interacted. The resulting amalgamation can be clearly seen in art forms, for instance the polychrome Celtiberian pottery which combines Celtic and Iberian traditions.

Something of the political and social organisation of the Celts and Celtiberians of the third and second centuries BC can be determined from Roman literary and epigraphic sources. Each region was controlled by a tribe (e.g. Vettones, Carpetani, Arevaci) whose territorial boundaries might undergo occasional adjustments as a result of intertribal warfare, and included a number of fixed settlements, usually occupying a hill-fort (*oppidum*). Despite the bellicose atmosphere implicit in these fortifications, tribes sometimes formed coalitions against a common enemy, and would elect a war leader chosen for his bravery and skill in battle. Each tribe had a class of nobles who presumably made up the cavalry element, attested by depictions of mounted warriors on reliefs and coins (Figure 1.2), by decorated harness fittings in tombs and by stone cavalry obstacles outside some forts. The nobility was probably hereditary, based on wealth transmitted from father to son. Related persons belonged to a common clan (*gens*), and there were also smaller divisions known as *gentilitates*, to be discussed in chapter 9. Animal and plant remains document the raising of sheep, cattle, goats and grain, and we know that in the northern Meseta there were sizable wheat harvests in the mid-second century BC.

If the Celts are a problem, the so-called Iberians are a total mystery. No one knows who they are – their practice of cremation inhibits craniometric study – or whence they came; we can transliterate their script but we cannot read their language(s). There is, moreover, a confusing tendency among scholars both ancient and modern to apply the term 'Iberian' to the cultures of both the eastern seaboard and southern Spain, whereas the archaeological evidence points clearly to two different cultural traditions. Around the same time that Catalonia was absorbing the urnfield culture, the south-western quarter of the Iberian peninsula came under the influence of the Atlantic Final Bronze culture. This influence is perhaps most easily seen in the 'carp's tongue' sword, a cut-and-thrust weapon which originated in western France. A shipment of such swords, recovered from a shipwreck at the mouth of the river Odiel, has been radiocarbon-dated to approximately 850 BC.[12] There are also regional traits, such as the stroke-burnished pottery and the Extremaduran engraved funerary stela (already betraying evidence of oriental influence), which are found in south-western Spain but not on the east coast. This south-western culture seems to be the home of the fabled realm of Tartesos – 'charming Tartesos, land of rich men', as the geographer Dionysius describes it – and shows increasing orientalising tendencies as a result of Semitic settlement along the Andalusian coastline.[13] Perhaps, then, we should refer to this culture as 'Tartesian', and restrict the 'Iberians' to the east coast.

Tartesos entered into contact at an early date (probably the mid-eighth century) with Phoenician merchants, who established a series of important trading and production centres on coastal sites such as Cadiz, Toscanos (Málaga) and Almuñécar (Granada). The Phoenicians introduced, among other novelties, iron, the potter's wheel, vase painting and the alphabet.[14] Though we do not yet understand their writings, we know from Strabo that the people of Turdetania (the later name for the Tartesian zone) possessed histories, poems and laws of great antiquity.[15] For the time being, our information about the history of Tartesos rests partly on archaeological discoveries, partly on stories in Herodotus and other ancient writers about the exploits of the Tartesian kings. The fame of Tartesos was chiefly attributed to its wealth in minerals, especially silver, and the Greeks were fond of propagating tall stories about the enormous quantities of silver the Phoenicians brought home from Tartesos.[16] The source of this metal, and of the copper which produced the two chambers of Tartesian bronze (of which the smaller weighed 500 talents) seen by Pausanias in the Sicyonian treasury at Olympia, was undoubtedly the rich mines of Riotinto (Huelva). Here excavation has revealed a stratigraphy dating back to at least the seventh century BC, and the finds include Phoenician amphoras and lamps.[17] Exploitation of these mines was resumed in Roman times, leaving millions of tonnes of silver and copper slag in the neighbourhood.

Although Phoenician pottery is also found in Catalonia, the principal foreign influence in this zone was Greek. Hellenic finds of the late seventh century BC (coinciding in date with the first appearance of iron in the region) suggest visits to the east coast by Greek merchants. The Phocaean colony of Emporion is dated archaeologically to about 580, and another station (of disputed ownership) was established at nearby Rhode (Roses).[18] The names of several other Greek posts are preserved but their locations have not been determined with certainty. The excavated site of Ullastret (Girona), formerly assumed to be one of these Greek foundations, is now recognised as a fortified indigenous settlement which traded heavily with Emporion; other large indigenous towns, such as Tournabous (Lleida) and La Bastida de les Alcuses (Valencia), as well as a host of smaller villages, show that native sites continued alongside the new Greek foundations. The Greeks maintained a healthy commerce with the towns of the east coast, and to some extent with Andalusia (to judge, for instance, by Corinthian amphora fragments of the second quarter of the fifth century found at sites near Seville, though these could conceivably have been brought by Punic merchants). In the end, the Spaniards became sufficiently acquainted with the Greek world that they are reported to have sent peace emissaries to Alexander the Great.[19] Greek cultural tradition remained strong on the east coast well into Roman times, as is apparent in the art of the region (Figure 1.3).

Phoenician commerce, and with it the fame of Tartesos, seems to fade out by the end of the sixth century, although 'Tartesian' warriors figured briefly in the Second Punic War.[20] The appearance of Punic (Carthaginian) materials in the fifth century raises the intriguing question of whether the Carthaginians somehow dislodged the Phoenicians from the western Mediterranean, or merely arrived to fill the power vacuum after some disaster. Justin indeed relates that Gades was attacked by the neighbouring Spaniards, jealous of the Phoenicians' success; the Carthaginians sent an expedition to help their Phoenician cousins but 'avenged the injury to the Gaditanians by the greater injury of annexing part of the province to their own empire'. This late story appears, however, to be a total fabrication. As a recent study demonstrates, the Carthaginians of this period had

Figure 1.3 A Greek mythological theme, the Labours of Hercules, on a mosaic from Lliria (Valencia). Late 2nd or early 3rd c. AD. (Museo Arqueológico Nacional, Madrid.)

no territorial ambitions in Spain; they were interested in trading, not fighting, with the Tartesians and Gaditanians. The idea of military intervention or of a Punic 'empire' in Spain before the third century BC is therefore untenable. Indeed, apart from a fifth-century trading settlement at Villaricos (on the east coast, not the south), there is no record of Carthaginian activity in Spain until the fourth century, long after the demise of the Phoenicians. Their decline may in fact be due not to the Tartesians but to troubles in the Phoenician homeland, which was overrun by the Babylonians in the 570s.[21]

Indigenous art and architecture in southern Spain continue to develop (with some evidence of Punic influence) until the Roman period. However, it may be possible to detect at least a symptom of the collapse of Tartesos in the cultural alignments of the south-east. This hypothesis is difficult to prove because art historians disagree over the chronology of the monuments; for instance, the 'Dama de Elche' has been assigned every date from Archaic to Roman, while verdicts on the *jinete* (horseman) relief from Osuna (Seville) range from the fifth century to the first! None the less, the south-east appears to have close cultural affinities with Andalusia until about the fourth century, after which its efforts are directed northwards. The Tartesian connection is most evident in the 'orientalising' (Phoenician and, increasingly, Greek) plastic art of the sixth to fourth centuries, especially the zoomorphic stone sculptures (bulls, lions, sphinxes etc.) and bronze ex-voto statuettes which occur both in Andalusia and in the south-east (Alicante, Murcia, Albacete).[22] The stone reliefs from La Albuferete and Alcoy (Alicante) also have Andalusian parallels, though those from Pozo Moro (Albacete) defy classification. Similarities can also be seen between the gold treasure of Villena (Alicante) and those of Aliseda (Cáceres), Evora (Cadiz) and El Carambolo (Seville). But during the fourth century, 'Turdetanian' writing is replaced in the south-east by the new 'Levantine' script, which eventually expands into Catalonia, the Ebro valley and southern France. Likewise, 'Iberian' pottery in the south-east follows Andalusian geometric canons at first, but at the end of the fourth century (or slightly later, according to some scholars) an innovative style appears at Arxena (Murcia) and La Alcudia (Alicante), with animal and human figures and floral motifs; this type spreads northward to Lliria (Valencia) by the second century and to Azaila (Teruel) by the first. The sum of this evidence suggests that the south-east not only transferred its cultural allegiance from Turdetania to Catalonia around the fourth century, but initiated new styles of writing and painting which set a precedent for the entire east coast. Whether the context for this apparent disaffection from the south was the diminution of Tartesian power at the hands of Carthage, we can only guess.

2

FROM FRONTIER TO PROVINCE

THE WAR WITH HANNIBAL

Carthage's inheritance of the Phoenician trade network in southern Spain was initially of scant concern to Rome; far from threatening Roman interests, it diverted Punic attention from potential expansion into Italian waters. After the First Punic War (264–241) it was indeed Carthage which felt threatened, by a peace treaty which cost her Sicily and a huge indemnity, and her bitterness was further exacerbated by Rome's peremptory confiscation of Sardinia and Corsica in 238. Deprived of these territories, the Carthaginians funnelled their efforts into Iberia. Under the able generalship of Hamilcar Barca, they expanded their domain from the south coast into central and eastern Spain. The peninsula provided not only silver to finance the war indemnity but a training ground for honing the military skills of the Africans and their Spanish mercenaries. Unknown to the Romans, Hamilcar's goal (or so later historians believed) was to construct a new Punic empire which might again challenge Rome. It was not until after Hamilcar's son-in-law and successor Hasdrubal founded the naval base of New Carthage (Cartagena) that the Romans, realising the impending danger of a Punic empire in Iberia – or, more frightening, the possibility that Hasdrubal might make common cause with Rome's old enemy the Gauls – effected a pact with him in 226, tacitly recognising Carthage's pretensions in southern Spain while receiving her promise not to cross the river Ebro. This river, while well beyond the extent of Carthaginian conquest thus far, offered a convenient and protracted boundary from the Cantabrian Mountains to the Mediterranean, allowing Carthage ample *Lebensraum*, yet preventing her from interfering with Greek colonies in Catalonia or from crossing the Pyrenees into Gaul.

The event which triggered the Second Punic War was the siege, in 219–18, of the city of Saguntum by Hamilcar's son Hannibal (Figure 2.1). Saguntum was located well south of the Ebro and was thus not covered by the treaty of 226, but it had appealed to Rome for help in 220, after it became obvious that Hannibal had designs on the town. The Roman response was unconscionably tardy. For eight months Saguntum was besieged and its starving inhabitants were driven to despair, cannibalism and suicide. Only after the town fell did Rome declare war on Carthage and assemble an expedition. In the meantime, Hannibal crossed the Ebro and the Alps to carry the conflict into the Italian homeland; with him went Spanish cavalry and infantry, who were to play their part in the battle of Cannae. His brother Hasdrubal Barca was left to defend Spain with 57 ships, 21 elephants, 2,550 cavalry and 12,650 infantry. The Roman expedition of 218 got off to a clumsy start. The consul Publius Scipio, sailing to Spain along the south coast of France, discovered that Hannibal had already ferried his army across the Rhône. Scipio then decided to return to Italy, entrusting the Spanish expedition to his brother Gnaeus. Meanwhile Rome's failure to defend Saguntum can hardly have earned her a good reputation in Spain, and although Gnaeus found a safe base at Emporion, many of the towns north of the Ebro had to be taken by siege. A Roman naval victory against Hasdrubal at the mouth of the Ebro in 217 encouraged the Senate to reinforce success by dispatching Publius Scipio with fresh troops, ships and supplies. The combined Roman army now pushed south to Saguntum, where a traitor to the Punic cause soon surrendered the Iberian hostages, whom Publius tactfully restored to their grateful families. Schulten professed to find the Scipios' camp near Almenara, 8 km north of the town, near the presumed temple of Aphrodite mentioned by Polybius. A stone wall with towers at intervals surrounds the trapezoidal encampment whose maximum dimensions are 500 × 300m;[1] this is less than half the size of the 'standard' two-legion camp described by Polybius and could thus have held only one of the Scipios' three legions.

Eager to retain their Spanish empire while detaining a Roman army, the Carthaginians not only provided Hasdrubal with reinforcements but sent a new army in 215 to hold Spain while Hasdrubal led his forces to Italy. The Scipios thwarted this move by crushing Hasdrubal's army in a pitched battle on the Ebro, which had the additional advantage of winning over the allegiance of the hitherto distrustful Spaniards.[2] Though short of provisions, the Romans followed up this victory by pushing south, eventually liberating Saguntum in 212. But luck was about to abandon the Romans. In the summer of 211 the Scipios rashly decided to terminate the Spanish war by defeating all three Punic armies. The success of this plan hinged on the loyalty of the 20,000 Spanish troops in Roman employ; but when Hasdrubal bribed the Celtiberians in Gnaeus' army to break camp, the Roman commander found himself outnumbered. Publius' army became fatally sandwiched between Numidian cavalry and the main Carthaginian force. When Gnaeus divined what had happened, he attempted a sortie but was attacked from the rear and forced into a hopeless last stand. Rome lost not only two generals with their armies but all of Spain south of the Ebro.[3]

While the survivors of the tragedy struggled (with unexpected success) to consolidate the Ebro frontier against Punic assaults, the Comitia at Rome took the unusual step of conferring proconsular *imperium* upon P. Scipio's 25-year old son, likewise named Publius. This younger Scipio arrived in Spain in 210 with 10,000 infantry and 1,000 cavalry. The three Punic armies were still operating separately, and Scipio surprised them by marching from the Ebro to New Carthage in seven days. Taking advantage of a sudden lowering of the water level in the lagoon north of the town (which Livy ascribes to a freak wind, though the text of Polybius suggests rather that the Romans seized and opened the basin's flood-gates), Scipio's forces were able to scale the walls from an unexpected quarter and thus captured the city in a single day. Though Roman hindsight interpreted this miraculous feat as a heaven-sent omen of Scipio's later victory at Zama, we may rather see in it the touch of a skilful tactician.[4] Moreover, by striking directly at the Punic military and naval headquarters, he not only captured ships, grain, military supplies, skilled manpower and silver to pay his troops – commodities which Rome could hardly afford to send him – but scored a stunning psychological victory over the Carthaginians, prompting the defection of many of their Spanish allies.

Realising that the fall of New Carthage opened the door to the rich Guadalquivir valley, Hasdrubal endeavoured to block the Roman advance at Baecula (near Castulo) as soon as campaigning resumed in the spring of 208. Hitherto, Roman legions had always fought in three ranks, but Scipio had been training his troops in fluid tactics.

Figure 2.1 The *castillo* or acropolis of Saguntum, whose siege precipitated the Second Punic War. The visible walls are medieval.

While half his force advanced to meet Hasdrubal's skirmish line, the remainder scaled the high ground unnoticed, suddenly attacking Hasdrubal's main body from either flank and forcing a retreat. With Andalusia exposed and Punic military credibility shattered, Hasdrubal decided to abandon the peninsula without giving his Spanish troops an opportunity of desertion, and to join his brother in Italy. Though Scipio dispatched a token force (which Hasdrubal easily eluded) to guard the Pyrenees, he concentrated the bulk of his effort upon the conquest of Andalusia and the defeat of the two remaining enemy armies, commanded by Mago and Hasdrubal, son of Gisgo. The crucial battle unfolded in 206, not far from Seville, near a town which Polybius identifies as Ilipa (Alcalá del Río, on the Guadalquivir) and Appian as Carmo, 30 km to the east. The conflicting toponyms and the considerable intervening distance can easily be reconciled if we suppose that the battle was fought somewhere between the two towns.[5] Wherever the site, the battle was won by Scipio's use of an unconventional and complex manoeuvre which has been compared with a parade-square drill movement. By swinging his legions and cavalry to fall upon Hasdrubal's Spanish auxiliaries from either wing and put them to flight, Scipio not only overcame the enemy's numerical superiority but outflanked the African troops in the centre. An opportune thunderstorm broke up the battle and the Carthaginians, abandoned by their Spanish allies, retreated. Slingbullets of the Roman Thirteenth Legion found at Gandúl on the left bank of the Guadalquivir may attest the pursuing force.[6] Finally, from his toehold at Gades, Mago unsuccessfully launched a surprise attack against New Carthage, only to discover upon his return that the Gaditanians had locked him out. Meanwhile, a series of lightning victories by Scipio over Spanish cities and tribes which had supported the Carthaginians ended all opposition. Eastern and southern Spain were now in Roman control; the Carthaginians would never return, though the remains of their cities could still be seen in the fifth century AD.[7]

THE CREATION OF THE SPANISH PROVINCES

By 206, Scipio had driven the Carthaginians out of Spain, but the Roman forces remained. Rome feared, perhaps rightly, that a withdrawal from the Iberian peninsula would only invite the Carthaginians to return. Yet if Rome was to maintain a long-term presence here, there was clearly a need for some form of organised government to replace the emergency arrangements of the Hannibalic War. Elsewhere Rome had relied on alliances or *clientelae*, but the Spanish tribes were recalcitrant and had proved fickle allies during the past war. They could not be trusted to keep the Carthaginians out, and the distance from Italy to Spain would prevent Rome from responding rapidly to crisis. Direct control by authorised Roman commanders on the spot was the only feasible solution. Thus in the elections of magistrates for 197 the Romans created two additional praetors whose *provincia* (which at this early date signified 'mission' or 'sphere of responsibility' rather than 'province' in the modern sense) was Spain. Except on rare occasions when a consul had to be sent out to handle a military crisis, Spain remained under the control of praetors throughout the Republic.

The curious geographic configuration of Rome's territory in Spain – a long coastal strip stretching from the Pyrenees to Cadiz – necessitated the double *provincia*. It may also have been deemed prudent to have one governor to deal with the rebellious northern tribes such as the Ilergetes and Sedetani, and another to defend Andalusia against Punic incursion or intrigue. In any event the decision was made to divide Spain into Hispania Citerior ('Closer Spain') on the north and Hispania Ulterior ('Farther Spain') on the south. The division was initially hypothetical and indeed the first two praetors were tasked to fix a boundary; we know from later evidence that the demarcation was established south of Carthago Nova, extending into the *saltus Castulonensis* (Sierra Morena?).[8] Each praetor also brought 8,000 infantry and 400 cavalry with which to relieve the veterans still serving in Spain. Major revolts racked both Spanish provinces in 197, with the result that the governor of Citerior was killed in battle, while his southern colleague became so ill that he had to remain in Spain an extra year after his replacement arrived.[9] By this time the Roman Senate was rightly worried about the precarious military situation in Spain and decided to send to Citerior in 195 a consul with an army comprising two legions, 15,000 Latin allies, 800 cavalry and twenty warships. The nominee was M. Porcius Cato, later famous as the censor of 184 and as a writer on agriculture.

CATO, *OPTIMUS IMPERATOR*

Cato contrived effective if unorthodox methods of exercising his command. He dismissed the contractors who were hoping to supply his army with food, on the parsimonious (and ambitious) grounds that the campaign would feed itself. When the Ilergetes sent envoys to his base at Emporion seeking military assistance to enable them to resist the rebels, Cato promised to send part of his force and even ordered it to board ship; after the ambassadors had departed for home with this news, he prudently disembarked his troops, relying on the rumour of the Roman approach to ensure the Ilergetes' loyalty. This prudent stratagem succeeded in keeping his army intact for the major clash which eventually followed. In the meanwhile he played for time, avoiding pitched battle while toughening his troops with forced marches and tactical exercises; and he can hardly have failed to appreciate that reports of these manoeuvres would reach enemy ears, producing apprehension at the prospect of encountering this well-drilled force. In the end it was Cato who seized the initiative, secreting his troops behind the camp of an enemy tribe, probably the Indigetes, thereby achieving surprise and ensuring that neither side could retreat until the engagement was completed. At daybreak a feint by three of his cohorts enticed the Spaniards to counterattack into a Roman cavalry ambush, with such vigour that the Romans were driven back on one flank until Cato resorted to psychological warfare. Sending a small, visible force towards the enemy's rear, he incited panic in their ranks and urged his own men forward, personally seizing those who attempted to run away and sending them back into the fray. Finally, Cato's reserve legion broke through the rebel fortifications and massacred the hapless defenders.[10]

The Romans followed up their victory by plundering the countryside. As Cato's army marched south towards Tarraco, towns and tribes quickly capitulated. It is as well that they did, for archaeology has revealed a relatively dense concentration of indigenous sites which might have been costly to capture by storm; Cato later claimed he had subdued over 300 'cities'.[11] After unsuccessfully inviting the natives to surrender their arms, Cato sent to the magistrates of each town a message demanding that they dismantle its walls that very day or be conquered and enslaved; they hastily obeyed the order, not realising that an identical letter had been dispatched to every town in north-eastern Spain. The few resisting towns were captured individually. Cato then led his troops southward to assist his praetor P. Manlius, who was battling a tribe whom Livy calls the Turdetani. 'Turdetania' properly refers to Andalusia, but is sometimes used loosely to refer to southern Spain generally (just as 'Celtiberia' often designates all of the interior, or even the entire peninsula). Considerations of time – it was now already autumn – and distance (not to mention the danger of fresh revolts in Catalonia) make it extremely unlikely that Cato's army marched to Andalusia, and Livy's 'Turdetani' are almost certainly the inhabitants of south-eastern Spain.[12] The combined Roman forces were handily able to defeat the 'Turdetani', and Cato concluded the season's campaigning by attacking the Celtiberian town of Seguntia. The following spring, Cato extended Roman influence by marching up the Ebro valley and defeating an inland tribe called the Lacetani (not to be confused with the coastal Laietani).[13] The consul is also credited with regulations providing the Roman government with revenue from the iron and silver mines of Citerior.[14] This not only reinforces Cato's policy of letting the war support itself, but is the first clear evidence of conscious exploitation of Spain's economic resources by the Romans.

The archaeological evidence for Cato's campaign is inconclusive; more precisely, there are remains which *might* refer to it, but none which can be clearly dated. At Emporion, in an arsenal near the south gate of the Greek city (Neapolis), was found a cache of weapons, sling ammunition and the metal fittings for an arrow-firing catapult, datable to the first half of the second century BC;[15] none of these stores need be as early as Cato's expedition. The fortified town where the rebels made their stand is possibly Ullastret, where occupation ceases at the end of the third century or beginning of the second; two sites near Girona which were abandoned in this same period are also possible Catonian victims.[16] Attempts have been made to identify Cato's winter encampment near Emporion as well as marching camps near Seguntia and even around Numantia; again, none can be securely dated. More recently, a small fort at Tentellatge (Solsones) has been ascribed to Cato, but the coins and pottery, vaguely dated by the excavator to the second or first century, hardly substantiate the connection.[17]

The flurry of revolts which erupted when Cato quit the province of Citerior was at last suppressed by Scipio Nasica in 194; the following year we find the governor of Ulterior campaigning in the northern Meseta while his colleague from Citerior is fighting in the south. It seems clear that the interprovincial boundary was confined to the coast; in the interior, commanders were at liberty to engage tribes at random, as opportunity or provocation demanded. There was apparently no grand strategy for the systematic conquest of the peninsula.[18] None the less, in 190 L. Aemilius Paullus was already battling the Lusitani in western Ulterior and eventually defeated them, bringing home a huge quantity of gold.[19] One surviving decree of Paullus, issued from his camp, liberates the slaves of the people of Hasta Regia living in the tower of Lascuta (presumably a fortified hill settlement in the territory of Hasta; such towered towns are well attested)[20] and permits them to keep the land and town which they possessed at that time. 'Slaves' presumably means dependants, since they are said to have property. It is interesting to note that the decree ends with the formula, 'so long as the Roman people and Senate are willing'. This is a reminder that a governor's agreements with the indigenes were subject to ratification at Rome, and that privileges might subsequently be revoked.

The 180s BC saw little significant change in the military situation in Spain. Three governors died (one of them killed by Ligurians before he could reach his province) and four others were awarded triumphs against the Lusitani and Celtiberi. The former appear to have been raiding settlements in the Guadalquivir valley and were merely driven out; in Citerior, the Romans won victories at Calagurris (Calahorra) in the upper Ebro valley in 186 and in the vicinity of Toledo in 185.[21] The governor of Citerior for 181, Q. Fulvius Flaccus, won a decisive cavalry battle over the Celtiberi the following year while awaiting his successor, Ti. Sempronius Gracchus, who arrived late. In consequence of this victory, Flaccus built a temple at Rome to Fortuna Equestris, dedicated in 173.[22] The record of military successes by Gracchus (father of the famous Gracchi brothers) and by his colleague in Ulterior, L. Postumius Albinus, is somewhat confused. Gracchus triumphed over the Celtiberi, Albinus over the Lusitani; but Livy contradicts himself over whether Albinus also defeated the Vaccaei.[23] Yet Gracchus was chiefly remembered for his administrative arrangements, which ensured peace in Celtiberia for the next quarter-century. Clearly defined treaties were enacted with each tribe in the region, incorporating mutual oaths of friendship between natives and Romans. The tribes were obliged to supply auxiliary troops to the Roman army, and a system of taxation was imposed. Although previous generals had brought back tonnes of plunder from the Spanish wars and Cato had introduced a tax on mine production, this is the first reference to a regular collection of revenue. It may be at this time, too, as part of Gracchus' treaties, that the *vicensima*, a requisition for five per cent. of the grain harvest, was established (it is definitely attested by 171 BC); this annual quota, which should have sufficed to feed the Roman and allied troops, represented a more efficient system of provisioning than either the hiring of contractors from Italy or Cato's hit-or-miss technique of living off the land. A final provision of the *pax Gracchana* was that the Celtiberi could fortify existing cities but not found new ones. Outside of Celtiberia, however, Gracchus may have founded at least two native settlements, at Gracchuris on the upper Ebro and Iliturgis on the upper Guadalquivir (though the inscription recording the latter *deductio* dates to the Empire); he also reorganised the Celtiberian town of Complega, giving land and local citizenship to the poor.[24]

The years 180–179 thus introduce a rare lull in Iberian history. The military successes of Albinus over the Lusitani and Gracchus over the Celtiberi, and the treaties concluded with the recalcitrant tribes of central Spain, ushered in a period of relative calm which endured until the mid-150s. This peaceful period is marked by an apparent reduction in the size of the army (one legion in each province instead of two) and a corresponding dearth of triumphs and ovations for returning governors.[25] The period was not entirely without military incidents, however: there were attempted revolts by the Celtiberi (possibly enticed by the cutbacks in Roman military strength) in 174 and 170, both quickly repressed; and operations against the Lusitani in the 160s. But the days of the Gracchan peace were enviously remembered as a sort of golden age in the tumultuous period which followed.[26]

VIRIATHUS AND THE WAR OF FIRE

The efforts of the Romans in pacifying Spain were largely undone by the revolts of the years 155–133 BC. The war with Viriathus in Ulterior and the even bloodier Celtiberian or Numantine War in Citerior – which Polybius appropriately dubbed the 'war of fire' – mark a watershed in the history of Roman Spain.[27] True, there would be other conflicts in the peninsula – the revolt of Sertorius in the 70s and the civil wars that sealed the doom of the Republic – but these would be led by Roman generals and their Spanish clients representing political factions opposed to the current government at Rome. The wars of 155–133, on the contrary, were the last-ditch attempt by the indigenous peoples of the peninsula to expel the conqueror and reassert their former independence. For a time they nearly succeeded.

The trouble began with a revolt by the Lusitani and Vettones in 155–154, which resulted in 6,000 Roman dead, including the quaestor of Ulterior. The governor of 153 was the praetor L. Mummius (later famed for his sack of Corinth in 146) who, after an initial and costly defeat – 9,000 dead, if we can believe Appian – rallied his forces and scored a great victory over the Lusitani.[28] The revolt in Citerior seems to have started in 154 as the result of a dispute between the Roman Senate and the Celtiberian town of Segeda, which formed a confederacy with neighbouring towns and refused to pay tribute or provide troops. The Senate's response seems exaggerated. They designated as governor of Citerior for 153 a consul, Q. Fulvius Nobilior, and moreover decreed that the consuls would henceforth enter office on the first of January instead of the first of March, 'because the Spaniards were rebelling'.[29] The intention, clearly, was to permit the consuls to finish their duties at Rome in time to reach their provinces by the beginning of the campaigning season. But it is unclear why the revolt of Segeda was deemed sufficiently grave to justify a drastic (and, as it turned out, permanent) change in the calendar and the dispatch of a consul to Citerior. The decision to send a consul perhaps lies, not in the internal situation in Citerior, but in a shortage of suitable provinces for military command at this time.[30]

Whatever the reason, Nobilior arrived with an army of nearly 30,000 men and moved against the Segedans. These latter, who had not finished fortifying their town, took refuge among the neighbouring Arevaci, who soundly defeated Nobilior on 23 August 153. That night the Arevaci regrouped at the fortress of Numantia; on the 26th, Nobilior pitched his camp 24 stades (4.3 km) from the town. Schulten claimed to have found Nobilior's camp (including the stables for his elephants) on the hill of Gran Atalaya near Renieblas, at almost double the recorded distance from Numantia.[31] Nobilior's attempt to storm Numantia backfired when his panic-stricken elephants trampled the Romans, and after another costly defeat near Uxama and the ambush of a Roman detachment sent to seek support from a neighbouring tribe, Nobilior retired to his camp for the winter, losing many men to frostbite. His more competent successor, M. Claudius Marcellus (152), lay waste the countryside until the Arevaci and their allies begged forgiveness and a return to the Gracchan peace. Marcellus dispatched their ambassadors to Rome, but the Senate was unwilling to make concessions to tribes which had refused to submit to Nobilior the year before. A display of clemency towards the rebels would only encourage other tribes to revolt. What the Senate wanted, therefore, was not an armistice but *deditio* – unconditional surrender. When the envoys returned empty-handed, Marcellus tried to persuade them to surrender voluntarily; after this bid failed, he laid siege to Numantia until, in early 151, the tribes placed themselves totally in his hands.[32]

The Senate clearly disapproved of Marcellus' magnanimity in granting the rebels a truce; accordingly they elected as governors for 151 two notorious hard-liners, L. Licinius Lucullus for Citerior and Servius Sulpicius Galba for Ulterior. Discovering that his predecessor had already received the Arevaci into *deditio*, Lucullus ('greedy for fame and in need of money', as Appian characterises him) wantonly invaded the territory of the peaceful Vaccaei to the west. After the Romans won a victory outside the walls of Cauca, the townspeople sued for peace. Lucullus demanded hostages, tribute and the admission of a Roman garrison; when these demands were complied with, he murdered all male citizens and sacked the town. He then attempted to make a treaty with the people of Intercatia, but news of his treachery had preceded him, and after an unsuccessful siege and the assurances of his lieutenant Scipio Aemilianus, the Intercatians purchased peace with meat, hostages and winter clothing. Lucullus continued his clockwise swing through Vaccaean territory, ending in Palencia province, where excavators have attributed to his campaign the earliest of three destruction levels at Tariego de Cerrato.[33] Finally, after a futile attempt to seize the wealthy town of Palantia itself, Lucullus had to retreat into Turdetania for the winter. The following spring he joined forces with Galba, who had been routed by the Lusitani the previous year. A pincer movement by the two armies constrained the Lusitani to seek a settlement. They approached Galba, who feigned sympathy and offered to resettle them on fertile land. When the people assembled at the rendezvous, Galba divided them into three groups, some distance apart. Then his soldiers surrounded and massacred each group in turn; thousands were slaughtered and the rest were sold into slavery in Gaul. On his return to Rome, Galba was tried for his misconduct but acquitted.[34]

Galba's treachery, while condoned at Rome, reaped further bloodshed in Ulterior, where Viriathus, one of the few Lusitanians to escape the massacre, organised a massive revolt. An initial victory at Tribola (147) and the slaying of the Roman governor C. Vetilius, further fuelled the uprising, and Viriathus proceeded to overrun the province until the consul Q. Fabius Maximus Aemilianus routed his army at Urso in 144. Sobered by this unexpected defeat, Viriathus incited the tribes of Celtiberia to renounce the peace they had concluded with Marcellus seven years previously.[35] The Romans reacted swiftly to this fresh rebellion. They replaced the scholarly governor of Citerior – the distinguished orator and philosopher C. Laelius Sapiens – with Q. Caecilius Metellus, a past conqueror of Macedonia and the first consul assigned to Citerior since Lucullus. Metellus successfully attacked the Arevaci while they were occupied with the harvest, but neither he nor his successors could capture the redoubtable fortress of Numantia, which in consequence became the symbol of Spanish resistance (Figure 2.2). The proconsul Q. Pompeius, repeatedly worsted by the Numantines, negotiated a disgraceful peace with the enemy at the beginning of 139. Two years later, C. Hostilius Mancinus was surrounded in Nobilior's old camp and surrendered. Both these treaties were repudiated by the Senate, and Mancinus was actually handed over, naked and bound, to the Numantines – who refused the bizarre gift.[36]

In Ulterior, meanwhile, the Romans were experiencing mixed fortunes. The consul Q. Fabius Maximus Servilianus arrived in 142 with elephants and cavalry from Africa. Viriathus was defeated near Itucca, but the disorderly Roman pursuit allowed him to counter-attack and force the Romans back to the town. It was, however, a Pyrrhic success for Viriathus, whose manpower and supplies were so exhausted that he temporarily had to withdraw into Lusitania. But while Servilianus was besieging Erisana, Viriathus (now with replenished forces) put the Roman army to flight and pinned them against a cliff, obliging the hapless governor to sign a peace treaty which the Senate (for once) ratified. None the less, Servilianus' brother and successor Q. Servilius Caepio considered the treaty a disgrace to Roman honour and repeatedly petitioned the Senate to renew hostilities. When permission at last arrived, he overpowered Viriathus in Carpetania, forcing the rebels to withdraw. In 139 he attacked the Vettones and Callaeci (neighbours of the Lusitani on the east and north), assisted by his colleague from Citerior, M. Popillius Laenas. Under pressure from two consular armies, Viriathus attempted to negotiate, first with Popillius (who demanded that the Lusitani lay down their arms, an unacceptable condition), then with Caepio, who managed to bribe the Lusitanian envoys to assassinate their leader.[37] This brought the Viriathan conflict to an end, but it was a victory won more by treachery than tactics.

The next governor of Ulterior, D. Iunius Brutus, conducted

Figure 2.2 Remains of a Celtiberian street and houses at Numantia.

mopping-up operations in Lusitania from his base at Moron (possibly to be identified with the earthen fortifications at Alto de Castilla, Alpiarça). He then crossed the river Lethe – which his superstitious troops mistook for the entrance to the Underworld and refused to cross until Brutus personally carried the standard to the far bank – and defeated a large army of Callaeci. The violent destruction of the hill-fort of Sabroso in northern Portugal has been plausibly dated to this campaign.[38] Eutropius' epitome of Roman history places Brutus' triumph over the Callaeci and Lusitani together with Scipio's triumph over the Numantines in 133, but this would give Brutus an incredibly long tenure in Ulterior. Other sources, including Eutropius' contemporary Festus, insert between the campaigns of Brutus and Scipio a 'consul Sylla', who pacified the insurgents in Spain. Since the *fasti* for Citerior in these years are full and the governors unsuccessful, this Sylla must have succeeded Brutus in Ulterior, as *praetor pro consule*. Only half the praetors in the mid-130s have been identified (assuming six per year); this one may be P. Sulla, who was a *monetalis* (mint official) in the 140s or early 130s.[39]

The protracted war with Numantia remained an embarrassment to the Roman government. M. Aemilius Lepidus, sent to replace Mancinus, stupidly attacked the Vaccaei (falsely claiming that they were helping Numantia) and after a long and unsuccessful siege of Palantia was recalled by the Senate for involving Rome in a new war while she was already hard-pressed by the old. None the less, Q. Calpurnius Piso (consul 135) renewed the attack on Palantia, either fearing to attack the Numantines or (worse) suffering defeat at their hands. The situation in Citerior was becoming intolerable; as Livy observes, the Numantine War had dragged on through the incompetence of Rome's generals and to the shame of her people.[40] The command was therefore offered to Cornelius Scipio Aemilianus, already famous for crushing Carthage in 146. From the moment of his arrival the army in Spain felt his iron hand. Merchants, prostitutes and fortunetellers were barred from the camps; beds were outlawed, rations cut, and the soldiers had to travel on foot. When his troops were sufficiently toughened by deprivation and training exercises, Scipio began laying waste the plains of the Arevaci and Vaccaei, gathering the ripe grain for his own force and burning the rest. Then, prudently declining open battle with the Numantines, he invested their town with a ring of siege works, intending to starve them into submission. The string of seven camps, linked by a wall nearly three metres high hermetically enclosing the rebels, was identified by Schulten and is still visible from the air. Towers at 100-foot intervals along the wall served as platforms for Roman artillery.[41] After several unsuccessful attacks against these defences, the Numantines sought a negotiated settlement, but Scipio would entertain nothing short of *deditio*. Only after being reduced to cannibalism did the Numantines agree to unconditional surrender in 133. Many of them (like the Zealots at Masada centuries later) committed suicide, confirmed by the large number of excavated skeletons; the rest were sold into slavery and their town, like Carthage, was razed by Scipio. Whether his motive was revenge or prevention of further uprisings, he was criticised by some senators for destroying the famous stronghold without Senate authorisation.[42] But doubtless there were others who agreed that 'Numantia delenda est', and Scipio was awarded the triumph he deserved.

The Lusitanian and Numantine conflicts had been not only embarrassing to Rome, but very costly. For instance, Roman casualties in Ulterior alone in the period from 147 to 141 exceeded 12,000,[43] and the total expense of the wars in manpower and money must have been staggering. In the end, however, Rome proved her military superiority, and the ultimate victories in both provinces helped negate or at least mask the blunders, defeats and unscrupulous conduct of previous commanders. The capture of Numantia was as effective a symbol of Roman supremacy as its resistance had been for Celtiberian autonomy, and the conquest of the entire peninsula, while far from accomplished, was at last beginning to appear feasible.

3

TO THE BOUNDARY
OF OCEAN

THE LATE REPUBLIC

The Numantine War ended with the dispatch of ten senatorial commissioners to organise the lands and peoples acquired by Rome under Scipio Aemilianus and Brutus. This presumably included the territory of the Arevaci as well as the lands in southern Spain recovered from Viriathus; there is no reason to believe that the lands of the Vaccaei, Lusitani or Callaeci had actually come under permanent Roman domination during the campaigns of these generals. Nothing more is heard of the commissioners, though we may speculate that they settled the terms of the peace (including a war indemnity and the creation of *ager publicus* in the captured zones). Whether the interprovincial boundary was extended to the new frontier may be doubted. We have no information on events or governors in the decade following the war, but the silence of our sources and the exhaustion of resources on both sides suggest peaceful coexistence of Roman and native. In 123 the consul Metellus was given a command against the foreign pirates in the Balearic Islands. It has been argued that these came from southern Gaul and Sardinia, a situation paralleled in Muslim times when pirates flourished in this region.[1] While there is no explicit evidence that Metellus' mandate included the province of Citerior, he must at least have used Spain as a base of operations. More significantly, he led 3,000 Roman citizens from Spain to settle his new colonies at Palma and Pollentia on the island of Mallorca; unless these men were already under his jurisdiction, this would have been a reprehensible act of interference. If we then accept Metellus as governor of Citerior, we must assign Q. Fabius

Maximus Allobrogicus (whom Plutarch calls a propraetor in Spain) to Ulterior. He was censured by the Senate for exacting grain from the cities and sending it to Rome without recompense.[2]

Another hiatus in the historical record brings us to 114 BC, when the governorship of Ulterior was given to one of the greatest figures in Roman history, Gaius Marius. Accused of bribery while praetor in 115 (and very nearly convicted), Marius redeemed himself by temporarily ridding the province of bandits, an endemic problem in Spain. He went on to hold the consulship an unprecedented seven times.[3] His successor was L. Calpurnius Piso Frugi (praetor in 113 or 112) who was killed there while attempting to suppress a revolt. Servius Sulpicius Galba, who replaced him, probably in 111, was son of the infamous Galba who had massacred the Lusitanians; how he dealt with the revolt is not known, but unlike his predecessor he survived to reach the consulship. Greater success was achieved by Q. Servilius Caepio (praetor 109) who triumphed over the Lusitani in 107. We have no *fasti* for Citerior in this period, but the governors should include the proconsuls Q. Fabius Labeo and M'. Sergius, recorded as building roads near Ilerda and Barcino respectively. We also know that Cn. Cornelius Scipio was refused the post because of immoral conduct, perhaps in 109.[4] A Roman army was defeated by the Lusitani in 105, but the next year the town 'Seanoc . . .' (near Alcántara in Lusitania) surrendered to the *imperator* L. Caesius.[5] As a holder of *imperium* Caesius must have been a praetor, presumably in Ulterior. The Lusitani were finally defeated and peace established in this province in 101; the event is usually associated with M. Marius (brother of the consul), who is attested fighting the Lusitani with the aid of Celtiberians, and settling the latter near Colenda five years before their slaughter by T. Didius.[6]

A further revolt in 99 was suppressed by L. Cornelius Dolabella (praetor 100) who triumphed over the Lusitani in 98. T. Didius, one of the consuls for 98, took command of Citerior, where he allegedly killed 20,000 Arevaci, moved the town of Termes to an unfortified site in the plain, and successfully besieged Colenda. Turning to the nearby town founded by M. Marius, he offered its people (who were poor and subsisting as brigands) the land confiscated from the Colendans; when the populace arrived to take up the offer he had them surrounded and killed, in the manner of Galba. On another occasion, when a battle with the Celtiberi lasted until nightfall, Didius sent men to bury many of the Roman dead under cover of darkness; at daybreak the Spaniards were so amazed at the comparative enormity of their own casualties that they sued for peace.[7] P. Licinius Crassus (consul 97, and father of the triumvir) continued the war in Ulterior, triumphing over the Lusitani in 93. A hoard of about 936 silver coins, found in a helmet at Orellana de la Sierra on the right bank of the Guadiana, seems to have been buried around the time of this campaign.[8] Didius, who triumphed over the Celtiberi at the same time, was replaced in Citerior by C. Valerius Flaccus (consul 93), who is reported to have killed 20,000 Celtiberians and to have executed the rebels of Belgeda who set fire to their own senate when the elders refused to join the revolt. Flaccus is subsequently recorded as governor of Transalpine Gaul c. 85–81, and the manuscript of Granius Licinianus has him triumph over both Celtiberia and Gaul in the latter year; but a dual governorship of Gaul and Spain is unprecedented and the editor of Granius is probably right to assume the intrusion of a marginal gloss in the text.[9] Flaccus no doubt triumphed over the Gauls in 81 and over the Celtiberi in the late 90s. We have, in fact, no surviving list of Spanish governors for the 80s.

SERTORIUS' REVOLT: THE 'NEW MAN' VERSUS THE 'OLD WOMAN'

Despite, or perhaps because of, being a distant province, Spain found herself embroiled in two major civil wars in the first century BC, in which provincial blood was spilled for the sake of political rivalries at Rome. A tough soldier named Q. Sertorius had already served under Didius in the 90s and had lost an eye in battle during the Social War. As praetor in 83 he supported the seven-time consul Marius against their mutual enemy Sulla, whose victorious army returned from Asia that year and landed unopposed in Italy. Sertorius, who sharply criticised the Marians for failing to take adequate precautions against Sulla, was conveniently dispatched to Citerior as proconsul for 82. While he was there, Rome fell to Sulla, and the following spring, outlawed and pursued, Sertorius was obliged to flee to Africa. Here he was approached by a delegation of Lusitani who invited him to become their leader and help them overthrow Roman rule. Sertorius accepted the offer, no doubt seeing it as a means of striking back at the Sullan regime. To defeat the Romans, however, the Lusitani needed not only a Roman general but a Roman army. From the Marian party Sertorius recruited experienced officers to train the indigenous troops to fight in the Roman manner. Moreover,

Sertorius was a master in the art of deceit, which could be directed at allies as well as foes. The story of the albino doe (allegedly given to him by a peasant with the suspicious name Spanus), from which Sertorius publicly pretended to receive secret messages from the gods, is so often repeated in our sources that it sounds more like popular myth than historical fact. Nevertheless, Sertorius was precisely the sort of leader to exploit native superstitions, to take advantage of *fides Iberica* (Spanish devotion to their leaders without regard for their own lives) and to romanise a people depending on him to free them from Roman control. In this he was only partly successful, since Lusitanian resistance to Rome would continue for many decades after his death. All the same, he was the only Roman general of the period to employ barbarians in his army, and received the praise of antiquity for his care in selecting the best recruits.[10]

In 79 Sulla responded to the news of Sertorius' revolt by sending an army under his fellow consul, Q. Caecilius Metellus Pius. Metellus came from a long line of aristocrats and had no respect for a 'new man' like Sertorius, a parvenu from a Sabine town and a traitor to boot. But Metellus was advancing in years – Sertorius reportedly called him 'that old woman' – was addicted to luxury, and even insisted on being worshipped like a god, while Sertorius was young, energetic and inured to deprivation. Moreover, the rugged Spanish terrain was better suited to the unconventional guerrilla tactics developed by Sertorius than to the pitched battles familiar to Metellus.[11] But if he could not defeat the rebel in combat, Metellus could at least wear down the resistance of his civilian supporters. Just as his father had used a scorched earth policy against the Numidians in 109, so Metellus set about burning the villages and hill-forts of the Lusitani and driving the farmers off their land.[12] Metellus' ineffectual campaigning against the superior generalship of Sertorius in the years 79–77 BC is reminiscent of the blundering British efforts against Rommel. Sertorius' greater mobility and competent intelligence network consistently permitted him to anticipate the old man's every move. For instance, learning of Metellus' plan to besiege Langobriga (just south of modern Oporto),[13] Sertorius first ensured that the town was well provisioned, then ambushed the Roman foraging party, so that Metellus soon had to lift the siege. In Citerior, Metellus' colleague M. Calidius (subsequently convicted of extortion) was so badly defeated by Sertorius' lieutenant L. Hirtuleius in 78 that L. Manlius, governor of neighbouring Gaul, had to intervene. Instead of averting disaster, Manlius precipitated it by losing a major battle to Hirtuleius near Ilerda. Retreating into Gaul with a fraction of his original force, he was again beaten by the Aquitani.[14] Encouraged by this success, and perhaps acting in concert with an insurrection by the anti-Sullan consul M. Aemilius Lepidus in northern Italy, Sertorius himself campaigned in Citerior in 77, defeating the cave-dwelling Characitani by the novel use of air pollution (using his horses to stir up a choking dust outside their homes). The tribes of the Ebro valley made common cause with Sertorius, who not only trained their men in Roman warfare but even established a school at Osca (Huesca) for sons of the indigenous aristocracy. By the summer, Lepidus' revolt was crushed and a large party (allegedly 53 cohorts) of Marianist refugees under M. Perperna fled to Sertorius. Sertorius was now at the height of his power, controlling nearly the entire peninsula.

This massive influx of trained Italian soldiery into his ranks gave Sertorius the potential to invade Italy from his base in Citerior, a worrisome prospect for the Roman Senate. Their panic may in part explain the award of proconsular command in Citerior to Cn. Pompeius, an *eques* still in his twenties who had never been elected to office, though their hand was undoubtedly forced by Pompey's refusal to disband his army after the defeat of Lepidus. By the autumn of 77, the eager Pompey was already in his province; Sertorius, who was occupied in organising the recently arrived Italian officers into a shadow senate, did not even attempt to block his entry. Sertorius' inaction and the presence of a Roman army on their doorstep prompted several tribes of the north-east to defect, though Sertorius prevented the rot from spreading into Celtiberia by successfully besieging the dissident town of Contrebia (Botorrita). The following spring, leaving Hirtuleius to picket Metellus' force, he sent Perperna to defend the Mediterranean coastline while he himself reduced the towns of the upper Ebro valley, perhaps hoping to lure Pompey into the hills to defend them. Pompey stuck to the coast, but his southward advance was sufficiently retarded by Perperna's operation that when the town of Lauro near Valencia declared its support of the young newcomer, Sertorius was able to outrace his opponent and besiege the town before the Pompeian column could arrive. He then fell upon Pompey's foraging party, obliging Pompey to commit further troops which Sertorius' cavalry then outflanked. In a single day Pompey is said to have lost 10,000 men with all their equipment. This humiliating defeat was avenged in midsummer by a successful manoeuvre by Metellus against Hirtuleius, who had unwisely engaged him in pitched battle near Italica.[15] Sertorius himself remained undefeated.

The defeat of Hirtuleius enabled Metellus to stage a breakout and join forces with Pompey. In the spring of 75, the two pro-consular armies converged on Valentia while Sertorius attempted to obstruct their rendezvous. A battle was inevitable, but Pompey had no intention of sharing the glory with his colleague. Perperna and C. Herennius had established a blockade on the river Turia (Guadalaviar). Pompey successfully breached it, killing Herennius and a large number of his men. Pompey then pursued Perperna southward to the Sucro (Júcar), where he was attacked by Sertorius himself. Since Metellus' likeliest route was up the Guadalquivir valley, north of the Sierra de Alcaraz and east towards the coast, Sertorius had presumably been waiting to ambush him either on the Sucro itself, or further south where the river Canoles cuts a defile between Enguera and Xátiva;[16] but his plan was altered by the unexpected prospect of destroying Pompey first. The resulting battle was as fierce and bloody as the recent engagement on the Turia, but with the very different result that Pompey's troops were put to flight while their wounded commander barely escaped with his life.[17] The arrival of Metellus prevented Sertorius from giving Pompey a thorough thrashing; as it was, each side suffered 10,000 casualties.

The Romans were short of money and supplies (as we know from a letter of Pompey to the Senate) and Sertorius was content for the moment to harass them, but eventually they provoked him into open battle – at Segontia according to Appian, at Saguntum accord-ing to Plutarch.[18] After inflicting heavy casualties on Pompey's army, Sertorius turned against Metellus. When the 'old woman' was wounded by a spear, however, his men instead of retreating fought with a vengeance and treated Sertorius to his first defeat. He withdrew into the hills and resorted to his beloved guerrilla tactics. While Sertorius delayed, the Senate acted, sending fresh troops and supplies (including wheat from Narbonensis) to its generals, and minting an unusually large number of *denarii*.[19] Thus reinforced, Pompey besieged the towns of the Vaccaei in 74, while Metellus returned to Ulterior as if in triumph. But the greatest menace to Sertorius was desertion from his own ranks, no doubt fuelled by impatience at his delaying tactics and by distrust between the Italians and Spaniards in his retinue.

His ranks depleted, Sertorius was driven out of Celtiberia in 73 and fought his last battles against Pompey in the north-east. In the midst of the campaigning season, his Italian officers, led by Perperna, turned against him. Inviting him to a banquet, they treacherously murdered him.[20] With Sertorius dead, most of the Spanish troops returned home and made their peace with the senatorial generals. The year 72 was spent subduing Clunia, Uxama, Calagurris and other towns which still resisted out of *fides Iberica* to the memory of Sertorius (sometimes to the point of cannibalism), until Pompey was master of all Citerior.[21] He returned to Rome and a triumph in 71, though he had never beaten Sertorius in battle.

Though Sertorius' revolt ultimately failed, its consequences were profound. For eight years it posed a military threat and political embarrassment to the Sullan and post-Sullan regimes at Rome. For the first time a Roman general had not only used foreign troops against Rome but employed guerrilla tactics against the pitched-battle approach of his enemies. Numerous caches of silver plate, coin and jewelry throughout the peninsula provide but a small index of the great economic upheaval and panic generated by the conflict. As Sallust records, Citerior was devastated to the point of ruin, except for the towns of the east coast, and not even all of them escaped damage.[22] In consequence the tribes of Citerior, having achieved nothing in this long and costly war, made no further attempt at revolt. The war was also significant for propelling into prominence Pompey, who would later preside over the last days of the Republic. Yet the most intriguing historical question is the position of Sertorius. He was not, as some would claim, an enemy of Rome, nor yet a champion of provincial independence, but a patriot who intended to use his victories in Spain as a power base for reinstating a democratic, Marianist government at Rome in place of the oligarchy revived by Sulla.

THE CAESARIAN CAMPAIGNS

With the conclusion of the Sertorian drama, the Spaniards for the most part returned to peaceful pursuits. There was still some sporadic fighting, enough to justify triumphs for the new governors but not enough to claim the attention of historians; as Appian succinctly notes, 'the war was over.'[23] Caesar, who had already

Figure 3.1 Iberian soldiers armed with the small shield (*caetra*), as shown on this stela from Urso (Osuna), fought for the Pompeians at Ilerda. (Musée du Louvre. Clichés des Musées Nationaux, Paris; © PHOTO R.M.N.)

served in Ulterior as quaestor with juridical power in 69, returned to that province as governor in 61. Seeking both military glory to further his career and booty to repay his creditors, he raised a third legion and launched a lightning campaign against the Lusitani and Callaeci, conquering the Atlantic coast with the aid of a fleet as far as Brigantium (La Coruña) and plundering even those towns which opened their gates to him.[24] Like Decimus Brutus in the 130s, Caesar apparently did not leave garrisons behind to consolidate the overrun territory, but the victory was sufficient to win him the consulship of 59.

The next decade was a relatively quiet one for the Spanish provinces, the sole recorded disturbance being a revolt among the Vaccaei in 56–55. Caesar himself noted, during a speech in 49, that Spain had been at peace for a long time.[25] In fact, the *Lex Trebonia* of 55 awarded a five-year command of both Spanish provinces to Caesar's arch-rival Pompey, who preferred to remain in Italy and to govern his province through legates. The increasing tension between the two generals may perhaps be reflected in Pompey's failure to send (or Caesar's to request) a relief force from Spain during the Gallic uprising of 52, though Caesar did purchase Spanish horses for this campaign. Caesar's crossing of the Rubicon and march on Rome in January 49 sent the Pompeians scurrying to the east as both sides prepared for civil war. Now master of Italy by default, yet unable to pursue his foe until a new fleet could be assembled on the Adriatic, Caesar took advantage of the delay to secure his rear. In Spain he faced what he called 'an army without a leader'[26] – or rather with three, for L. Afranius and M. Petreius had established a well-fortified, if isolated, defensive position at Ilerda (Lleida), while the scholarly M. Varro provided troops from Ulterior, equipped with diminutive round shields (Figure 3.1). Caesar's operations were beset with difficulties: shortages of grain and timber, and a flash flood which washed out the bridges he had constructed over the river Sicoris (Segre). When he eventually overcame these difficulties and secured food supplies from neighbouring tribes, the Pompeians decided to make a dash for the Ebro. Harassed by Caesar's cavalry and outraced to the protective high ground by Caesar's better-disciplined infantry, the Pompeians were trapped in an unenviable position far from water. Finally, surrounded, they were obliged to capitulate on 2 August 49.[27] News of this victory swayed the loyalty of the cities of Ulterior, who without exception complied with Caesar's edict to send their delegates to a conference at Corduba. Several cities expelled their Pompeian garrisons, and one of Varro's two legions – significantly, a legion of native troops – mutinied, prompting his surrender. Caesar left in charge of Ulterior the propraetor Q. Cassius Longinus, as recently confirmed by an inscription from the outskirts of ancient Ulia, a town conspicuously loyal to the Julian clan.[28]

The pacification of Spain placed all of western Europe in Caesar's hands, leaving him free to prosecute the war in the east. But he could hardly have chosen a worse governor for Ulterior. As quaestor of this province in the 50s, Longinus had nearly been assassinated for his rapacity. Now, as governor, he imposed heavy taxes on the populace while purchasing his troops' loyalty with donatives. A second plot was soon hatched by the provincials, whereby Longinus would be stabbed to death by a host of conspirators while holding court in Corduba. The description of the assassination attempt in the anonymous *Alexandrian War* (written after Caesar's death) bears a suspicious resemblance to that of Caesar's murder in 44, except that whereas Caesar had dismissed his Spanish bodyguard beforehand, Longinus' bodyguard saved his life. His reprieve was temporary: several days later the native legion revolted, followed by the Second Legion and most of the Fifth. A miniature civil war thus erupted between the two factions (both loyal to Caesar) until the governor of Citerior intervened with a large force. Longinus was replaced as governor by C. Trebonius and conveniently perished in a shipwreck on the way home.[29] His successor had to face a new crisis. After the defeat of Pompey the Great, his son Cn. Pompey sailed to the Balearic Islands, allegedly at the request of the legions of Ulterior who feared reprisals by Caesar for the recent mutiny. Declaring in favour of the Pompeians, these legions had expelled Trebonius and driven Ulterior into revolt by the time Pompey arrived on the mainland in 46 to seize control. Many cities opened their gates; others, like Carthago Nova, resisted and were besieged.[30] Caesar was therefore summoned once again. As in 49, word of the great general's arrival sparked defections among some native communities, notably Corduba. By advancing to this city, Caesar obliged the Pompeians to lift the siege of Ulia. Despite several days of costly skirmishing, however, he was unable to lure Pompey into open battle, and moved on to besiege Ategua, a town near Corduba, where large supplies of grain were stored; Caesar's siege works are still visible from the air.[31] The town fell on 19 February 45, despite harassment of Caesar's troops by Pompey, and Caesar was able to 'liberate' several other towns. Pompey at last offered pitched battle on the plain of Munda, where he drew up his forces on high ground in front of the town on 17 March.[32] Caesar wrongly calculated that they would descend into the plain once the attack began; but Pompey held his ground, forcing Caesar to fight uphill. At one point (as numerous sources delight in telling us) Caesar thought the battle lost and even contemplated suicide, but finally won the day by personal example. Cn. Pompey, wounded, hid in a cave but was discovered and beheaded. Even after winning this desperate battle, Caesar had to spend the spring and summer besieging Munda itself, Urso (Osuna) and other towns which continued to resist, before he could return to Rome and a hero's welcome. Slingballs from Osuna and Utrera (Sevilla) inscribed 'Cn. Mag(nus)' and 'Imp(erator)', as well as remains of iron weapons, provide material confirmation of these battles.[33] Reliefs from Osuna depict Iberian warriors similar to those encountered by Caesar (Figure 3.2).

After Caesar's departure, Cn. Pompey's younger brother Sextus, who had commanded the Corduba garrison in the recent war, remained in Spain to organise a resistance movement, using guerrilla tactics in the manner of Sertorius. Twice Caesar sent generals against Sextus, without success. By the time news arrived of Caesar's assassination in 44, Sextus had an army of six legions with which he had captured the towns of Carteia and Baria (Villaricos). Finally the incoming governor of Citerior, M. Aemilius Lepidus, persuaded Pompey to leave Spain in exchange for a bribe of 50 million denarii, ostensibly in compensation for his father's confiscated property.[34] Spain played little part in the ensuing conflict between Caesar's successors, Marc Antony and Octavian. Octavian succeeded Lepidus as governor of Spain in 42 but, like Pompey in the 50s, preferred to govern through legates.[35] The army of six legions which he dispatched to the province in 41 was prevented by Antony's forces from crossing the Alps,[36] but in 40 Antony conceded to Octavian control of all the western European provinces. In this moment of reconciliation Octavian awarded the Spanish governorship to Antony's brother Lucius. The following year, however, it passed to Cn. Domitius Calvinus, who had to suppress a revolt by the Cerretani (a tribe inhabiting a region of the Pyrenees, now known as Cerdanya). For this victory Calvinus triumphed in 36, rebuilt the Regia in the Roman Forum with Spanish gold, and erected an altar, still extant, recording the dedication of the spoils of war.[37] Five of the next six governors were also awarded triumphs, but for what achievements we have no idea.[38] Ironically, the one governor for whom no triumph is recorded is credited with subjugating the Cantabri, Astures and Vaccaei in 29.[39] Marc Antony took little interest in Spain: it is questionable whether he ordered Bogud the Moor's hapless raid on Ulterior in 38. Nevertheless, after losing the battle of Actium in 31, Antony and Cleopatra were allegedly planning to sail to Spain and stir up a revolt there. In retrospect this sounds fantastic; yet Octavian was clearly expecting some threat, for he appointed C.

Figure 3.2 Another Urso relief, showing a warrior armed with the long shield (*scutum*) and *machaera Hispana*, a sword type used in the battle of Munda. (Museo Arqueológico Nacional, Madrid.)

51

Baebius to the unprecedented post of 'prefect of the seacoast of Hispania Citerior' at this time.[40]

THE CANTABRIAN WAR

As uncontested ruler of the Roman world, Augustus was able to redirect his generals' efforts to extend the empire to the Atlantic Ocean, 'from Cadiz to the Elbe' as he records in chapter 26 of his *Res Gestae*. Three regions of Spain had yet to be conquered, Cantabria, Asturias and Galicia, though the war which began in 26 is usually named after the first of these. To what extent the war was actually provoked by the Cantabri, rather than an act of Roman aggression, is unclear; however, both Dio and Plutarch list them among various tribal groups causing 'disturbances' (*tarachai*) in 29 BC, while Florus credits them with raids against their neighbours in the Roman zone.[41] Yet it is difficult to believe that Augustus did not have his eyes on the rich mineral resources of the north-west, from which the natives had long been producing gold torques, bracelets, diadems and other jewelry; indeed, a cache of gold and silver jewelry at Arrabalde (Zamora) has been plausibly linked with Augustus' invasion of Asturias.[42]

The chronology and strategic details of the conquest are problematic.[43] In 26 BC, Augustus' seven legions marched northward in three columns through the rugged Cantabrian landscape. After a preliminary battle, the defeated Cantabri fled to Mons Vindius (location unknown) where they were starved into submission. Campaigning conditions were gruelling: the Roman camps were overrun by rats, and supply trains from Aquitania were barely able to negotiate the rough trails.[44] Augustus himself fell sick and had to be evacuated to Tarraco. His general P. Carisius continued the invasion westward into the country of the Astures, again advancing in three columns. The Astures shrewdly sent three columns of their own to attack the three Roman marching camps simultaneously. However, the Brigaecini disclosed their plan to Carisius, who saved the day by arriving with reinforcements. The Astures were beaten and their chief town, Lancia, was constrained to surrender. The final phase of the operation was the advance into Galicia, apparently in 25. This time the Romans advanced in two columns, one of them commanded by C. Antistius Vetus, the governor of Citerior. Once again the natives were forced to seek refuge in a hill fort, the Mons Medullius (of disputed location). The Romans were obliged to encase the stronghold with an 18-mile circumvallation, but the defenders evaded capture, in Numantine fashion, by committing suicide.[45]

The victory (if it may so be termed) at Mons Medullius was sufficient token of conquest, in Augustus' view. Returning to Rome at the end of 25 he closed the temple of Janus to show that the war was finished, and commissioned the construction of a temple to Jupiter the Thunderer (completed in 22) to commemorate his narrow escape from death during an electrical storm in Cantabria.[46] But in Spain the storm was far from over. Revolts by the Cantabri and Astures are recorded in 24, 22, 19 and 16 BC.[47] The revolt of 19 was serious enough that Augustus' right-hand man Agrippa had to take charge. Discovering to his chagrin that some of the soldiers were afraid of the Cantabri, Agrippa had first to rebuild their morale, then to defeat and disarm the enemy and resettle them on level ground. Returning to Rome in 13 after a second tour of Gaul and Spain, Augustus ordered the construction of an altar of peace – the famous Ara Pacis – for provinces which he had prematurely declared pacified in 25.

Expansion demands reorganisation. Augustus himself informs us that, during his tour of Gaul and Spain in 16–13 BC, 'I successfully organised these provinces', and it is to this period that the creation of the third Spanish province should be assigned. Ulterior was subdivided into Baetica (Andalusia) and Lusitania, and to the latter province Augustus initially assigned Galicia and Asturias. However, he subsequently transferred this potentially rebellious zone to Citerior, the only Spanish province to retain legions. Baetica was deemed so thoroughly romanised that Augustus entrusted its administration to the Senate. The inscribed base of a golden statue of Augustus dedicated by that province thanks him for bringing peace to the region.[48]

CONCLUSIONS: THE CONQUEST IN RETROSPECT

'Spain, although it was the first mainland province to be entered by the Romans, was the last to be completely subdued, and held out till our own times', writes Livy in the age of Augustus. Livy ascribes the slowness of the conquest to two factors: the rugged nature of the country and the recalcitrant character of its people.[49] In chapter 1 we saw that, while the coastal areas of the peninsula are relatively accessible, the rocky Meseta which dominates the interior is a barrier to communications and a zone of climatic extremes which would make campaigning arduous. Here food and water were often scarce, transport of supplies was difficult, and the uneven terrain facilitated ambushes. The stubbornness of the inhabitants, particularly the Celts and Celtiberians, who were inured to hardship, adept at guerrilla warfare and who preferred certain death to capitulation, was notorious. But the land and its people were not the only factors that impeded the conquest. Equally important was the lack of an overall strategy for conquering the peninsula. The Hannibalic, Viriathic, Celtiberian and Sertorian wars accounted for only 40 years out of the two centuries needed to subdue the peninsula. Except for these periods of intense activity, Spain was little more than a sideshow as far as the Roman Senate was concerned. Two recent writers have ably demonstrated that in both war and peace the Senate entrusted affairs in Spain to the commanders on the spot, who were often politicians first and soldiers second.[50] Brilliant generals like Scipio Africanus were rare; more often it was the Spaniards who seized the military initiative, forcing the Romans to react. Rome had no Schlieffen Plan, no blueprint for victory; most governors waged war less by strategy than by crisis management. In the end, with the resources of most of the Mediterranean world behind her, Rome won; but it was a war of attrition, long, costly and largely inefficient. It is particularly difficult to accept the view that Rome owed her success in Spain to 'the aggressive policy of the senate',[51] when it is clear that the Senate had no real policy on Spain, and showed little interest in it except when embarrassed by repeated military disasters. Moreover, by relying entirely on the governors – who were often inexperienced, incompetent or dishonest – not only to take the necessary actions but to report them, the Senate was sometimes the recipient of misinformation. Triumphs were awarded again and again for the supposed conquest of tribes like the Lusitani and Celtiberi by generals who submitted inflated reports of successful campaigns, which were often little more than reconnaissance expeditions or retaliatory raids. The ephemeral 'victories' had to be repeated many times before the tribes were truly subdued. In the meantime, a large contingent of Roman troops – at least 20–25,000 per year, according to a recent estimate[52] – were tied up in Spain, obliging Rome to develop the standing army which eventually helped build the Roman Empire.

Part II

ASSIMILATION

Assimilation, acculturation, romanisation . . . Though different historians have their own preferred word (and may pretend, by using one in preference to another, that their approach has greater sociological or anthropological validity), all these expressions refer to the same process, whereby the behaviour, customs and lifestyles of the conquered population gradually became compatible with and, in the ideal model, indistinguishable from those of the conqueror. None of these terms necessarily implies that this metamorphosis was, on the one hand, part of a deliberate policy of the conqueror, or, on the other, a voluntary imitation of a more advanced culture by a less sophisticated one, though 'romanisation' is used by some writers in the former sense. In reality the process, by whatever name we call it, requires the participation of both conqueror and conquered, though the proportion and result of their involvement may vary. The degree of variation is most evident in the different regional 'patterns' of romanisation found in the Iberian peninsula. The eastern and southern coastal strips became the most thoroughly assimilated, for three reasons: the early date of their incorporation into the Roman world, their previous exposure to Phoenician and Greek civilisation, which helped bridge the transition to Roman culture, and the enthusiasm of Roman merchants, colonists and entrepreneurs for the lucrative economic potential and amenable Mediterranean climate of these zones. The regions bordering on these coasts – the Ebro valley, the southern Meseta and Portugal south of the Tejo – had less claim to these three catalysts of romanisation, and as we move further west and north, the level of assimilation declines accordingly.

Though the story of assimilation properly begins under the Republic, it is only under the Empire that we see it in full flower. Indeed, our observation of this process is facilitated by the assimilation itself: although we lack for this period the literary chronicles that characterised our study of the Republic, there survive the inscriptions, buildings, reliefs and artifacts of daily life, all of which reveal the extent to which the indigenous people were borrowing the material trappings of Roman culture. In this part of the book we shall begin by considering the means by which Rome endeavoured to control the peninsula. We shall then see how Roman influence was felt in social relations, in urban and rural life, in commercial organisation and even in spiritual beliefs. A final chapter tackles the difficult question of what some scholars inelegantly call 'indigenism': the extent to which native traditions withstood the trend to romanisation.

4

THE MACHINERY OF CONTROL

PROVINCIAL ORGANISATION

In the early second century BC, Hispania – at that time consisting essentially of the southern and eastern littorals – was established as two provinces, Ulterior and Citerior. Under Augustus, when the entire peninsula had been conquered, Ulterior was partitioned into Baetica (named after the river Baetis or Guadalquivir) and Lusitania, with the emperor retaining control of the latter. Galicia, at first assigned to Lusitania, was soon transferred to Citerior, presumably for military convenience. Citerior, by far the largest of the three provinces, was also called Tarraconensis after its capital city. Pliny (who was probably procurator of this province) informs us that either name is acceptable and uses them interchangeably, though Ptolemy prefers Tarraconensis. However, as we learn from inscriptions, the provincial governors and priests retained in their titles the formula 'provinciae Hispaniae Citerioris', suggesting that this was still the official name. Moreover, since Tarraconensis was also the name of a *conventus* (judicial district), confusion is best avoided by referring to the province as Citerior.

Although the *conventus* system can trace its origins to the Republican period, the meaning of *conventus* underwent a gradual transformation. A *conventus civium Romanorum* was originally an unofficial association of Roman citizens in a distant land, who banded together for matters of common concern such as trade and defence. These *conventus* naturally tended to be located at major towns, where Roman citizens regularly congregated to conduct business and exchange news. Since these towns thus acted as central

57

meeting places, they were convenient locations for the provincial governor or his delegate to visit and dispense justice during his annual circuit through the province. For instance, as quaestor of Ulterior in 69 BC, Julius Caesar was sent by the governor to conduct the assizes, and one of his stops was Gades. Twenty years later, Caesar tells us, the *conventus civium Romanorum* at Corduba shut their gates against the Pompeian governor Varro, on their own initiative.[1] It is thus clear that in Caesar's day the *conventus* was still an association of Roman citizens, in a town which might be a stop for the circuit court. Under Augustus, however, the purpose of the *conventus* became primarily judicial, and while still centred in a major town it referred not to an association but to a geographic region comprising many lesser towns, whose inhabitants would travel to the central town (or conventual capital, as we may call it) to engage in lawsuits. In addition to this judicial function, the conventual capital retained its importance as a commercial centre, and was now also an administrative centre, with its own *concilium* or 'parliament', and a religious centre, as shown by conventual dedications to the Imperial Cult and the fact that the *conventus Asturum* was originally called '*conventus* of the Altar of Augustus'.[2] There were four *conventus* in Baetica, three in Lusitania, three in the north-west and four in the rest of Citerior (see Map 3); we shall be looking in greater detail at each of the 14 conventual capitals, three of which coincide with provincial capitals, in chapter 6.

From 193 to 155 BC the two Spains, Citerior and Ulterior, were governed by praetors or propraetors, but the intense warfare in the peninsula from 155 to 133 necessitated the appointment of governors of consular rank. In the Late Republic, Citerior was usually consular and Ulterior was usually praetorian, though exceptions are recorded (e.g. Caecilius Metellus as proconsul of Ulterior during the Sertorian war). From 55 to 49 BC Pompey was nominally governor of both Spains, but remained in Italy and governed his province through legates. This practice served as a precedent for Augustus, who appointed a legate of consular rank (commensurate with his control of three legions) in Citerior, and a legate of praetorian rank in the new province of Lusitania. Even the legates were sometimes absentees, most notably L. Arruntius, who was governor of Citerior from AD 23 until probably 37 (the year of his death) but was prevented by Tiberius from going to his province. Baetica, the part of Ulterior which Augustus returned to the Senate, remained proconsular, though the emperor's influence can be seen in some of the appointments, and occasionally he intervened directly by appointing a proconsular legate.[3] Although governors had a wide range of powers, important decisions were subject to approval by the emperor or Senate. Even under the Republic when governors had a relatively free hand in their province, agreements made with the Spaniards required ratification by the Senate, and on rare occasions this was withheld (for example in 137 BC, when the Senate repudiated Hostilius Mancinus' treaty with the Numantines). Also, as we saw in chapter 2, Scipio Aemilianus was criticised for destroying Numantia without senatorial authorisation. Improved communications under the Empire allowed governors to consult with the emperor before making a decision: this can be seen from Pliny's correspondence with Trajan, as well as from preserved rescripts and instructions of the emperors to various other legates, and even to the proconsuls of senatorial provinces.

Much of a governor's time was devoted to the administration of justice. Strabo informs us that the governor of Citerior held assizes in the coastal *conventus* in the winter and in the interior ones in summer. Several inscriptions show the governor arbitrating disputes over property or water rights between cities, tribes or individuals.[4] Each governor also issued a 'provincial edict', essentially a booklet of regulations, which relied in large part upon the edicts of his predecessors. He had sweeping powers of punishment over the provincials, except that Roman citizens had the right of appeal to the emperor. Even this provision was overruled by the future emperor Galba, who as governor of Citerior in the 60s AD crucified a Roman citizen for murder; when the man protested that he was a citizen, Galba ordered him to be placed on a higher cross.[5] In view of the size of his province, the governor of Citerior was allotted a *legatus iuridicus*, appointed by the emperor, to cover part of the assize circuit. These juridical legates are first attested under Tiberius, and in the Antonine period they were explicitly assigned to 'Asturia et Callaecia' (Asturias and Galicia). Quaestors (provincial treasurers of senatorial grade) are found only in the senatorial province of Baetica; in the two imperial provinces (Citerior and Lusitania) finances were controlled by procurators of equestrian grade, whose job included not only taxes but revenues from mines and lands owned by the *fiscus*. There were also subordinate procurators in charge of individual mines, and procurators of Asturia and Callaecia are attested from the principate of Nerva through the Severan period.

TRIBUTE

'Tribute is the price of peace', declared the Spanish cleric Orosius, no doubt aware that the Romans had exacted it from his countrymen with alacrity. The attested booty in gold and silver recorded between 206 and 169 BC brought to the Roman treasury amounted to about 188 million sesterces. The treaties concluded by Ti. Sempronius Gracchus with the Celtiberian tribes in 179 included provision for payment of tribute. Eight years later the Roman Senate, in response to complaints from both Spains, ruled that prefects could not be placed over the towns to collect money, and shortly thereafter the payments seem to have lapsed, for Livy records no tribute after 169 BC.[6] Indeed, when the Senate tried to collect tribute and troops from the Celtiberi in 153, the demand was refused on the grounds that the Romans had released them from this obligation 'after Gracchus'; and Appian concedes that this was true. The Lusitanian war had already begun, and it has recently been suggested that the series of Iberian bronze and silver coins on the *denarius* standard, minted in Catalonia, the Ebro valley, and (in bronze only) in Ulterior, should begin in 155/4, as a means of paying a tax imposed on cities to help finance the war.[7] It is questionable whether this coinage could be organised quite so soon, or whether the cities of Citerior would be liable to subsidise a campaign in Ulterior; but once Celtiberia joined the insurrection and Rome sent in additional troops, the need for funds became acute. After the abortive peace arrangements of 152 the war resumed with vigour in both provinces the following year, which would seem a likely occasion for the Romans to squeeze the loyal cities for money, and hence a plausible date for the commencement of the Iberian *denarius* coinage. We hear nothing further about tribute until 70 BC, when Cicero informs us that the Spanish provinces pay a fixed tax, called tributary, as war reparation: 'vectigal . . . certum, quod stipendiarium dicitur . . . quasi victoriae praemium ac poena belli'. It is reasonable to assume that this was paid in cash and collected on an annual basis. Much of the money in fact never reached Rome, for the governor needed a large sum to pay his troops and to meet other expenses. Indeed in the 50s BC, Pompey drew thousands of talents from the Roman treasury to finance his proconsulship of Citerior.[8] Another imposition, which has sometimes been misinterpreted as a tax, was the requirement for Spaniards to sell five per cent of their grain to Rome. At first they were obliged to accept whatever price the provincial government set, until the Senate in 171 BC abolished this artificial price-fixing. But later in the century the Spaniards were again being cheated. When the governor Q. Fabius Maximus Allobrogicus sent Spanish grain to Rome in 123 BC, Gaius Gracchus persuaded the Senate to sell it and remit the money to the cities of Spain, which Fabius had apparently not paid.[9] Not all of the grain went to Italy: some was undoubtedly used to feed the provincial army, and in AD 44 the governor of Baetica was dismissed for not sending enough grain to the army in neighbouring Mauretania. But there is no evidence that the Spaniards were not reimbursed, and indeed the younger Pliny in AD 100 stresses that harvests are not confiscated from the provinces but are willingly paid for by the treasury (though perhaps this represents Trajan's cancellation of a Flavian confiscation).[10] Whether the Spanish cities were still obliged to sell five per cent of their harvest to Rome is unclear; the availability of Egyptian grain under the Empire may have made this regulation obsolete.

THE EMPEROR AND THE PROVINCES

A crucial factor in our understanding of the role of Spain under the Empire is the relationship between the emperor and the provinces. To begin, we should consider why the Spanish provinces were particularly important to the emperor. An obvious reason was the revenues which accrued to the *fiscus* from mines and taxes in the two imperial provinces, and to the emperor from his personal estates. (We know very little about the extent of such estates, except that the emperor owned property in all provinces, and that Nero's properties in Spain were profitably sold by the rebellious Galba.)[11] But financial gain was not the sole or necessarily the greatest importance of Spain to the emperors. The peninsula held a strategic position, guarding Mediterranean access to the Atlantic and hence the security of Roman trading routes to Britain, western Gaul and the Rhine. In addition to this commercial advantage, a foothold on the Atlantic was of great psychological significance because Ocean (as the ancients called the Atlantic) was thought to have been established by the gods as the boundary of the earth; thus, by conquering the very shores of the Atlantic, the Romans could claim that their empire extended to the edge of the world. As one of the major regions of the empire, Spain could also serve a propaganda purpose, as is shown by its frequent appearance on coins. During the civil war of 68–9, Galba (who had been proclaimed emperor in Spain) issued seven coin types labelled 'Hispania' or 'consensus Hispaniarum', and his example was followed by Vitellius and Vespasian. Some years later, Hadrian issued coins to commemorate his visit to the peninsula, on which he is called the restorer of Spain ('restitutor Hispaniae'). A final importance of Spain was as a power-base for prospective emperors. After Galba revealed the *arcanum imperii* that an emperor could be created in the provinces, various pretenders attempted either to initiate their bid for imperial power in Spain (for example Cornelius Priscianus, governor of Citerior, in 145) or to include Spain in a western support bloc for a revolt begun in Britain or Gaul (Clodius Albinus in 197, Bonosus in 280, Magnus Maximus in 383, Constantine III in 408).

The emperors often had direct, personal contacts with Spain. Some were Spanish by birth or at least had family origins in the Peninsula. Trajan, for instance, was born at Italica, Hadrian either at Italica or at Rome of a family from Italica. The family of Marcus Aurelius came from Ucubi in Baetica, while Theodosius in the fourth century was a native of Cauca in Citerior. Moreover, some emperors had previous service in Spain. The young Octavius (later Augustus) had been there with Caesar in 45 BC, and Tiberius had served as a military tribune in the Cantabrian war. Galba had been governor of Citerior, and Otho of Lusitania, to which distant province he had been sent because Nero coveted his wife. Trajan was commander of the Seventh Legion in 89 and led it from Spain to Germany to help quell the revolt of Saturninus. Septimius Severus also served in Spain, apparently as *legatus iuridicus* of Asturia and Callaecia, *c.* 178–80. The only emperor who actually campaigned in Spain during the Early Empire was Augustus, who seems to have spent less time at the front than at Tarraco, where he held court and received embassies. Tarraco was also the focus of a visit by Hadrian, the travelling emperor, in the winter of 122–3. Here he narrowly escaped being assassinated by a madman, and was gently rebuffed by the provincial council on the question of conscription. He may also have toured Baetica, since coins commemorating his visit display an olive or olive branch, symbolic of the prosperity of this oil-rich province, and an inscription records his *liberalitates* to

Baetica. Perhaps, in accordance with his practice of touring military installations, he also visited the base of the Seventh Legion at León. The visit of the emperor (who was virtually a demigod) was a rare event which must have drawn and impressed large crowds. It enabled both emperor and subjects to view each other at first hand. Imperial visits entailed considerable trouble and expense for the host cities, which had to provide for the emperor's every need, but their diligence might be repaid by a grant of special favours. It is difficult to believe that Italica was not on Hadrian's itinerary, and indeed the mention in the *Historia Augusta* of an address by Hadrian to the 'Italici' (Italians) may be a misunderstanding for 'Italicenses'. At any rate, Italica was granted the status of colony and apparently received financial assistance, for the city was nearly doubled in size and endowed with magnificent public buildings.[12]

The emperors also had indirect contacts with the peninsula. Virtually all the emperors of the Early Empire, and many under the Late Empire, are named on milestones as authorising the construction or repair of public roads. Various cities received favours from the emperor, such as municipal status (primarily under Augustus and Vespasian), public works, or additional settlers (such as when Otho sent new colonists to Emerita and Hispalis). The public works provided by the emperors may be more numerous than we realise: Hadrian, for instance, is said to have built public monuments in all places without putting his name on them.[13] When a city went into debt, the emperor appointed a *curator rei publicae* to oversee its finances; in Spain such curators are first attested in the Antonine period. The emperors could also bestow citizenship, either by a *viritim* grant to individuals, or by conferring *ius Latii* on a community. Claudius, who allegedly wanted to see all Spaniards in the toga, is recorded making a *viritim* grant to a local magistrate of the unprivileged town of Ammaia. *Ius Latii*, which was already widespread in Baetica in the Augustan period, was bestowed lavishly by Vitellius and especially by Vespasian, who allegedly conferred it upon all of Spain ('universae Hispaniae').[14] This phrase is either an exaggeration or is to be interpreted as meaning, 'in all parts of Spain', for it is certain that not every town received this privilege. Under the terms of *ius Latii*, all citizens of the town became Latin citizens, and the annual magistrates and their families became Roman citizens. Another privilege which could be granted by the emperor was adlection, whereby prominent individuals were appointed into the Roman Senate. Vespasian was active in promoting Spaniards, and those elevated to the Senate in his reign included the future emperor Trajan. Trajan and Hadrian in turn recruited new senators, so that Spaniards made up about 25 per cent of the Senate.[15] After Hadrian, this proportion dwindled as an increasing number of senators were admitted from the eastern provinces.

Provincials could request the emperor's assistance by means of a petition (*libellus*), normally delivered by an embassy; the emperor had a special secretary, the *a libellis*, to help handle these documents. The petition would be sent by the local senate (*ordo decurionum*) of a city, or by the council (*concilium*) representing a *conventus* or a province. Often these petitions resulted in action or advice from the emperor: for instance, when the Balearic Islands appealed to Augustus for help against a plague of rabbits, he sent in troops, and when the *concilium* of Baetica inquired about the appropriate punishment for cattle thieves, Hadrian replied that they should be condemned to the arena or, in the case of notorious offenders, to the mines.[16] The emperor's rescript or reply to a municipal petition was sometimes engraved and posted publicly. Two such inscriptions survive, both from the Flavian period, and are worth quoting to illustrate the variety of issues which could form the subject of petitions, and the varying degrees of sympathy accorded them by the emperor. Both are of particular interest in that they come from Baetica, a senatorial province where the emperor, in theory, had no authority, but in practice, seems to have intervened freely. The first document, dated AD 77, is from Sabora, a hill fort in the interior of the province, which wanted to move to a more favourable location and to adopt the Flavian name (thereby becoming a *municipium Flavium*):

> The emperor Vespasian . . . to the quattuorvirs and decurions of the Saborans. Since you allege that your town is burdened with many difficulties, I authorise you to build a town under my name on the plain, as you wish. I confirm the revenues which you say you were awarded by the deified Augustus. If you want to add any new ones you must approach the governor about them, for I cannot make a decision without his recommendation. I received your decree on 25 July and sent your envoys home on the 29th. Farewell.[17]

In the second rescript, dated two years later, the citizens of Munigua receive a less charitable reply from the popular emperor Titus, whom they had petitioned for exemption from paying a debt. Unlike the request for new revenues foreseen in the previous example, which would be forwarded through the governor to the emperor for a decision, the Muniguans were trying to overturn a judgement by the governor himself. Such an appeal, as Tacitus informs us, was illegal and carried a penalty, which the Muniguans narrowly escape in this rescript:

> The emperor Titus ... sends greetings to the quattuorvirs and decurions of Munigua. Since you appealed in the hope of not paying the money which, according to the judgement of Sempronius Fuscus [the previous governor], you owed to Servilius Pollio, you should have been assessed the penalty for wrongful appeal. But I have preferred to answer with my forgiveness rather than with your rashness, and I have written off the 50,000 sesterces [penalty] to the public poverty that you claim. I have furthermore written to my friend Gallicanus the governor, that should you pay the money which was awarded to Pollio, he should absolve you from the calculation of interest from the day the judgement was given. It is only fair that the revenue from your local taxes, which you declare that Pollio had contracted, should be taken into consideration, so that your city will lose nothing on this count. Farewell. Issued on 7 September.[18]

Whether through flattery or genuine gratitude, the provincials set up numerous memorials to the emperor. Sometimes these appear on important public works, such as the bridge of Alcántara, dedicated to the emperor Trajan in AD 105. Sometimes too the motive is relatively transparent: at Munigua, Vespasian is hailed as censor, in which capacity he had granted the city *ius Latii* in AD 73–4, while at Hispalis, the volunteer firemen's association thanks Antoninus Pius for his 'indulgence' in allowing them to form a *collegium*, though limited to 100 members.[19] Several of the Julio-Claudians were patrons or honorary duovirs (chief magistrates) of various Spanish cities, and an inscription from Aritium in Lusitania contains a detailed oath of loyalty to the new emperor Gaius (Caligula) in 37, in which all the citizens swear vengeance against his enemies, under threat of punishment by the gods.[20] We shall defer until chapter 8 the question of whether the imperial cult involved true worship of the emperor or was simply a political instrument for ensuring the loyalty of the provincials.

LOCAL GOVERNMENT

For most people in Roman Spain, the level of government which had the greatest impact on their daily lives was that of the city in whose territory they resided. Even the taxes paid to Rome were collected by the cities and forwarded to the provincial authorities. In rural areas – and it should be borne in mind that most people lived in the country – the taxes were probably collected by the local village (*vicus*) or district (*pagus*) on behalf of the city to which it was attributed. Most important towns held the privilege of being a colony (mostly dating to the time of Caesar and Augustus) or *municipium* (a status distributed liberally in Spain by Vespasian). In principle a colony was a settlement of Roman citizens, usually army veterans, founded on a new site and under the control of Rome, while a *municipium* was an indigenous community which had been granted *ius Latii* (Latin citizenship for the townsfolk and Roman citizenship for the magistrates) but retained its local autonomy. In practice we know of colonies which were established on the sites of indigenous towns (e.g. Urso) or which included natives as well as Romans (e.g. Corduba). Moreover, the charters of the Flavian *municipia* reveal that Rome imposed a great many administrative regulations on the *municipes* and made them subject to Roman law, so that local autonomy was in many respects limited. Indeed, the surviving charter fragments from several Baetican *municipia* (notably Malaca, Salpensa and Irni) are virtually identical in wording, leaving little doubt that they are copies of a prescribed Flavian municipal law imposed uniformly on all such towns. One special privilege enjoyed by colonies was *ius Italicum* (exemption from land tax), and it was perhaps for this reason that the *municipium* of Italica requested from Hadrian a change of status to the theoretically more dependent rank of colony.

Local authority was in the hands of the *ordo decurionum* or senate. This body, analogous to the Senate at Rome, consisted of members of the local elite who were able to meet the five criteria for admission: free birth, age between 25 and 55 years, residence in the city, lack of moral or legal taint, and a property qualification. The property qualification probably varied from town to town, as did the number of decurions. The municipal charter of Irni specifies 63 members and the Flavian senate-house at Conimbriga could similarly have seated up to 60, whereas in larger cities the number of decurions might be several hundred.[21] In some cities, two senates are attested, voting separately on some matters and collectively ('in universum') on others. At Singilia and Valentia, one of these is called the 'old order' (*ordo vetus* or *veteres*), and we know from Italian parallels that the other *ordo* was sometimes called *novi* or *novani*. To judge from these titles, the two *ordines* do not represent upper and lower houses (in the sense of decurial and plebeian 'orders'), but are rather the result of the city being dramatically expanded in population through annexation of new territory or the arrival of additional settlers. The newly incorporated citizens would want political representation, but the old *ordo* would not be willing to surrender half its seats: hence the creation of a second senate. Thus at the colony of Valentia the second *ordo* is called the 'veterans', implying the arrival of a new wave of discharged legionaries, perhaps after the civil wars of the 40s and 30s BC.

As at Rome, magistrates were elected on a yearly basis by the people, who were divided into a limited number of voting units (*curiae*). Whether these units were equivalent to geographic 'wards' or were allotted in some other manner is unclear, but the provision in the Flavian municipal law that all resident aliens (*incolae*) will be arbitrarily assigned to a single *curia* tells against a strictly geographic division. Since magistrates were elected in pairs, each *curia* voted for two candidates, and the two who carried the most *curiae* won the election. In most cities, whether colonies or *municipia*, there were two chief magistrates called duovirs, two deputies called aediles, and two treasurers called quaestors. The duovirs and aediles were sometimes collectively designated as quattuorvirs (meaning 'board of four'), though this title is not found everywhere and its use seems to have been a matter of local preference. Although quaestors are provided for in the Flavian municipal law and also occur in substantial numbers at colonies like Tarraco and Valentia, there are many other cities where no quaestors are attested at all. This may mean either that some cities did not have this type of magistrate, or that for some reason (such as the lowness of the office compared with the other magistracies, or the unpopular role of the quaestor as tax collector) mention of a quaestorship was frequently omitted from inscriptions outlining the careers of local aristocrats.[22] In a few towns we find magistrates with unusual titles, such as decemvirs ('board of ten'), praetors or censors; since most of these date to the first century BC and none is later than the Julio-Claudian period, they tend to suggest that cities under the Republic were allowed greater flexibility in choosing titles for their magistrates than was later the case.

Each of the magistrates had a prescribed set of duties. The duovirs presided over the local senate, consulting with the decurions on a variety of religious, financial and administrative matters. They also served as local justices in civil suits involving amounts up to 1,000 sesterces, as we learn from a recently discovered copy of the Flavian municipal law. Every fifth year the duovirs acted as *quinquennales*, responsible to conduct the local census of citizens and their property, from which poll- and property taxes were calculated. Our understanding of the duties of aediles and quaestors was largely conjectural until quite recently, when the chapters dealing with these magistrates were unearthed in southern Spain. As we now know, the aediles had the same juridical powers as the duovirs. In addition they were in charge of the grain supply, temples, streets, sewers, baths, markets, the fire department, weights and measures, and any other duties assigned to them by the decurions. Clearly the aediles were very busy men, but were assisted by slaves belonging to the *municipium*. A similar situation applied in the colonies; a water pipe from Caesaraugusta, for instance, is inscribed with the names of the aedile and the public slave who installed it. The principal duty of the quaestors was, in the words of the municipal law, the 'collecting, disbursing, safeguarding, managing and controlling' of public funds, as directed by the duovirs. The quaestors also had public slaves to assist them, who presumably included book-keepers and guards. In Republican times, when many Spanish towns were issuing their own coinage, the quaestors may also have been in charge of the local mint, though the coin legends often name the duovirs of the year.[23]

The city's expenses were covered in part by the magistrates and decurions themselves, who are frequently attested donating monuments, distributing grain to the people, or sponsoring public entertainments. There may also have been a requirement for a *summa honoraria* (cash donation to the city in exchange for being made a magistrate), though the surviving evidence is inconclusive. However, the bulk of local revenues came from rentals (e.g. of public lands), fines awarded by the magistrates, and various kinds of local taxes (*vectigalia*). Contractors were hired locally to collect the *vectigalia*, like Servilius Pollio at Munigua, and were apparently subject to a fine if collection was deficient.[24] Under the Empire, towns were not allowed to initiate new *vectigalia*, as we learn from Vespasian's rescript to Sabora. The revenues were probably modest, but with sound financial management a community could balance its books. If, however, a city fell hopelessly into debt (as occurred fairly often from the Antonine period onward), the emperor would appoint a *curator rei publicae* of senatorial or equestrian rank to monitor the town's finances and curb unnecessary spending. Curators are attested in only a handful of Spanish cities, but the list includes all three provincial capitals as well as such famous towns as Italica and Urso.[25] The financial demise of the provincial capitals may have been attributable in part to the inescapable burden of supporting the governor and his retinue.

THE PEACEKEEPING FORCE AND ITS BASES

After Augustus' Cantabrian war there were no major revolts in Spain, though we do hear of a campaign against the Astures in the late 50s, for which a centurion of the Sixth Legion was decorated, and there may have been other, unrecorded disturbances.[26] Certainly the potential existed for an uprising among the peoples of the north and north-west, hence the need for constant military vigilance. By maintaining a physical presence in northern Spain, the well-trained and strategically positioned legionary strike forces acted as an effective deterrent to revolt. Moreover, in the absence of a police force, the responsibility for protection of mines and roads against bandits, of the governor against assassination, and of government installations against sabotage, devolved upon the army. Augustus' pacification of the north-west allowed the reduction of the Spanish garrison from seven legions to three – the *IV Macedonica*, *VI Victrix* and *X Gemina* – and the transfer of the remainder to the Rhine-Danube front, where the military need was greater. One of these, the *II Augusta*, is sometimes supposed to have been posted to Germany after the Varian disaster of AD 9, but there is no evidence that it remained in Spain so late, and a likelier context for its departure is the preparation for Drusus' German campaigns of 12–9 BC.[27] There was simply no justification for four legions in a province where all fighting had ceased. Augustus' final tour of Spain in 13 BC enabled him not only to reassure himself that its conquest was complete, but to earmark idle legions for the German and Pannonian offensives being planned for the following year.

By the end of the Julio-Claudian period the number of legions was further reduced to one, an indication that the conquered peoples were adapting to Roman rule and that the danger of revolt appeared small. The Fourth Legion was moved to Germany, probably in preparation for Gaius Caligula's abortive invasion of Britain in 40; it is definitely attested at Mainz in 43 (being excluded, ironically, from Claudius' British invasion). The Tenth Legion was sent to Carnuntum in 63 to replace the Fifteenth, recently dispatched to the Parthian front. Five years later Galba, governor of Citerior, revealed an important secret of empire: that an emperor could be created not only in the provinces, but by a provincial army.[28] Not only did Galba rely on the Sixth Legion, hispanised by nearly a century of service in the peninsula, and including Spanish-born recruits, but he raised a new legion of provincials, the *VII Galbiana* (or *Hispana*), as well as several auxiliary units – of which we know of two cohorts of Basques and an *ala Sulpicia civium Romanorum*.[29] In fact, Galba left the *VI Victrix* to hold Spain (though he took its commander, T. Vinius, with him), and thus it was his Spanish levies which really swept him to power. After reaching Rome, the Seventh Legion was posted to Pannonia and later participated, with heavy casualties, in the battle of Cremona.[30] To protect Spain from an invasion by the pro-Othonian governor of Mauretania, Vitellius sent *X Gemina* to Baetica during his march to Rome, and later reinforced the Spanish garrison with *I Adiutrix* (conscripted from the fleet by Nero), of which a member seems to be attested at Emerita. All three legions were withdrawn from Spain by Mucianus in 70 to deal with the revolt of Civilis.[31] The new emperor Vespasian reconstituted the Seventh Legion under the name *VII Gemina* (twin), presumably because it combined the remnants of *VII Galbiana* and of some other legion which had suffered heavily. The reconstituted legion was stationed at León, probably the former home of *VI Victrix*, and remained there for virtually the rest of the imperial period, though it was temporarily withdrawn in 89 under its commander, the future emperor Trajan, to deal with the revolt of Saturninus, and it sometimes sent vexillations to other provinces. In fact, Citerior was one of the quietest provinces to boast a legion, fitting perfectly with Josephus' description of the army as an 'ornament of peace-time', and its command would be a 'safe' posting for an untested general.[32]

Recruiting patterns, too, illustrate the provincialisation of the army in Spain. During the Julio-Claudian period, although the army was still largely Italian,[33] we find a substantial number of legionaries from Spain, chiefly under Claudius and Nero. The majority of these came from Baetica, which was the most romanised of the three provinces, already contained many Roman citizens and was thus a logical province for a *dilectus* or recruiting drive. The practice of enrolling peregrines in the legions was not widespread in the western provinces in this period,[34] and as will be seen below, even the auxiliary cohorts consisted of Roman citizens. If we then assume that the recruits from Spain were mostly Roman citizens, at a time when few indigenes had been granted such citizenship, it follows that many of these 'Spanish' recruits were of Italian stock. In the Flavian period we find a few Italians in the Seventh Legion, but the bulk of the Spanish legionaries, whether serving in or out of Spain, come from Citerior and Lusitania, and there are no Baeticans attested in the Seventh Legion. This change of geographic focus suggests that recruiting efforts were now concentrated in the two imperial provinces. The trend becomes even clearer in the second and third centuries when there are virtually no Italian soldiers in Spain and the bulk of Spanish legionaries (serving nearly exclusively in *VII Gemina*) come from Citerior, and more specifically Galicia, the legion's home ground.[35] The Seventh Legion, then, which origi-nated in a levy of Spaniards, remained a predominantly provincial, and ultimately regional, organisation. Citerior, the senior armed province in the empire, thus became the prototype of military provincialisation, of local recruitment and local attachment, which was emulated in Africa, Germany and Syria (though not in Britain, where indigenes are not attested in the legions).

In addition to the legions there were several auxiliary cohorts stationed in Spain. In the period from Augustus to Gaius there were four infantry cohorts (*cohortes civium Romanorum quattuor in Hispania*) under the overall command of an equestrian prefect, and at least one cavalry squadron, the *ala II Gallorum*.[36] A *tessera hospitalis* of AD 40 from Clunia, extending friendship to C. Terentius Bassus, prefect of an *ala Augusta*, is most easily explained if this unit was stationed in northern Spain.[37] But the grant of hospitality need not imply that the squadron had been in Spain for a long time; on the contrary, its intent could have been to welcome a squadron recently arrived to replace the *legio IV Macedonica*. Under Claudius, the *ala II Gallorum* was sent to Upper Germany, and the only auxiliary unit attested in Spain (though there were probably more) is a *cohors IV Gallorum*, whose boundary stones have been found about 20 km south-east of Astorga.[38] Less secure is a *cohors Thracum*, attested by a single epitaph of Claudian date at Astorga, yet reminiscent of Tacitus' account of the Thracians in AD 26 balking at being conscripted and sent to the far corners of the empire. On the other hand, we know that in 68 the governor of Citerior controlled two *alae* and three cohorts.[39] The overall impression, then, is that the number of cohorts had been reduced from four to three since the time of Augustus, while the number of *alae* had either been increased from one to two (perhaps in compensation for the reduction in legions) or had been two throughout. We thus arrive at the following *schema* for the Julio-Claudian period:

Augustus to Gaius:
4 *cohortes civium Romanorum*
ala II Gallorum
[*ala Augusta?*]

Claudius to Nero:
cohors IV Gallorum
cohors [*Thracum?*]
cohors . . .
ala [*Augusta?*]
ala . . .

After the civil war of 68–9, the auxiliaries were again rearranged. The *ala II Flavia Hispanorum civium Romanorum*, 500 strong, moved into the camp of Petavonium recently abandoned by *legio X Gemina*. The squadron is still attested here in a third-century inscription, and the *Notitia Dignitatum* (written in the fifth century, but apparently using outdated information)[40] records a *cohors II Flavia Pacatiana* at Petavonium which, if *cohors* is not an error for *ala*, suggests that the unit had been converted from horse to foot. The *Notitia* lists several other auxiliary units in Spain, namely a *cohors Lucensis* at Lucus Augusti, *cohors Celtibera* at Iuliobriga, *cohors I Gallica* at Veleia and *cohors II Gallica* at a site unhelpfully named after the cohort. Of this last unit we have no further news, but *cohors I Gallica equitata civium Romanorum* (i.e., mounted infantry) is epigraphically attested in Spain as early as the second century AD. A decurion of 'coh. I Celtib.' is named on a dedication at Villalís in the gold-mining region of León, and a *cohors I Celtiberorum* which may be the same unit is attested in other texts. A lost inscription of the first century AD from Lucus Augusti seems to refer to a soldier of *cohors III Luce(n)s(ium?)*, but since five Lucensian cohorts are known, there is no guarantee that this is the same unit mentioned in the *Notitia*, nor indeed that *cohors III* actually served in Spain.[41]

The stability of the 'imperial peace' permitted the establishment of permanent camps for both legionaries and auxiliaries, with the possibility of more comfortable accommodation than in Republican times. This meant the construction not only of stone buildings (a great asset in the biting winter winds of northern Spain) but also of baths and recreational facilities for the soldiers, and of civilian-operated *tabernae* outside the camp gates. Disgracefully we have only succeeded in finding a few of the camps used by various legions and auxiliary units of the early Empire, though in some cases legions and auxiliaries may have been collocated. One of the known camps is Petavonium (Rosinos de Vidriales), occupied by *legio X Gemina* until 63 and reoccupied by the *ala II Flavia* probably after the civil war, though the earliest datable finds are second-century. The camp, which is said to cover 4.7 ha, has long been recognised as too small to accommodate more than a small detachment. More recently, aerial photography confirmed by field survey suggests that this camp was surrounded by a larger one of 442 × 285 m, or 12.6 ha.[42] Even this is only half the normal size of a legionary base (about 25 ha for 5600 men). However, the smaller camp would be more than adequate for the roughly 500 men of a cavalry squadron. Examples from Britain average 3.1 ha (7.7 acres), while those in Germany and Raetia range from 3.1 to 4.2.[43] On the basis of the reported dimensions it would appear that the larger camp, base of *legio X Gemina*, actually only accommodated half the legion at any time, the remainder being detached as vexillations to towns, mines or forts, and that when the *ala* was assigned to the same site it built the smaller but more than ample camp. This camp, surrounded by a wall at least 1.5 m thick, contained foundations and construction materials of numerous buildings. One investigator reported finding, adjacent to the east wall, a tank-like compartment with thin, concrete walls coated in red plaster (perhaps hydraulic cement?), but provided with an entrance.[44] The description is too vague to allow us to conclude that this pool is part of the baths donated by the squadron commander L. Versenus Aper, which, together with the temple of Hercules erected here by another squadron commander, M. Sellius Honoratus, might help account for the unusual size of the camp.[45] More recently, however, Patrick Le Roux has recalculated the dimensions of the large camp as 540 × 345 m and of the small camp as 255 × 210 m. If these measurements are correct, they would yield an area of 18.6 ha for the larger camp (just big enough to house a legion) and 5.3 ha for the smaller (sufficiently large for both an *ala* and a cohort: compare, for a similar combination of troops, camps of 5.2 ha at Echzell and Frankfurt).[46]

Identifying the base of *legio IV Macedonica* has proved to be more problematic. It was long assumed to be in the vicinity of Aguilar de Campóo in the upper valley of the Pisuerga, well within Cantabrian territory. However, the boundary stones of the legion's grazing lands (*prata*) cover a distance of about 55 km, from the limits of Iuliobriga (Retortillo) to those of Segisamo (Sasamón), and the legionary base might be anywhere within this zone. Moreover, the discovery of *terra sigillata* and tiles bearing the stamp 'L.IIII.MA' at Herrera de Pisuerga (ancient Pisoraca, as we learn from nearby milestones) suggested that the legion's pottery was produced here, and apparent confirmation arrived in 1983 with the excavation of a rectangular kiln of stone and mud brick at the nearby site of La Jericó. It was of course possible, if curious, that the legion's pottery was manufactured at a distance from the base (Herrera being 23 km south-west of Aguilar). But in 1984, four trenches sunk at the suspected site of the camp – ironically adjacent to the present barracks of the Civil Guard – unearthed not only stone walls but a large quantity of first-century AD pottery, glass, bone, stucco and metal, including a cache of iron lance heads and daggers, bronze and silver coins and a strigil. These new finds, together with the legion's stamped pottery, the importation of South Gaulish *sigillata*, and milestones attesting a road to Pisuerga under Tiberius, make a strong though not definitive case for locating the legionary base at Herrera, and postulating that the *canabae* which sprang up around it formed the nucleus of the town of Pisoraca, which survived the legion's departure for Mainz (c. AD 40).[47] Also, if trouble was expected from the Cantabri, the legion would be more securely sited on their outskirts than surrounded by them.

But the principal legionary base is that at León, named after *legio VII Gemina* but perhaps earlier (to judge from a fragmentary inscription with the tantalising suffix '. . . trix') the home of *legio VI Victrix*.[48] It is located at the confluence of the river Bernesga and its tributary the Torio, at an elevation of some 820 m. Measuring 570 × 350 m, it encloses an area of slightly under 20 ha and is thus comparable in size with many other legionary bases.[49] The site was amply furnished with water, both from the two rivers

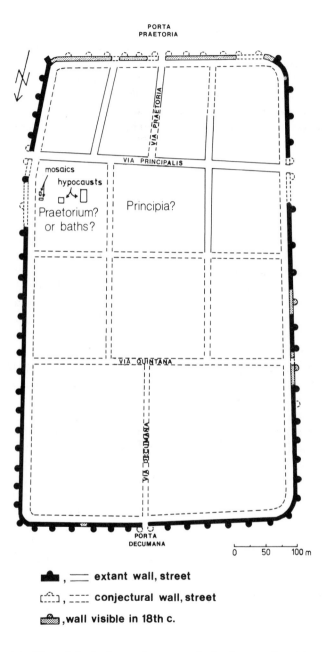

Figure 4.1 Plan of the legionary fortress at León. Source: Based in part on Risco (1792) and García y Bellido (1970).

and from the *fons Amaevus*, a local spring whose nymphs the legion's commandant commemorated on two identically worded altars, early in the reign of Antoninus Pius.[50] The outline of the camp is still preserved in the Late Roman fortification wall, most of which is still visible except on the south, and even this side could largely be seen in the eighteenth century (Figure 4.1).[51] Immediately inside this massive (5.25 m thick) circuit wall is an earlier wall, much lower and narrower (1.8 m) and built of dressed and cemented blocks, the top courses of which were obviously robbed to build the grand, fourth-century version with its seventy-odd projecting towers.[52] Like all legionary fortresses, the wall of León was punctuated with four gates, each of which would have been flanked by towers. Although Roman camps were usually rectangular, minor adjustments sometimes had to be made to conform with the terrain, e.g., at Nijmegen in Germany (home of *X Gemina* from 70 to 104) where the north-east corner of the walled camp bulges to skirt the edge of a cliff.[53] In the case of León, the ground slopes away sharply in the south-east corner of the camp, necessitating an inward bending of the east wall at a 10 degree angle to its theoretical course. Just inside the wall (as we know from other legionary bases) would be a circuit lane.

The principal east-west corridor through the camp was the Via Principalis, which must correspond, as Richmond realised, with the present Calle de Generalísimo Franco, the only street to pierce both the east and west walls.[54] The Via Principalis should pass through both walls at right angles; however, because of the improvised angle of the east wall this could not be done without bending the Via. To avoid this, the Via seems to have been laid at a 94 degree angle to the west wall, so that the street would remain straight yet appear to cross both walls at right angles. The Via Praetoria, joining the Principalis to the south gate, could have run either parallel to the west wall or perpendicular to the Principalis; the angle of the present Cardiles Street suggests the latter solution. The Via Praetoria passed out of the camp through the Porta Praetoria or main gate. From here it was only a few miles' march to the Tarraco-Asturica highway described in the Antonine Itinerary. At Asturica the road split into three forks, one leading to Lucus, one to Bracara, and one south to Emerita with a branch passing through Clunia to Caesaraugusta. The camp was thus strategically positioned to allow rapid 'strike routes' to almost any trouble spot in the peninsula. The position of the other east-west street in the camp, the Via

Quintana, cannot be identified with certainty, especially since it was an internal street only and did not pierce the circuit wall. From this street the Via Decumana ran at right angles towards the Porta Decumana, securely identified with the modern Puerta del Castillo, the only gap in the middle of the north wall. From here a local road presumably continued northward into Cantabria. The standard layout of the interior buildings of legionary bases is well known,[55] though minor variations do occur. The *principia* (headquarters) should be just north of the Principalis-Praetoria intersection, but its limits cannot be traced with any semblance of accuracy because the winding medieval streets generally ignore the Roman camp grid. However, Cervantes Street, parallel to the west wall at one-third the width of the camp, conceivably perpetuates the lane on the west side of the *principia*. The *praetorium* (commandant's house) ought to stand behind the *principia*. However, García y Bellido excavated a building with mosaics and hypocausts to the east of the *principia* (beneath the present Cathedral), which might belong to the *praetorium*. Alternatively it could be a bath building: nearly all legionary bases have baths within the camp boundaries, some of them exceeding 100 m in length.[56] The location of other buildings within the camp can only be guessed. Nearest to the wall would be the soldiers' barrack blocks, while the centre of the camp would contain tribunes' quarters, granary, storehouses and workshops.

5

SOCIAL STATUS AND SOCIAL RELATIONS

THE ELITE

Like all agrarian societies, the Roman Empire was characterised by conspicuous social inequality and imbalance of wealth. Even the 'upper class' of Roman society was not homogeneous but comprised three elite strata, based on wealth and free birth. In descending order these were the senatorial class (men with property worth 1,000,000 sesterces), the *equites* (worth 400,000 sesterces) and the decurions or local aristocrats, whose property value is attested as 100,000 sesterces at Comum in northern Italy, but may have varied from town to town throughout the Empire.

Two important observations need to be made at the outset. First, the widespread assumption that the pre-Roman elite was 'supplanted' by a 'ruling class' of Romans and Italians, can no longer be supported.[1] Instead we must recognise the development of an 'Hispano-Roman' elite, composed of a combination of Italian settlers and romanised indigenes. The former category are mostly to be found in towns established by Rome, such as the veteran colonies; the indigenous towns, many of which had received municipal status by the Flavian period, remained in the control of local families which gradually became romanised. We can see this transformation clearly in the coinage and inscriptions of the Late Republic, in which local magistrates still bear indigenous nomenclature like Iskerbeles and Deivorix, and sometimes titles like *princeps*, which are Latin translations of pre-Roman tribal appointments. An inscription from Contrebia in the Ebro valley, dating to 87 BC, shows that the town was governed by a *praetor* with the delightful name 'Lubbus Urdinocum, son of Letondo', and a council of five men vaguely titled *magistratus*. As time

Figure 5.1   The career inscription of Q. Iulius Maximus and his sons; 3rd century AD. From Nossa Senhora da Tourega; now in the Museu Regional de Evora.

goes on, local magistrates abandon the ancestral nomenclature and adopt Roman names: we see this transition in examples of the type 'Granius Silo, son of Elaesus', where the son's name is Latin but the father's is not. The significance of Vespasian's grant of *ius Latii* to 'all' of Spain was that it extended Roman citizenship to the local magistrates: these men were clearly indigenes, not Italians, for the latter had been awarded Roman citizenship in 89 BC. Many local magistrates in fact belonged to the voting tribe Quirina, in which new citizens were enrolled in the Flavian period, and several of them explicitly state that they received the citizenship *per honorem* in this period. Nor were indigenes restricted to municipal office-holding. Of the ten known Roman senators from Lusitania, seven came from the indigenous town of Ebora.[2] The careers of three of these, Q. Iulius Maximus and his sons Clarus and Nepotianus, are recorded in an inscription from their villa at Nossa Senhora da Tourega (Figure 5.1).

The second point to note is that social mobility is closely linked to the level of romanisation. Only persons from deeply romanised areas of the peninsula – primarily Baetica and the east coast – could hope for much social advancement. We know of nearly 100 senators from Baetica, of both Italian and indigenous descent; more than 50 of them held the consulship, beginning with L. Cornelius Balbus of Gades in 40 BC. The Baetican senators are represented by only 32 *nomina*, suggesting a relatively closed elite controlled by certain

79

families. In Citerior there are some 30 known senators, virtually all from the east coast or the Ebro valley.[3] The shortage of senators from the interior and from the north-west is striking. In both provinces, the period of maximum accessibility to the Senate runs from Vespasian through Hadrian; after this, there is a marked increase in new senators from the eastern Mediterranean, at the expense of the western provinces. One of the Baetican senators, Trajan, was the first emperor from a provincial family (the Ulpii, of Umbrian origin but resident at Italica). However, it should be noted that although Trajan entered the Senate under Vespasian, his family had long been senatorial, and his father, M. Ulpius Traianus, had served as a legionary commander and proconsul of Baetica before Vespasian's accession. A certain M. Traius, a magistrate and benefactor of Italica in the first century BC, is possibly an ancestor of the Trajan family.[4] A similar geographic pattern applies to the equestrian ranks. There are only a handful of known *equites* from Galicia and the interior, but a large number from Baetica and the east coast. An Augustan census recorded the presence of 500 *equites* at Gades, a figure matched only by Patavium in Italy. Baetican *equites* achieved the highest equestrian posts, including two prefects of Egypt and one praetorian prefect.[5] In Citerior, the office of *flamen provinciae Hispaniae Citerioris* was often given to those who had held positions in the equestrian *cursus honorum*, such as military appointments or service on the equestrian jury panels at Rome.

Probably the most famous elite family from Spain was the Annaei of Corduba, whose ancestors were probably Italian. L. Annaeus Seneca (*c.* 55 BC–*c.* AD 39), whose father was almost certainly a rich equestrian landowner, was sent to Rome to be educated, during the troubled period of the civil wars. At Rome he met and married Helvia, a wealthy lady of ancient family, whose step-sister was married to C. Galerius, a future prefect of Egypt. Seneca divided his time between Spain and Rome, where he moved in intellectual circles and wrote books on rhetoric. Of his three sons, two advanced into the senatorial ranks. The eldest, Annaeus Novatus, was probably admitted to the Senate in AD 38, and was soon afterwards adopted by his father's friend, the senator and orator Junius Gallio. Taking the name Gallio Annaeanus, he served as *praetor pro consule* in Greece in 51–2 and dismissed the charges against St Paul, thus acquiring mention in the Bible (Acts 18:12–16). He became consul in 55 but was forced to commit suicide under Nero. His brother, L. Annaeus Seneca the Younger, was a student of philosophy. As a sickly young man, Seneca moved to Egypt for relief from asthma, and invested in large tracts of land there. He was adlected to the Senate around the same time as his brother, but was condemned to death in 41 for an alleged affair with Julia Livilla. The emperor Claudius commuted the sentence to exile on Corsica, where Seneca remained for eight years until recalled to Rome as tutor for the young prince Nero. As Nero's advisor and ultimately victim, Seneca is immortalised in the writings of Tacitus, but he was also famous for his wealth, which totalled 300,000,000 sesterces, and was alleged to have sucked Italy, Britain and other provinces dry by lending money at exorbitant interest rates. The third son of the elder Seneca was M. Annaeus Mela. Talented but complaisant, he declined admission to the Senate and was content to be a wealthy procurator. A disastrous marriage produced a son, Annaeus Lucanus, the greatest Latin epic poet after Vergil. Lucan held the favour of Nero and was made quaestor while still under age, but he and his father were implicated in the conspiracy of 65 and forced to commit suicide.[6]

While it is correct to say that the provincial elite played a leading role in romanisation, we must be careful not to think of the elite solely in terms of senators and equestrian officials. These successful men, whose service and activities often removed them from Spain, were to a large degree the beneficiaries rather than the agents of provincial romanisation. Though they provide sterling examples of social mobility, they were not realistic role models for the average Spaniard. The focal point of romanisation was the city, and it was the local aristocracy – the town councillors and priests – who set the example for each community. They adopted Roman dress, Roman speech, Roman names, Roman manners, in short a Roman lifestyle. Their elegantly decorated town houses and country villas disclosed the luxury and comfort which Roman technology, artistry and consumer goods made accessible to those who could afford them. This local elite consisted of the most affluent free-born men in the town, some of whom probably met the equestrian census. The available evidence points strongly to landowning and agriculture as the basis of their wealth. Though decurions were required to maintain a residence within one mile of the town, municipal regulations permitted the suspension of local government business for up to 60 days per year for the purpose of harvest and vintage. Since these activities were the climax of the agricultural year and the prime source of decurions' income, it behoved the landowner to supervise the work personally, regardless of rank or dignity. We read, for instance, of a 'leading man' (*princeps*) of Citerior, the father of a Roman praetor, routinely supervising the winnowing of wheat in his barns. Membership in the local 'senate' (the *ordo decurionum*) was both a privilege and a duty. In some towns, decurions may have been required to make a cash donation as an entrance fee (*summa honoraria*), and elected magistrates were formally required to provide entertainments or other services out of their own pockets. At Tarraco and Barcino, the presence of a number of wealthy outsiders among the local magistrates suggests that offices were being sold.[7] In addition to obligatory expenditures, decurions, magistrates and priests often made donations of buildings, statues or handouts (*sportulae*), both as a service to the city, as a means of enhancing their own prestige and as a way to win the gratitude of the electorate. Several Spanish magistrates are attested as subsidising the high price of grain or distributing it free of charge, or handing out gifts of olive oil for use in the baths. Elite women were ineligible for political office but could serve as priestesses, and several female *sacerdotes* are attested donating shrines, porticoes or spectacles. One lady who bears no title at all built baths on her own land for the people of Tagili, and provided circuses, a banquet and an endowment of 10,000 sesterces to maintain the baths in perpetuity.[8]

The degree of social mobility into the ranks of the local elite varied from town to town. At Saguntum, an Iberian settlement which was already flourishing prior to the war with Hannibal, Latin epigraphy reveals a closed, hereditary elite dominated by a handful of families such as the Baebii, Aemilii and Fabii, with a regular *cursus honorum*.[9] In other towns we have evidence for the advancement of new blood (including the wealthy sons of freedmen) into the decurial class. Although the number of decurions in each town was fixed, the departure of sons of the elite to pursue careers outside of Spain, together with the well-attested inability of closed aristocracies to reproduce themselves, led to vacancies which had to be filled by *novi homines*. Thus it was possible for local citizens to gain admission into the ranks of the elite, provided that they had proved their merit through financial success – wealth being a criterion for entry – and had built up a network of supporters in the local senate through business dealings, marital ties or a patron-client relationship. Despite such opportunities for advancement, however, the decurions were not elected by the people (as magistrates were) but remained an exclusive club of 'socially acceptable' families who controlled membership in the *ordo*.[10]

THE LOWER CLASSES

The *plebs* or commons, although comprising the vast majority of the population, is not easily subdivided. In principle, the rich enjoyed higher status than the poor, and the free-born enjoyed higher status than the freed. In practice, these two value systems were incompatible, since free-born people were often poor, while ex-slaves could be as wealthy as senators yet lacked social mobility. 'Rich' and 'poor' are in any event relative designations, for there was no agreed sum that constituted a 'poverty line'. One educated guess estimates that the poor comprised at least one-third of the population of the Roman Empire. Possibly this figure is a little high; in the Montes de Toledo settlements in the seventeenth century, pauper burials made up 15–20 per cent of the total. The urban poor lived largely in apartment blocks (*insulae*) similar to those at Ostia. Little remains of these archaeologically, since the upper storeys were made of wood and were notorious fire-traps; but an inscription from Carthago Nova records a purchase of *insulae* by a freedman, C. Plotius Princeps.[11] Occasionally paupers and debtors received some relief from the governor. Sempronius Gracchus in 179 gave land to poor people from the town of Complega, and Julius Caesar as governor of Ulterior precluded creditors from foreclosing on the property of debtors, by allowing the latter to pay off the debt in annual instalments amounting to two-thirds of their income. Under Hadrian, the governor of Baetica awarded 2,000 sesterces to a pauper whose son was killed at a dinner while being tossed in a blanket; though the amount of compensation seems small, the son's death was accidental. Few plebeians could hope for even this much help. In straitened circumstances they relied on the mercy of a patron or on the *sportulae* distributed by local magistrates. One desperate Spaniard supposedly travelled all the way to Rome in hope of the emperor's *sportula*, and turned back only a mile from the city upon hearing that it had been cancelled.[12]

Liberti (freed slaves) were an important component of the plebeian population, though not as prominent as at Rome, where tombstone evidence suggests that freed persons outnumbered free-born ones. Out of perhaps 10,000 Spanish inscriptions (the majority of them epitaphs) which had been published by 1971, approximately 700 mentioned freedmen, while some 300 mentioned slaves. These figures, though by no means an accurate guide to the actual proportion of slaves and freedmen in the population, are none the less remarkably low. In central Spain, less than one-tenth of inscriptions mention slaves or freedmen. However, a stronger showing of persons of servile origin may be seen in large towns. At Tarraco, for instance, 10 per cent of persons named in inscriptions were definitely slaves and 19 per cent definitely freedmen, and the true percentages for each group were probably much higher because the status of a further 58 per cent could not be determined. Thus it would not be an unreasonable conjecture that slaves and freedmen constituted at least a third of Tarraco's population.[13] The social mobility of *liberti*, beyond the initial leap from slavery to freedom, was limited. Wealthy freedmen could purchase the position of *sevir Augustalis*, an official of the imperial cult, but could not hold political office. None the less, prominent local freedmen were sometimes made honorary decurions or magistrates, and the sons of freedmen had full access to real magistracies. *Liberti* sometimes improved their social position through marriage with someone of higher rank, such as the freedwomen of local magistrates who married their patrons, though male *liberti* were not allowed to marry their patronesses.[14] A group enjoying special, almost elite, status was the *liberti Augusti*, freedmen of the emperor, who were a major component of the imperial civil service. These officials had their own hierarchy of offices and some became exceptionally rich. Although many imperial freedmen are attested in Spain, it is very rare for them to indicate their province of origin. On the other hand, we know of an imperial freedman of Spanish birth, C. Iulius Hyginus, who was a prominent scholar, a friend of the poet Ovid and curator of the Palatine Library at Rome.[15]

It is an irony of history that the people who made up the bulk of society in the Roman world are those about whom we know least: the *plebs rustica* or rural lower class. Rarely do they make an appearance on the historical stage, their sole aim in life being subsistence – producing just enough to pay taxes and rents yet still provide their families with the necessities. Poverty was a cruel fact of life for these folk, especially in the barren highlands, as our sources occasionally record.[16] To add to his discomfort, the stalwart, honest peasant, though praised by Cato and other extollers of Republican virtue, was in practice liable to be scorned as an uncultured bumpkin by his city cousins. Peasant production, which essentially means food production, demanded intense physical labour from the entire family, not only on their own land (whether owned or rented) but by hiring themselves out as part-time workers on more prosperous farms.[17] Peasant families lived in cramped conditions in rude cottages, often with their animals. Their diet included milk and cheese, vegetables, goat's meat and bread, which in mountainous regions was made from crushed acorns.[18] They could not afford to erect epitaphs, nor to experiment with new technologies. A farmer who fell into debt was liable to lose ownership of his land forever, though he might be permitted to remain as a tenant.

Not much is known about slaves in Spain, apart from their mass employment in mines and on estates (see chapter 7). Whereas working conditions in those environments could be extremely unpleasant, domestic slaves had a more comfortable existence. They received a *peculium* or allowance, which we sometimes see them spending to erect memorials to deceased fellow-slaves. They were also permitted to take a slave partner (properly known as *contubernalis*, though the inscriptions often use terms like *uxor* or *maritus* as if the couple was legally married) and raise a family, thus providing the master with a new generation of slaves.[19] From the fragments of the Flavian municipal law unearthed in Spain we learn a great deal about the manumission of slaves. For instance, whereas Roman legal writers state that manumission in the provinces was the prerogative of the provincial governor, the municipal law allows slaves to be manumitted before a local magistrate, the duovir. Manumission of slaves belonging to the municipality required the approval of two-thirds of the town council; the slave had to pay a fee to the local treasury – which shows that even public slaves had a *peculium* – and after manumission he would still owe services (*operae*) and his inheritance to the municipality. Public slaves of both *municipia* and colonies are attested in Spanish inscriptions. They acted as clerks, policemen and construction workers, and were fed and clothed at the expense of the town council.[20]

WOMEN AND THE FAMILY

In contrasting the civilised lifestyle of the Romans with the barbaric customs of the indigenous tribes, ancient writers are fond of portraying Spanish women, particularly those of Galicia, Cantabria and Celtiberia, as tough and unfeminine. They perform every sort of menial task, give birth while working in the fields, and are not above killing or even eating their children in time of war. Against this unflattering stereotype we must weigh the tender sentiments expressed by and about women on tombstones, and the portrayal of women in relief sculpture in activities requiring sensitivity and skill, such as weaving or playing musical instruments.[21] Women were also fond of personal adornment, as shown by the quantity and quality of excavated jewelry, though the Baetican lady who ordered her statue to be smothered in pearls and gems displayed more vanity than taste. Though child-rearing and other domestic chores occupied many women's lives, we also find women employed in the labour force, working either in their husbands' or fathers' shops or for hire. Most of the employments attested for women are in exclusively or typically 'female' jobs, such as hairdressers, wet-nurses, prostitutes, seamstresses and barmaids, though we also find women working in industry (for example, tile-makers at Conimbriga).[22]

Spanish epigraphy, which consists predominantly of epitaphs, reveals a strong sense of family affection. There are particularly touching funerary memorials of young children, set up by their parents, and tombstones which record a family burial plot. The terms of endearment used in epitaphs are so varied and personal that they surely represent genuine sentiment rather than mere stock formulae. Some children bear different *nomina* from their fathers or even from both parents, suggesting the possibilities of remarriage, illegitimacy and adoption. The abandonment and subsequent discovery of unwanted children may be evidenced by mentions of *alumni* and *alumnae*, 'foundlings'. Though teachers and schools existed for the sons of the well-to-do, other children are attested working, for instance in the mining towns of Vipasca and Carthago Nova.[23]

PATRONS AND CLIENTS

Patronage was a conspicuous and essential mechanism in both Celtic and Roman societies, a partial mitigation of the inequalities of the class hierarchy. The rich and powerful patron gave financial and legal assistance to his dependants, who reciprocated by waiting upon him, voting for him or performing various other services (*operae*). An aristocrat's importance was judged in large measure by the size of his client network. The client, though sometimes humiliated or disgusted by the relationship, recognised and exploited his dependence: 'it's shameful, but I'm after your dinner invitation,' the Spanish poet Martial admits to his patron.

In Celtic Britain the clients would fight and die in defence of the nobles;[24] in Spain we find the same principle under the name of *devotio Iberica*. The transition to Roman rule merely substituted Roman for Iberian patrons: the Sertorian war, for instance, was essentially a conflict between the clients of Sertorius and those of Metellus and Pompey. The cliental attachment of the indigenous lower classes to Roman or romanised patrons no doubt accelerated the process of assimilation through personal contact and example. *Clientela*, however, was not limited to personal subservience: tribes, towns or corporations could equally appoint a prominent individual as their patron, in return for favours already performed or in expectation of future gifts or lobbying on behalf of the client body. Having a patron to whom one could turn in time of need was an obvious asset, whose potential later found expression in a Spanish proverb ('a service not yet rendered is worth more than a hundred thousand million already rendered'). Patronage was often combined, associated or confused with *hospitium*, a guest–friendship which did not necessarily involve a patron–client relationship. For instance, Diodorus records that the Celtiberians strove to outdo one another in their hospitality towards strangers, though they were cruel to their enemies. The Romans sometimes offered *hospitium* to Celtiberians, as exemplified in the story of Q. Occius, legate of Q. Metellus in 142 BC and nicknamed Achilles for his valour. After winning a duel against Pyrresus, the noblest and bravest of the Celtiberians, Occius 'asked that they might be joined by the law of hospitality once peace was restored between Romans and Celtiberians'.[25] Both *hospitium* and *clientela* were mutual, reciprocal and hereditary relationships, and being similar, often overlapped.[26] However, the two were not identical. Under Tiberius, for instance, we find pacts of *hospitium* between Ucubi and two other towns, Iptuci and Baxo, where patronage is not at issue, and as late as 408 the emperor exhorts the troops billetted at Pamplona to show due respect to their hosts (*hospitiis obsequamini*).[27]

At the personal level, a client would either seek the patronage of a social or financial superior, or in the case of a freedman, would be automatically bound to the patronage of his or her former master. To judge from his poems, Martial, although of equestrian status, was often short of money and turned to a number of patrons for handouts (*sportulae*) and, he hoped, dinner invitations. After 34 years of rising before dawn to line up at patrons' houses in Rome, he returned to his native Bilbilis, where he boasted he could sleep till nine in the morning; but news of his arrival soon spread, and he was again forced to rise early – by local clients knocking at *his* door! Freedmen and other clients sometimes received free tenancies from their patron, and in Spain tenants' costs for sacrifices were apparently remitted until the early fourth century. But the client remained in the patron's debt, and the Flavian municipal law is quick to point out that patrons will retain their traditional rights over freedmen, even though one or both parties may receive Roman citizenship in the new *municipium*.[28]

Patrons represented a wide variety of social and professional backgrounds, as is clear from the large selection of Spanish inscriptions involving freedmen. One prominent freedman claimed as patron the Spanish-born consul L. Licinius Sura, to whom he was an aide (*accensus*) as well as a *sevir Augustalis* at both Tarraco and Barcino; he is commemorated in a series of honorific inscriptions erected by Barcino and other towns and by his fellow *seviri* and friends.[29] Others were freedmen of members of the local elite – municipal magistrates and priests – and occasionally of provincial priests or priestesses. In some cases a magistrate's freedwoman was also his wife. Another group of freedmen had army officers (legionary tribunes, centurions) or other ranks as patrons, reminding us that soldiers sometimes kept slaves; one *liberta* is a veteran's wife, another an heir. A considerable number of clients were freedmen of other freedmen, many of the latter being *seviri Augustales*. In one such instance, the libertine patron held the civil service position of provincial archivist (*tabularius*). Another patron, whose *nomen* Aelius suggests descent from an imperial freedman, was a grammar teacher.[30]

Several features of the epigraphy suggest that freedmen and their patrons had a warm and close relationship. One is the fact that personal patrons are most frequently represented on epitaphs, either commemorating their deceased freedmen or (oftener) being commemorated by them. Moreover, it is sometimes specified that the freedman erected the monument at his or her own expense (*de suo* or *de sua pecunia*) or out of benevolence (*secundum voluntatem*).[31] The epitaph frequently includes a laudatory adjective characterising the deceased as well-deserving, excellent or the like. While these are mostly conventional formulae, we occasionally find an unusual epithet (such as *obsequentissima*, 'most compliant') or a longer eulogy in verse. A freedman who refers to his deceased teenage ex-master as *dominus* rather than *patronus* is either unashamed of his servile origin or, more likely, has just been manumitted by testament and still thinks of his posthumous patron by his former title.[32] But the clearest sign of affection is the interment of patron and freedman together in a family tomb – or deposition of their ashes in the same niche of a *columbarium*, for the monuments include plaques as well as tombstones – as indicated by the formula 'et sibi' (referring to the dedicant) on the epitaph. In most of these cases the patron is explicitly or probably a freedman himself; the sole freeborn patroness died, presumably childless, at age 15.[33] This feeling of *familia* may also appear on a votive inscription, which L. Antonius Avitus, his children and the freedwoman Zozima jointly dedicate to Tutela. While it is not explicitly stated that Zozima is the freedwoman of Antonius, the omission of her *nomen* makes this relationship highly probable.[34]

Entire tribes or cities might also appoint a patron who could help them in much the same way as a personal patron helped a client: namely, by providing financial assistance (e.g., underwriting the cost of monumental buildings or public banquets), legal or political aid (representing the civic body in a lawsuit, or lobbying at Rome for special privileges, or protesting against unscrupulous officials). Such a patron would need to be a wealthy and influential man such as a senator (though *equites* also occur), and provincial governors often filled this role. The elder Cato, for instance, after his consulship in Spain, represented the Spaniards at Rome. Later, both Pompey and Caesar acquired larger *clientelae* in Spain as a result of their governorships and military successes, and these played a role in the bloody civil war of the 40s. The banquets to which Caesar invited important provincials afforded them an opportunity to advertise their cliental ties, which were amply repaid when Caesar endowed their cities with magnificent public works. The emperors were the natural successors to this tradition, and the *obsequium* of the towns they founded or promoted is reflected in their nomenclature: Pax Iulia, Emerita Augusta, Baelo Claudia, Clunia Sulpicia and the numerous *municipia Flavia*. Hadrian's patronage of Italica led not only to a boom in the construction of public monuments (anticipating that at Lepcis Magna under Septimius Severus) but a change of status and name (*colonia Aelia Augusta*). Inscriptions and coins hail members of the imperial family as patrons: Augustus, Agrippa, C. Caesar and Tiberius at Ulia, Agrippa (with the additional title 'municipi parens') at Gades.[35]

Since not every community could claim the emperor as patron,

governors and consulars were obvious candidates. The patrons of
Emporiae in the period *c.* 32 BC to AD 15 included (in addition to
Augustus and one of his grandsons) several leading senators, some
of them governors of Hispania Citerior. Several other towns of
Citerior, including Carthago Nova, Uxama, the *civitas Bocchoritana*
in the Baleares and *civitas Lougeiorum* in Galicia, appointed known
or presumed governors as their patrons between 19 BC and AD 14, but
only the first of these cities refers to the patron by his gubernatorial
title, 'pro pr(aetore Augusti) leg(atus)'.[36] The omission of the title
could indicate that patronage was being extended to the individual
and was not a precedent for his successors, but a likelier explanation
is that the honour was granted after the governor's term expired.
This is definitely the case with the Uxama example, which postdates
Augustus' proclamation in AD 11 that provincial governors could not
be granted honours by provincials until 60 days after their departure.
No more governors are attested as patrons until the third century,
when we find a spate of (apparently serving) governors as patrons
of Emerita, Valentia and Tarraco.[37] In addition to governors, patronage could be offered to other senatorial officials who had served
in the province. Thus Munigua in Baetica conferred the title upon
a provincial quaestor under Augustus or Tiberius, while Calagurris
appointed two *legati iuridici* of Citerior in the late first and early
second centuries AD; and in AD 222 the commander of *legio VII
Gemina* was made patron of the entire *conventus Cluniensis*. On
the other hand, the appointment of the Gaditanian senator L.
Cornelius Balbus Minor (*cos. suff.* 32 BC) as patron of Norba in
or after 19 BC shows a certain amount of 'patronage' on the part
of the town, since Balbus' daughter was married to the son of the
colony's founder.[38]

Prominent equestrian officials could also be useful patrons. Thus,
two procurators of Baetica became local patrons, at Italica and
Singilia Barba. In the latter case the appointment was recognition
for relieving a lengthy siege of the town by the Moors, probably
in the reign of Septimius Severus.[39] Another equestrian patron at
Italica was a procurator of Mauretania who had also commanded
one of the three Parthian legions under Septimius Severus. The
appointment of an *eques* did not necessarily prevent a town having
higher-ranking patrons; we know from the roll-book of the local
senate at Canusium in Italy that the town had 31 senatorial and
eight equestrian patrons in AD 223. The absence of such a document
from Spain makes it difficult to prove that Spanish towns also had

several patrons at once, though the appointment at Ulia of four patrons from Augustus' family makes simultaneous appointments probable. Multiplicity of patronal positions would also facilitate the appointment of local notables to this honour. Several towns appointed their own magistrates and priests as patrons; in one case the motive for the appointment of an ex-duovir as patron is suggested by his description as 'munificentissimus civis'.[40] The 'P. Turullius P., f. Mai(cia)' named on a hospitality plaque (Figure 5.2) belonged to a family of lead exporters at Carthago Nova; no doubt such rich businessmen were in demand as patrons.

Professional associations (*collegia*) also frequently appointed patrons. In the second century AD we find an honorific inscription

Figure 5.2 (a) and (b)   Bronze hospitality token in the shape of joined hands, with inscription on the reverse. (Museo Arqueológico Nacional, Madrid.)

erected to their patron by the association of *seviri Augustales* at Tarraco, on account of his numerous benefactions. Among commercial associations honouring patrons are the boatmen (*lyntrari*) from three towns along the Guadalquivir, the interior builders (*fabri subidiani*) of Corduba and the Syrian and Asian merchants at Malaca. An inscription from Rome in the mid-second century records that the patron of the merchants of Baetican oil was a top equestrian official, a former prefect of Egypt. Finally, a bronze plaque dated AD 239 commemorates the 'very deserving, happy, distinguished and benevolent patrons' of a *collegium* of textile and shoe manufacturers at Segisamo, which includes women and slaves.[41]

SOLDIER AND CIVILIAN

While in the field, the Roman Republican army lived in pitched camps of the type described by Polybius. During the inactive winter months, however, soldiers were often billetted in or around native towns. In the case of towns on the frontier or of dubious loyalty, billetting might take the form of an armed garrison, but the impression given by the literary sources is that Republican generals often simply moved their troops into a town for the entire season. This practice was resented throughout the Roman world and caused insufferable havoc and depredation. For Spain, Plutarch informs us that troops wintering at Castulo in the 90s BC lived in luxury and were intoxicated most of the time, much to the disgust of the natives; and that Sertorius later won the sympathy of the Spanish people by quartering his troops in the outskirts instead of the centre of towns. A garrison is also attested at Ilipa in the first century BC.[42] Even in the Imperial period, when the legions (after AD 63, a single legion) and auxiliary troops had permanent encampments of their own, there was a military presence in the towns. At least one cohort of the Laietanian coast guard was stationed in the city of Tarraco in the late first and early second centuries AD. In the provincial capitals, governors were attended by a sizeable military staff.[43] Former soldiers held local magistracies and were thereby expected to sponsor games and other benefactions. One retired centurion at Barcino (Barcelona) donated 30,000 sesterces to provide bath-oil for the citizenry. Some cities had a *collegium iuvenum*, a sort of paramilitary cadet corps for teenagers; the future emperor Hadrian apparently belonged to one such organisation at Italica, where he is said to have undergone military training (*militia*) at age 14. In times of civil war (for example in 31 BC and AD 69), and then regularly under the Flavians and probably after, there was a shore patrol commanded by an equestrian *praefectus orae maritimae* and comprising two or three cohorts. These units, labelled *cohors I et II* and *cohors nova tironum*, hardly sound like legionary or even auxiliary cohorts, and are probably a local militia. The prefect's forces are not known to have included ships: Spanish coastal waters were a responsibility of the Misenum fleet.[44]

The local economy was clearly stimulated by contracts to supply goods (notably food and utensils) to the legions. In Republican times, when supplies were arranged by contractors (*redemptores*), goods could be obtained either by local purchase or by importation from Italy. In time of war, of course, food could be confiscated from the enemy without scruple. Thus Scipio demanded six months' supply of grain from the defeated Ilergetes in 205 BC, while Cato sent the contractors home in 195 BC with the boast that his campaign would feed itself. Numerous references attest the continuation of this practice in the Sertorian and civil wars of the first century BC.[45] Under the Empire it is unclear whether Spain was subject to an *annona militaris* (grain levy for the army), but since from the Flavian period there was only one legion and a cavalry squadron in Spain, the burden could not have been heavy. It has been calculated that a legion in peacetime consumed about 26,000 bushels (945,000 litres) of grain per year, which would be stored during the winter months in the legion's own granary (such as the Republican example excavated at Castillejo, one of Scipio Aemilianus' camps outside Numantia). If this grain was provided entirely by civilian resources (rather than grown by the legionaries) it must have kept the local farmers busy – and possibly affluent, again depending on whether grain was purchased or requisitioned.[46] One could argue that if compulsory provision of grain was regarded as a punishment for enemies, its continued imposition in peacetime would hardly provide much incentive to remain peaceful. Moreover, since the obvious source of grain for Spain's sole legion at León would be the surrounding Tierra de Campos (the 'breadbasket' of Spain), the burden of such requisitioning would fall inequitably on a single region. Despite these logical objections, the *annona militaris* was a fact of life in some parts of the Empire, and the high cost of transporting grain overland made a local source of supply imperative. The only mention of Spanish grain provision to the army is recorded in AD 44, when Umbonius Silo, governor of Baetica, was recalled and expelled from the Senate on the grounds that he had failed to send enough grain to the Roman troops in Mauretania, where a native revolt which had begun in 41 was apparently still simmering.[47] However, it is unclear whether the Baetican grain was requisitioned or purchased, and in any event this was not a regular exaction but an extraordinary measure to meet a military emergency in a neighbouring province. The army could not live by bread alone, and the legions had supply NCOs (*a rationibus*) to purchase other foodstuffs. Inscriptions on wooden tablets or clay seals attest military purchases, for instance of cattle from Frisia and (presumably) wine from Lyon to supply the legions in Germany. Unfortunately there is no comparable evidence from Spain itself, but we do know from references to the wars of the second century BC that the diet of Roman troops in Spain included both meat and wine.[48]

Although the legionaries carried utensils for grinding and baking grain as well as assorted pots, pans, cups and roasting-spits, such items could easily be lost or broken, especially when the army was on the march. Purchase of locally manufactured goods offered a much cheaper and faster means of replacing this equipment than importation from Italy. Celtiberian coarse pottery and hand-mills found in the Republican camps around Numantia suggest that Scipio's army was supplied with the products of itinerant artisans, though fine pottery still had to come from Italy.[49] It is, however, possible that these indigenous artifacts were used primarily by Spanish auxiliary troops (who comprised an estimated two-thirds of Scipio's force), as further suggested by the discovery not only of Iberian pottery but Iberian fibulas in the early first century BC camp at Cáceres el Viejo.[50] The legion's camp followers might include Italian pottery merchants or itinerant potters, though it is questionable whether these could produce fine wares with local clays and makeshift kilns while the army was on the move. The establishment of more permanent garrisons under the Empire permitted a stable environment for production and supply. We do not know whether the L. Terentius who produced *terra sigillata* for the *legio IV Macedonica* at Herrera de Pisuerga in the early first century AD was a soldier or civilian, but the recent discovery of his kiln shows at least that this pottery was produced locally, and not imported from Italy as previously conjectured.[51] Although some military outposts were still being supplied with Italian and South Gaulish *sigillata* into the Flavian period, the development of the Spanish *sigillata* industry assured a local, probably civilian, supply network thereafter. The legionary base at León was on a major east-west route passing through Tritium Magallum (Tricio), the premier production centre of Spanish *sigillata*, thereby facilitating the supply of Ebro valley wares to the army. Spanish *sigillata* has indeed been excavated within the camp of *legio VII Gemina*. More prominent in these excavations was the large quantity and variety of tiles stamped with the name of this legion, ranging in date from about AD 70 to 270.[52] The use of these stamped tiles in a luxury villa at Navatejera (3 km south of León) in the mid-third century as well as bricks with the legion's stamp in a (possibly) third century villa at Quintana del Marco (León) and as far south as Castrobol (Valladolid) suggests the provision, official or clandestine, of surplus bricks and tiles to civilians (in the case of Navatejera, perhaps a retired officer of the legion) either as a cash sale or, as MacMullen plausibly suggests for similar cases elsewhere, in barter for produce from the villa.[53] Whether the actual manufacture was in the hands of legionaries or civilian employees, this long-lived tile production was clearly under military control.

In the absence of military emergencies, the army undertook a wide range of civilian jobs. Each military unit had its *territorium* where soldiers – mostly of peasant stock anyway, whether Italian or Spanish – may have grown crops and herded sheep and cattle to supplement the legion's diet. The territory of the *legio VII Gemina* has not been delineated, but we know from numerous boundary stones of the early first century AD that the *legio IV Macedonica* controlled extensive grazing lands (*prata*) between Iuliobriga (Retortillo) and Segisamo (Sasamón), while *cohors IV Gallorum* had *prata* south of Asturica, between the unidentified towns of Baedunia and *civitas Luggonum*. Since Iuliobriga and Segisamo were 60 km apart and some of the boundary stones were found only 15 km from the former, the legion appears to have had surprisingly large *prata*, to say nothing of lands other than pasturage. However, the early date of the camp, the lack of intense urbanism in this region and the probable confiscation of large tracts of *ager publicus* after Augustus' Cantabrian war may account for this spacious allocation of terrain.[54] Once again, the possibility of civilian labour is not excluded, especially considering the extent of the *prata* and the occasional need for the legion to leave its camp to deal with an uprising by northern tribes. Arable, unlike grazing, land would probably be near to the camp in order to facilitate tending and preclude pilfering of the crop. The cultivation terraces visible outside the Romano-British fort at Housesteads suggest the configuration such farming might adopt. There is furthermore the possibility – indeed likelihood, given the normally inactive role of the army in Imperial Spain – that soldiers purchased or rented their own farms or plots in the neighbourhood. This practice, though technically illegal, was widespread even on active frontiers, providing the soldier with at least a hobby and at best a source of nourishment.[55]

The army played a more official role in another civilian activity, mining. In some cases army engineers may have acted as technical advisors on the sinking and shoring of shafts (which in Roman times were dug horizontally into a mountain side, and worked by slaves because of the cramped conditions and the danger of collapse). The chief contribution of the army, however, was in guarding the mines and the transportation routes of the extracted minerals. This was especially necessary in the case of the precious gold and silver of the north-west, but in fact it began much earlier. A series of forts in southern Portugal occupied from the first century BC to the second century AD protected the overland shipment of minerals from the mines of the Alentejo to the river port of Myrtilis, while another line of fortifications in Extremadura guarded the 'Vía de la Plata' or silver route between Asturias and Emerita. Moreover, the second-century mining regulations from Vipasca, allowing soldiers free admission to the baths, imply not only the presence of troops but some service entitling them to special privileges.[56] The Roman camp at Valdemeda (León), strategically situated to guard the busy gold-mining district between the rivers Duerna and Eria, is plausibly conjectured to have been established in the first century AD when serious mining got underway; and in the second century there is ample epigraphic evidence of the presence of Roman soldiers at the gold-mines of Villalís and Luyego in Asturias and Três Minas in northern Portugal. These troops came from detachments of the *legio VII Gemina, cohors IV Gallorum* and possibly *cohors I Celtiberorum*. There was also a cohort stationed at Castulo in the mineral-rich Sierra Morena, as well as a garrison at Las Merchenas (Salamanca) in a tin-mining district.[57] Though evidence is lacking, soldiers may also have been involved with quarries, guarding them and possibly working them if the legion needed stone for building. Military quarry work is attested in other provinces, and the cold winter of northern Spain demanded stone buildings for permanent garrisons, as on the Rhine-Danube frontier. Even for stone buildings a timber framework was needed, and soldiers had to become lumberjacks.

Parallels from Britain (where ancient timbers are better preserved) suggest that although the Romans were aware of the properties of various types of wood, military construction usually relied on local timber, even if inferior; from this we may infer that army units were probably cutting their own lumber. Vegetius (writing in the fourth century, but the statement may be true for earlier periods as well) confirms that 'the legion also has carpenters . . . and the other artisans necessary for the building of winter quarters.'[58] Moreover, soldiers were undoubtedly utilised to assist in civil construction; we know for instance that the Fourth and Sixth Legions built roads in Navarra under Augustus, while the Seventh Legion helped construct the bridge at Aquae Flaviae in 79. Similarities in the chronology and building technique of several town walls in northern Spain also suggest the assistance (in planning and possibly in construction) of the Seventh Legion.[59] There are also records of benefactions and *tesserae hospitales* involving army officers, attesting military interaction with the civilian populace.[60]

Whatever the impact of the Roman army on the indigenous population, there was clearly some native impact on the soldier. Caesar, reporting on the civil war, notes that the men of the Second Legion had served in Spain for so long that they had become hispanised, acquiring property, maintaining quasi-marital relations with indigenous women, and indeed regarding themselves as Spaniards.[61] Under the Empire this trend continued, and was indeed fostered by the increasing enrolment of genuine Spaniards into the Seventh Legion, including no doubt the sons of successive generations of legionaries. Soldiers (whether Italian or Spanish) retiring from service often preferred to settle close to the camp, near their old haunts and old friends, rather than return to their home towns. The attraction would be all the stronger if they had acquired families and property in the vicinity. Spanish epigraphy attests several veterans who died at Legio or neighbouring Asturica, and others at Tarraco, which had a detachment from the Seventh Legion. Spanish legionaries serving outside Spain similarly retired near their legion's base, as we know from inscriptions at Deva (Chester) in Britain, Carnuntum in Pannonia, Colonia (Köln) and Mogontiacum (Mainz) in Germany and Lambaesis in Africa. Veterans sent to Spain as colonists not infrequently discovered that their colonies were collocated with existing native settlements, providing possibilities for social or commercial interaction, though Romans and natives seem to have lived in different quarters of the city.[62]

But the place where the soldier was likeliest to make contact with the outside world was the *canabae*, the civilian shops and homes which grew up around a legionary base. Here the soldier could find wine, prostitutes and other commodities on which to spend his pay. At León, where it is generally conceded that the rectangular Late Roman wall encloses the camp of the Seventh Legion, the *canabae* should initially have been situated near the four gates (whose location is known) and then gradually expanded to form the plan of the modern city. If we accept Vittinghoff's calculation that the number of soldiers stationed permanently at León was between 2,500 and 3,000, and MacMullen's thesis that for every soldier there were two or three civilians, we get a rough idea of the population of the *canabae*.[63]

The civilian population which sprang up around a camp invariably included women, in Roman as in later times. The 2,000 harlots expelled from Scipio's camp at Numantia find a revealing parallel in the 'veritable battalions of prostitutes' accompanying Spanish armies in the sixteenth century – though in both cases the arbitrary labelling of female camp-followers as prostitutes may reflect less the genuine state of affairs than the moralising outlook of the chronicler. Since serving soldiers could not legally wed until the reign of Septimius Severus, their conjugal relations were confined to quasi-marital unions. After the soldier's discharge the woman could legally become his wife, and in the late first to early second century AD, auxiliary troops (including several known Spaniards) were regularly granted *conubium* with peregrine women in their discharge certificates.[64] Several *uxores* and *coniuges* are attested in the inscriptions of soldiers in Spain before Severus. Most are explicitly, and others arguably, veterans, though one serving soldier of the Seventh Legion, who died at age 37 in the early second century, already claimed a *coniunx*. The children of Roman soldiers by indigenous women were originally regarded as illegitimate, and by the *ius naturale* followed their mother's status. An exception was made in 171 BC when some 4,000 offspring of soldierly unions with Spanish women were granted Latin rights by the Senate and settled in a colony at Carteia. From the reign of Claudius until Antoninus Pius, however, the grant of citizenship and *conubium* to time-expired soldiers also conferred citizenship upon their children born during service. This retroactive grant of legitimacy was suspended in AD 139, so that soldiers' sons could acquire Roman citizenship only by following in their fathers' footsteps and serving 20 years in the legion or 25

Figure 5.3 Funerary stela of M. Valerius Celerinus, a native of Astigi.
(Römisch-Germanisches Museum, Köln; Rheinisches Bildarchiv 33517.)

in an auxiliary unit.[65] Septimius Severus' legalisation of soldiers' marriages, and his son Caracalla's grant of Roman citizenship to all free persons in the Empire, eliminated the problems of legitimacy and citizenship.

Soldiers' family life is illustrated in the inscriptions, which show a variety of relationships and terms of endearment; the latter were to some extent formulaic, but the choice of epithet is often revealing. The epitaphs of soldiers and ex-soldiers of the Seventh Legion include 13 erected by wives, who describe their spouses as worthy, pious, dear, incomparable or indulgent; 6 from sons and daughters; 4 from brothers; 3 from mothers (one portraying herself as *misera*); 5 from fellow soldiers; and one from a foster-son. One soldier is described as 'dear to his kin' (*carus suis*), another is remembered as excellent and honourable (*homo optimus et honestissimus*). Several soldiers erect tombstones to wives (variously described as sweet or chaste), to a faithful son, to an innocent daughter.[66] The decorated tombstone from Köln of M. Valerius Celerinus (born at Astigi and veteran of the *legio X Gemina* which was transferred from Spain to Lower Germany *c.* AD 70) depicts the deceased in his citizen's toga, reclining on a couch with refreshments at hand, and flanked by two persons, sometimes interpreted as servants (Figure 5.3).[67] The larger of these, comfortably seated on a *cathedra* (high-backed lady's chair), with her feet on a cushion and a basket of spindles conspicuous at her side, is more likely the veteran's dutiful, wool-working wife, Marcia Procula (also named on the epitaph), while the smaller figure is perhaps their son.

SPANIARDS IN THE LARGER ROMAN WORLD

The warlike Spaniards had a long history of mercenary service in foreign armed forces, and eventually made their impact on the Roman army as well. At the same time, military indoctrination helped to romanise the recruit, qualified him for Roman citizenship upon discharge and could serve as an avenue to a future career. 'All that is sound in the army is foreign', observed Tacitus, and the superior physical strength and excellent fighting ability of Spanish troops, both cavalry and infantry, were readily admitted by Roman writers.[68] Iberian mercenaries fought for Carthage at the battle of Himera in 480 BC, and are frequently attested in Punic service thereafter. Speaking in 415/4, Alcibiades expressed Athens' desire to hire Iberian mercenaries because of their aggressiveness, and the unexpected discovery of fifth-century Celtiberian belt buckles on the island of Corcyra (assembly area of the Athenian allies for both Sicilian expeditions) suggests that Athens may have found some.[69] In the early fourth century they also appear in the pay of Syracuse, and during the First Punic War a large number were employed by Rome. Livy claims that Hannibal's Spanish troops were the best in his entire army: this we may doubt, given the prominent role played by the African contingent in Hannibal's battles, but he did take 8,000 Iberians across the Alps.[70] With Carthage eliminated, the Spaniards henceforth worked exclusively for Rome. It has been calculated that two-thirds of Scipio Aemilianus' army at the siege of Numantia were Spaniards, and Spain was the only province where the Romans employed indigenous troops in the early first century BC.[71] A bronze tablet of 89 BC records an unprecedented grant of Roman citizenship to an entire troop of Spanish cavalrymen – the *turma Salluitana*, from Salduvia (later Caesaraugusta) – who fought with distinction in the Social War under Pompey's father.[72] Slingers from the Balearic Islands fought for Caesar in the Gallic War, and against him at Massilia. During Augustus' Cantabrian campaign, the mounted enemy apparently taught the Romans some new and enduring tactics, for we find Syrian cavalry rehearsing the 'Cantabrian manoeuvre' at Lambaesis in AD 128.[73]

The increasing percentage of Spaniards in the legions from Claudius onward, and especially in *VII Gemina* in the second and third centuries, amply illustrates the continuing and integral role of Iberian manpower in the Roman military machine. A few natives of Spain are even attested in the praetorian and urban cohorts at Rome.[74] Spaniards also served in auxiliary units, often bearing 'ethnic' names. There were cavalry squadrons of Arevaci, Astures and Vettones, plus infantry cohorts of Cantabri, Lusitani, Celtiberi and so on. There were also numerous generic units, both cavalry and infantry, of 'Hispani'. These units served on every frontier in the empire, though once established, their numbers would be replenished by local recruits so that they remained Spanish in name alone. Northern Spanish tribes like the Astures and Varduli, who provided some of the *auxilia* for Hadrian's Wall, were presumably selected for that frontier because they were accustomed to cold, damp climates.

Though military service was a prominent cause of Spaniards leaving Spain, it was by no means the only one. A number of Spanish merchants are attested at various cities in Gaul and Italy, including

Burdigala (Bordeaux), Nemausus (Nîmes), Ostia and Rome. The famous dancing girls from Gades are often mentioned in Latin literature, and occasionally in epigraphy. Spanish gladiators are attested in Gaul and Italy, and a Lusitanian charioteer named C. Appuleius Diocles acquired fame and fortune (35,000,000 sesterces) at Rome in the second century.[75] Another important group of émigrés consisted of writers and orators. There were many Spanish rhetoricians and poets at Rome in the time of Augustus and Tiberius, including the elder Seneca, whose family has already been discussed. The agricultural writer Columella (a contemporary of the younger Seneca) and the grammarian Quintilian, who was probably suffect consul under Domitian, are among those Spaniards whose writings have survived. The poet Martial was only one of several literary figures from Bilbilis who flourished at Rome. There were also what might best be described as literary tourists, Spaniards who travelled to Rome to see the epic poet Saleius Bassus or the historian Livy, and having seen them, returned home.[76]

6

TOWN AND COUNTRY

URBANISATION

Whether the Iberians and Celtiberians can be said to have had cities prior to the Roman period is largely a matter of definition. Posidonius ridiculed Polybius for alleging that the cities destroyed by Ti. Gracchus numbered 300, while Strabo suggests that those who claim the Iberians had more than 1,000 cities are calling the large villages cities. In fact it seems prudent to view the indigenous *oppida* as towns rather than cities, reserving the latter designation for the grander communities established by the Phoenicians (Gades), the Greeks (Emporion) and the Carthaginians (Carthago Nova). One possible exception to this rule is Saguntum, an indigenous town so strongly influenced by Greek urbanism that popular etymology falsely considered it a colony and namesake of the Greek island of Zakynthos. According to Livy it had a forum, and turreted walls strong enough to withstand Hannibal's siege for eight months.[1] But if coastal cities served as the urban model in the pre-Roman period, it was Rome's inland colonies like Norba (Cáceres) and Caesaraugusta (Zaragoza) that made cities a visible and viable concept for Spain as a whole. These colonies were theoretically new foundations, manned by army veterans, who were allotted land to till but in an emergency could take up arms to defend the colony's territory – as envisaged, for instance, in the charter of the Caesarian colony of Urso in Baetica. In fact the colony of Corduba, founded in the first half of the second century BC, contained from its inception a mixture of Roman and indigenous settlers, while colonies like Urso were established on the site of indigenous predecessors.[2] Colonisation reached its zenith under Julius Caesar and Augustus, largely through the need to settle the numerous veterans of the civil wars, though it is impossible to give an accurate list for each founder, since places named Colonia Iulia could belong to either. In addition to colonies, the Romans founded a few other towns, either for Romans (Italica, 206 BC) or for indigenous settlers (Gracchuris, 178 BC). Most of the indigenous towns in the territories seized by Rome seem to have been tribute-payers (*civitates stipendiariae*), but a few towns such as Tarraco and Malaca were *civitates foederatae*, allies rather than subjects of Rome. The elder Pliny informs us that in Baetica there were also six 'free' cities (*civitates liberae*), a status which was presumably granted as a reward for wartime loyalty, and which conferred protection against interference from the provincial governor, but not immunity from taxation. Beginning with Julius Caesar, another status was available to deserving indigenous towns, that of *municipium*. Grants of municipal status seem usually (though not necessarily) to have been concomitant with the privilege of *ius Latii*, 'Latin right', which gave Latin citizenship to the town's citizens and the more prestigious Roman citizenship to the annual magistrates upon completion of their term in office. Again according to Pliny, this privilege was granted by Vespasian, as censor in AD 73–4, to 'all of Spain' – which seems to mean towns in all *parts* of Spain, for not all communities were so honoured.[3]

Much has been written about the purpose, development, daily life and architecture of cities in the Roman world, but inadequate attention has been paid to their role in romanisation. Cities were in fact the focal points of provincial assimilation, thanks primarily to the leadership shown by the local elite. It has been claimed, somewhat cynically, that urbanisation was a deliberate attempt by Rome to rechannel the efforts of the Iberian elite from rebellion into community projects,[4] but this assumes a premeditated intent by Rome to impose cities on the conquered. Apart from the handful of colonies, however, Rome could claim little credit for the establishment of provincial cities, except insofar as these were inspired by the colonial model. Most cities in Roman Spain originated as pre-Roman towns – tribal capitals for instance – whose local leaders seized the initiative in upgrading their community's status and services. Cities were universally acknowledged as the hallmark of civilisation. Iberian towns in southern and eastern Spain were already on the way to urbanism under Greek influence before the Romans arrived. By the end of the Republic these towns were effectively romanised, and the towns of the interior were endeavouring to catch up. In Augustus' day the inhabitants of the interior (Celtiberia and the Ebro valley) 'are already called *togati*, that is to say, peaceful; and being garbed in the toga, they are now converting to the Italian lifestyle'.[5] The *togati* were of course the elite, who ambitiously competed for municipal honours and the coveted Roman citizenship, which gave them superior social and legal status. They constructed richly decorated townhouses (*domus*), hired teachers to instruct their children in the classics, watched Latin plays in the theatre and aspired to the priest-hoods of Roman cults. Just as in the 'potlatch' culture of North American tribes, whose elite attempted to surpass one another in giving away wealth, Spanish aristocrats competed with their peers to finance lavish public buildings and donate grain and cash to the populace. Under the peaceful conditions of the Early Empire, the cities became sated with monumental buildings and statues.[6] Not only the elite but the lower classes could enjoy the benefits of urban life, frequenting the public baths and receiving free 'bread and circuses'. Moreover, all citizens of the town were entitled to participate in local government through the popular assembly, by which the magistrates were elected. Even ex-slaves, though ineligible for magistracies, could become *seviri* (officials of the imperial cult) if they were able to afford an entrance fee.

Accidents of preservation tend to obscure our perception of the relative importance of Roman cities. The ruins of Italica and Conimbriga, extensively explored and publicised, have yielded finds of great value. Though important archaeologically, neither town was a major administrative centre (though Italica did enjoy the favour of Hadrian), and both sites were deserted after the Roman period, leaving their ruins intact and accessible to modern excavation. Other cities of greater importance in Roman times have produced fewer remains, precisely because they were more successful: their Roman constructions have been destroyed, buried or remodelled, and explo-ration is impeded by modern occupation. The siting of these ancient cities at major confluences, road junctions or other strategic points has been an important factor in their survival. While tourists judge sites by their glamour, the historian has the more demanding task of viewing cities from the ancient perspective. For this reason I have chosen to focus on the chief cities of the Roman administration, whose ruins, though sometimes scant, none the less suffice to convey their importance.

PROVINCIAL CAPITALS

Augusta Emerita (Mérida)

Ancient sources vary in calling this city Augusta Emerita, Emerita Augusta or simply Emerita. Its name (from *emeritus*, 'veteran') reflects the colony's origin as a settlement for Augustus' soldiers after the conquest of Galicia. The city occupies a strategic location on elevated ground (250 m) overlooking the plain of Extremadura. Situated at the highest navigable point of the river Guadiana, it was the chief communications junction of western Spain. Indigenous remains (a bronze cult-wagon, deer's-head jar, stone lion, bone idols) suggest the possibility of a small pre-Roman settlement here.[7] The oldest Roman monument is the bridge (still in use), whose 60 granite arches stretch 792 m across the valley of the Guadiana. An island in the middle of the river accommodated wharfs, warehouses and shops, while extensive breakwaters upstream helped retard the current, protecting the bridge from flood damage. The highway from Baetica crossed this bridge into the city, where it became the *decumanus maximus*, the principal east-west street. The main cross street, the *cardo maximus*, led northward across a small bridge over the Albarregas river in the direction of Asturica and Caesaraugusta. The other streets of the city were laid out on a rectangular grid, parallel to the *decumanus* and *cardo*. Although many of these streets were realigned in later times, the stone sewers of the Roman period still survive, allowing us to reconstruct the Roman grid (Figure 6.1). The Augustan colony was probably enclosed by a circuit wall, of which the only preserved traces are the wrongly named Arch of Trajan (the north gate) and a stretch of wall on the west flank of the Alcazaba citadel. The two-arched city gate depicted on the Augustan coinage of Emerita (Figure 6.2) was presumably positioned on this side, where a traveller crossing the Guadiana bridge would enter the city. In the late third century, a much larger rampart was built, enclosing the amphitheatre and showing that the city had greatly increased in size. Water was supplied to the city by three main aqueducts: Los Milagros, fed by a reservoir six km north of town; Aqua Augusta (so named in an inscription), fed by the Cornalvo reservoir 15 km east of town; and San Lázaro, fed by a system of underground channels. Though not the longest, Los Milagros is the most conspicuous, with its 38 surviving pillars of *opus mixtum* (alternating layers of granite and brick), 25 m high and linked by arches (Figure 6.3).

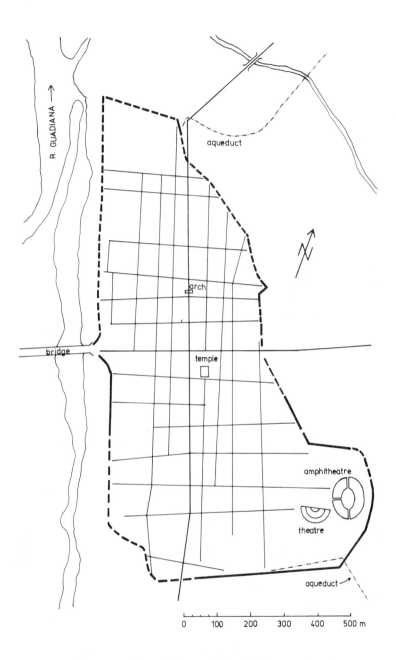

R. GUADIANA →

aqueduct

arch

bridge

temple

amphitheatre

theatre

aqueduct

0   100   200   300   400   500 m

Figure 6.1 Plan of Augusta Emerita. Source: Based
on Almagro Basch (1979) and Alvarez Martínez (1985).

Figure 6.2 The city gate of Emerita, as depicted on coinage
from the reign of Tiberius.

The civic forum was apparently located at the south-east corner of
the *umbilicus*, the junction of the main *decumanus* and *cardo*. This
zone contains the so-called Temple of Diana (shown by inscriptions
to be a temple of the imperial cult) as well as a bath complex supplied
by the San Lázaro aqueduct, and other public structures tentatively
identified as a basilica, portico and fountain. The supposed portico is
decorated with caryatids and roundels portraying Jupiter Ammon,
recalling the similar adornments of the Augustan forum at Rome.
Although the senate house has not been identified, the finds from the
'Diana' temple include a bronze statuette of the Genius of the Senate.
Further north, near the Plaza de la Constitución, is another public
zone (perhaps the provincial forum) including a temple podium,
inscriptions of the imperial cult, and another possible basilica.
The podium, partly unearthed in 1983, measures 24.9 m long by
3.2 m high and is thought to be a Capitolium, though a temple of
the provincial cult might rather be expected here.[8] Other religious

Figure 6.3 Los Milagros aqueduct at Emerita.

edifices in Emerita include a small temple of Mars (identified by an inscription erected by Vettilla, wife of the Hadrianic senator L. Roscius Paculus), as well as shrines of Mithras and other oriental deities.

The city also boasts places of entertainment, all in the south-east quarter. The circus (433 × 114 m) to the east of the city was restored between AD 337 and 340 but is now poorly preserved, unlike the theatre and amphitheatre. The theatre, 86.8 m in diameter, bears an inscription of 16 BC above the stage entrances, though the building gives evidence of later renovations. The seating, in three tiers according to Vitruvian canons, could hold an estimated 6,000 persons. The two-storey stage building, fronted by monolithic columns of coloured marble (Figure 6.4), replaces the original wooden structure, destroyed by fire in the late first or early second century. The adjacent amphitheatre is not a standing colosseum but is dug into a hillside. With maximum dimensions of 126.3 × 102.6 m it would have accommodated up to 15,000 spectators. Three inscriptions suggest a construction date of 8 BC. Excavations in and around the city have also revealed cemeteries and richly decorated houses.

Corduba (Córdoba)

The capital of Baetica was founded by M. Claudius Marcellus in either 169/8 or 152/1 BC, probably as a Latin colony. Under Caesar and Augustus it became a veteran colony. Although no pre-Roman occupation can be proved here, the town comprised from the beginning both Roman and indigenous settlers. But it was not so much a mixed as a divided community, for there is architectural and epigraphic evidence of an east-west wall separating the city into a 'forum' (Roman) sector and a 'Spanish' sector.[9] The colony was strategically sited at the highest navigable point of the Guadalquivir, with olive farming in the lands to the south and the silver and copper mines of the Sierra Morena to the north. The Republican town, enclosed by a rampart and laid out on a roughly square grid, was established about 500 m north of the river and covered about 30 ha. Under Augustus a further 20 ha were added on a different orientation to bring the city and its walls down to the river. The wooden bridge built by Caesar was later replaced by a stone one, whose foundations still support the

Figure 6.4   The stage building of the theatre at Emerita.

modern bridge. Several aqueducts delivered water to the town from the Sierra Morena; one of these, on the east side of the city, bears an inscription labelling it as the Aqua Nova built under Domitian. Remains of the forum have been discovered in the north sector of the town, and part of its paving has recently been unearthed on Eduardo Quero Street.[10] Attempts have been made to locate the basilica and senate house, without certainty. Although various deities are attested epigraphically, the only secure temple is that excavated on the corner of Claudio Marcelo and Capitulares Streets, dating to the late first century AD and perhaps dedicated to the imperial cult. Neither circus, amphitheatre nor theatre has so far been found, though four baths are known. There are scattered traces of town houses with mosaics and frescoes, and several cemeteries lie outside the city. Corduba was also a cultural centre, the home not only of noted poets like Lucan, but also of sculptors, as shown by the large quantity of local statuary.[11]

Tarraco (Tarragona)

Capital of the largest Roman province in Europe, Tarraco was described in antiquity as 'fortunate' (*felix*) and 'the most powerful city (*urbs opulentissima*) on these shores'.[12] Originally the chief city of the Cessetani tribe, it was captured and turned into a Roman town by the Scipios, and later became a Julian colony. Although not centrally located within its province, Tarraco was only five days' sail from Rome and gave access to the Ebro valley by a road ascending the Francolí valley, the swiftest route through the Catalan hills. Tarraco was surrounded by a rampart, perhaps 4 km in length, begun in Cyclopean masonry by the Cessetani and completed in Roman construction technique in the early second century BC (Figure 6.5). The city was divided into an upper and lower town, separated by the circus; the orthogonal layout is preserved in the modern street grid. The upper town, subdivided into two terraces, contained the large (300 × 150 m), porticoed provincial forum of the first century AD, and presumably a temple of the imperial cult which has not been found.[13] A much smaller porticoed area (58 × 13 m) in the lower town, traditionally identified as the colonial forum despite its miniscule size, has recently been interpreted as the main hall of a basilica, and the supposed senate house (13 × 11 m) on its north side is now seen as a shrine of Augustus, conforming to Vitruvian canons.[14] If this

Figure 6.5 The Roman circuit wall of Tarraco,
with pre-Roman stone courses at the base.

interpretation is accepted, the forum must lie to the south, beneath modern buildings.

The circus, dating to the second century AD, is 277 m long, with seating for an estimated 27,000 spectators. The amphitheatre, located close to the sea, was begun in the Flavian period and completed in the early second century; it measured about 93 × 68 m and could accommodate 11,000 persons (Figure 6.6). On the west slope of the lower town was a theatre, 70 m in diameter, with a seating capacity of 5,000.[15] Baths are mentioned in an inscription. A Paleochristian necropolis has been excavated west of the city.

CONVENTUAL CAPITALS

Astigi (Ecija)

The official name of this town, Colonia Augusta Firma, shows that it was not only founded by Augustus but considered a stronghold, originating no doubt as a settlement of army veterans. The indigenous name Astigi and an urn burial on the Alcázar hill are the only evidence for pre-Roman occupation. The site lies at the highest navigable point of the river Genil and would have been the export centre for local olive oil. The Alcázar acropolis which overlooks the surrounding countryside is guarded on the south and east by the Genil and the Matadero stream, though saved by its altitude (100 m) from their notorious floods. The Roman road from Corduba crossed the Genil over an eleven-arched bridge (remodelled in the eighteenth century but depicted in earlier engravings) to the east of the city. This road became the *decumanus maximus*, meeting the *cardo maximus* at the forum (the present Plaza Mayor). The medieval wall probably overlies a Roman predecessor, while the Palma (north) and Osuna (south) gates mark the Roman roads to Emerita and Urso. The remains of an amphitheatre, 133 × 106 m – slightly larger than those at Emerita and Tarraco – lie beneath the modern bull ring. No temples have been discovered, but one of the numerous mosaics in private houses portrays the triumph of the god Dionysus. Several cemeteries, streets and sewers have also been explored.[16]

Asturica Augusta (Astorga)

Hailed, with some exaggeration, as *urbs magnifica* by Pliny, the city owed its foundation to Augustus. Present evidence is inadequate

Figure 6.6 Interior of the amphitheatre at Tarraco.

to determine whether the town began as a legionary base for the conquest of the north-west, or whether a pre-Roman settlement marked the site. The town occupies a hill (height 850 m) on the boundary of two contrasting geographic zones, the infertile Teleno massif to the west, and the alluvial plain of the river Tuerto to the east. Asturica was the principal crossroads of north-western Spain, giving access to Galicia through the narrow corridor between the Teleno highlands and the Cantabrian Mountains. The medieval walls overlie Late Roman ones, of which traces (6 m thick) can be seen. A gate in the Roman wall stands behind the apse of the cathedral. Remains of the Roman sewer system provide some idea of the street grid. A well preserved series of hypocausts adjacent to Postas Street may indicate a bath house. A wide range of Roman deities is attested in local epigraphy, though no temples have yet been identified. There are also several private houses, some with mosaics.[17]

Bracara Augusta (Braga)

According to Pliny, this was an Augustan *oppidum*, unprivileged until the Flavian period when it received municipal status. There are traces of pre-Roman material, insufficient to show continuous occupation. The town was sited on a high (190 m) hill, 6 km south of the river Cavado, which provided access to the Atlantic Ocean 30 km downstream. The central location of Bracara made it a logical market and administrative focus for the Minho region, and by the fourth century it could be called 'rich Bracara which dominates an inlet of the sea'. The layout of the town is difficult to reconstruct, but the evidence suggests that it lay slightly to the south of medieval Braga. Traces of the (late?) Roman rampart, 4.5–5 m thick, were reportedly still visible at the beginning of this century, and the siting of the five cemeteries, which ought to lie outside the *pomerium*, tends to confirm the line of the wall. The location of the streets and forum is uncertain, archaeology being impeded by the modern town. The *decumanus maximus* is possibly Hospital Street, the *cardo maximus* Santa María Street. Several Roman deities are named in local inscriptions, but their temples cannot be located. However, the extramural shrine of two indigenous deities, Nabia and Tongo Nabiagus, has been discovered east of the town. In the west end of the city (the Maximinos quarter) a bath house has been excavated, and a theatre or amphitheatre was reported in the eighteenth century. There have been numerous casual finds of mosaics and other components of houses.[18]

Caesaraugusta (Zaragoza)

Successor to the Iberian town of Salduvia, Caesaraugusta was an Augustan colony and the chief city of the Spanish interior. As the principal inland crossing-point of the river Ebro it formed a nexus in the Spanish road system as well as being an agricultural and shipping centre, a mint and a conventual capital. The colony was laid out on a rectangular grid enclosed by a circuit wall with four gates, one at each end of the *cardo maximus* (Don Jaime Street) and *decumanus maximus* (Mayor and Espoz y Mina Streets). An inscription names one of these gates – presumably that facing Tarraco and Rome – as the Porta Romana.[19] The Roman bridge across the Ebro, which entered the *cardo* from the north, was destroyed in the ninth century. The modern city prevents excavation of the civic forum, believed to lie in the south-west corner of the *umbilicus*; there may also have been a commercial forum alongside the river. Some of the Roman drains were still in use in the early nineteenth century. The *cloaca maxima* was located near the north end of the *cardo*. Possible basilicas have been identified at the Casa Palacio de los Pardos and in Plaza de la Seo. Temples of the imperial cult are portrayed on the city's coinage, but none has been discovered. Although the Chronicle of Zaragoza records that a circus was seen here as late as AD 504, its site cannot be identified. The only place of public entertainment so far discovered is the theatre of the first century AD, at the corner of Verónica and Soler Streets; its external dimensions are 104 × 54 m, slightly larger than than of Emerita, with capacity for some 6,000 spectators. Public baths have been excavated in San Pedro y San Juan Street, and remains of private houses with mosaics are known.[20]

Carthago Nova (Cartagena)

Founded by the Carthaginians in 223 BC, 'New Carthage' was, at the time of the Second Punic War, 'the richest of all the cities in Spain', thanks principally to its excellent Mediterranean harbour, which is still an important base for the Spanish Armada. Mining, fishing and cultivation of *esparto* grass were the principal industries. Carthago Nova was also the site of a mint which coined both in the Punic period and under the Julio-Claudians. Protected by a lagoon to the north, the city was huddled amidst five hills, named by Polybius as Hasdrubal's Citadel and the hills of the gods Saturn, Vulcan, Asclepius and Aletes, the last being the deified discoverer of the local silver mines. The hills were ringed by a rampart with gates, one of which we know by name: the Porta Popilia, perhaps named after M. Popilius Laena, governor of Citerior in 139 BC.[21] The forum was centrally located near the modern Plaza de la Merced, at the *umbilicus*. The paving at the west end of the *decumanus* has been excavated in Plaza de los Tres Reyes, while the *cardo* led southward to the ovular amphitheatre, underlying the present bull ring. In addition to the temples of Saturn, Vulcan, Asclepius and Aletes (on the hills now known as Sacro, Despeñaperros, Concepción and San José, respectively), there was probably a temple on the site of the present cathedral, whose crypt is paved in Roman mosaic. Another public building was located in Moreria Baja Street, where a colonnade of monumental proportions has been unearthed. Remains of private houses with mosaics have been discovered in Duque Street.[22]

Clunia Sulpicia (Peñalba de Castro)

Promoted to the grade of colony by the emperor Galba (AD 68–9), Clunia must already have been a *municipium*, since its citizens belonged to the Julio-Claudian tribe Galeria, and its quattuorvirs and aediles were issuing coins under Tiberius. The site occupies a lofty (1,023 m) plateau called Alto de Castro, overlooking the rivers Arandilla on the east and Espeja on the south. The pre-Roman settlement, where Sertorius was besieged in 75 BC, apparently occupied the neighbouring hill, Alto del Cuerno. The hub of an extensive road network, as well as a production centre for Roman pottery (both *sigillata* and painted wares), Clunia must have been the chief market town of the northern Meseta. Two Roman bridges cross the Espeja, and a winding road leads up the hill to the town. The main *decumanus* and *cardo*, of which only traces survive, meet at the Flavian forum, which lies on a different orientation and is perhaps built over a Julio-Claudian forum. Measuring 140 x 100 m, it is flanked by shops, a tripartite basilica and a temple, possibly that of Jupiter, whose cult here is mentioned by Suetonius. Though the imperial cult is attested in inscriptions, its shrine remains unidentified. A small rock-cut theatre (95 × 63 m) is perched on the north-east edge of the plateau (Figure 6.7), and two public baths are

Figure 6.7 Rock-cut theatre at Clunia.

situated along the *decumanus* between theatre and forum. Of private houses the most impressive is the so-called Palace with gardens, occupied from the Augustan period until the fifth century.[23]

Gades (Cádiz)

The oldest city in Spain, founded by the Phoenicians (allegedly *c.* 1100 BC), Gades concluded a treaty with Rome in 206 BC. In 49 BC Julius Caesar granted Roman citizenship to the Gaditani, but its legal status remains controversial: Columella refers to the 'municipium Gaditanum' and an inscription records a 'duovir mun(icipii) Aug(usti) Gad(itani)', but local coins call it 'col(onia) Aug(usta) Gad(itana)'. In fact, we know that Cornelius Balbus founded a new city of Gades near the old one, so it may be that Augustus granted a different status to each of them, thus distinguishing the colony of Gades from the homonymous *municipium*.[24] Strabo claims that Gades had 500 Roman knights (citizens worth 400,000 sesterces), their wealth presumably derived from fishing and shipping, the two chief local industries. The most famous Gaditane monument, the temple of Hercules (on which see chapter 8), was located not in the city but 19 km to the south-east, on what is now the island of Sancti Petri. Traces remain of the aqueduct which brought fresh water to Gades from the vicinity of modern Algar, 60 km to the east.[25] Continuous occupation has impeded exploration of Cadiz itself; the notable monuments have been discovered near the Puerta de Tierra, the only land entrance to the city. Here stood a Punic necropolis, a Roman amphitheatre visible in the sixteenth century, and a Roman villa with mosaics, discovered in 1986. Spectacles in the amphitheatre featured wild beasts imported from Africa. Nearby, at the Posada del Mesón, the city's theatre is in course of excavation; according to Cicero, 14 rows of its seating were reserved for knights. The Saturn temple mentioned by Strabo has not been located.[26]

Hispalis (Seville)

Still one of Spain's premier cities, Hispalis is first attested in Caesar's war commentaries as a shipbuilding centre. This incident may have prompted Isidore's statement that it was Caesar who founded Hispalis and named it Iulia Romula. Although no other source calls the town Iulia, the colony was certainly in existence by

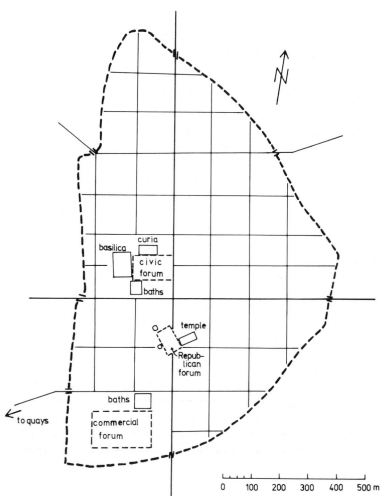

Figure 6.8 Plan of Hispalis, with hypothetical street grid.
Source: Based in part on Campos and González (1987).

the time of Augustus, when it struck coins labelled 'Col(onia) Rom(ula)'; the enrolment of its citizens in the Roman voting tribes Sergia and Galeria also points to a foundation by Julius Caesar or Augustus. The city gained prominence as a major river port on the Guadalquivir; Strabo makes it the third most famous city of Baetica, after Corduba and Gades, while Silius Italicus calls it 'renowned for commerce and for its alternating tides'.[27] Sufficient fragments of the Roman rampart, 2.5–3 m in breadth, have been discovered to permit

121

its course to be traced with reasonable accuracy (Figure 6.8). The road from Corduba passed through the San Esteban gate on the east side of the city, where it became the *decumanus maximus*. The Caños de Carmona aqueduct, bringing water from Alcalá de Guadaira, also entered the city at San Esteban and perhaps followed the line of the *decumanus maximus* to the forum. The location of the *cardo maximus* is more problematic; the solution adopted in Figure 6.8 would place it on the east flank of the fora. Three such fora have been proposed. The temple in Mármoles Street, of which five columns survive, as well as the remains of two early buildings to the west of it (one of the second century BC) are thought to mark the outline of the Republican forum, located at one of the highest points of the city. The temple lies at an angle to the later fora, suggesting that the city was resurveyed on a north-south orientation when it became a colony. The Republican forum was then replaced by a larger forum further north, near the *umbilicus*, in the vicinity of the present Plaza Pescaderia. Roman baths have been found here, and a basilica is thought to underlie the Moorish mezquita (now the Church of the Saviour). Numerous honorific inscriptions appropriate to a civic forum have also been unearthed here. A third forum, whose dimensions are less definable, has been postulated in the south-west corner of the Roman city (that corner nearest the river) in the vicinity of the cathedral. Baths have been excavated beside the Archbishop's Palace, and several inscriptions of professional associations, notably the *scapharii* (riverboat operators), suggest the presence of a commercial forum, similar to the Forum of the Corporations at Ostia.[28]

Lucus Augusti (Lugo)

The name of this town means the sacred grove of Augustus, the town's founder. It is situated on a hill (485 m) overlooking the river Miño, which waters the surrounding plateaus. The limits of Lucus in the Late Roman period are clearly marked by the extent of the extant rampart (restored in 1976) with approximately 85 semi-circular towers. The wall, more than 10 m high and *c.* 6 m thick, forms a rectangular circuit of 2,130 m. The *decumanus maximus* presumably ran from the Puerta del Miño to the facing gate on Generalísimo Franco Street; the position of the *cardo maximus* is not apparent. The forum was probably located in the Plaza del Campo, where a colonnaded building 12.4 x 5.5 m is clearly a public monument.

There are traces of an aqueduct and of water conduits within the city, as well as a bath house on the river bank.

Pax Iulia (Beja)

Although called Pax Augusta by Strabo, this colony was minting coins of Octavian before he became Augustus, and its foundation should therefore date to Julius Caesar or the subsequent civil war. The site, on a lofty (275 m) hill commanding an extensive agricultural plain, was a logical site for a conventual capital. The medieval and modern town has destroyed or covered most of the Roman constructions, but the medieval circuit wall rests on Roman foundations, and three of the ancient gates could be seen in the nineteenth century. The forum coincided approximately with the present Praça da República. The foundations of a temple, 29 × 16.5 m, were excavated in 1939 but subsequently reburied. Dedications to Isis and Serapis suggest that the city had shrines of these oriental cults, probably outside the rampart. Corinthian capitals and the granite foundations of a building on a north-south axis, discovered in the Rua dos Infantes in 1983, represent a temple or other public structure. A bath complex has been partly excavated, and the epitaph of an actor hints at the existence of a theatre.[29]

Scallabis (Santarém)

This town's origin as a pre-Roman stronghold is reflected in its official name, Praesidium Iulium. The enrolment of its citizens in two voting tribes, Sergia and Galeria, is consistent with a grant of colonial status under Julius Caesar or Augustus. The ancient site stood atop a high (100 m) cliff called the Alcáçova, the Moorish citadel of later times. It overlooks the river Tejo, on which there were presumably port facilities. Limited excavation on the Alcáçova has revealed Campanian ware, *terra sigillata*, and African and Phocaean Red Slip pottery, suggesting occupation from the second century BC to fifth century AD.[30]

VILLAGES AND COUNTRY DISTRICTS

While we can glean much information about Hispano-Roman cities from the preserved charters and the fruits of excavation, our knowledge of smaller settlements is scanty. Archaeological surface survey in the countryside can identify human agglomerations of differing sizes which may be consonant with villas or villages, but relatively few of the former, and almost none of the latter, have been excavated. On the other hand, chance epigraphic finds do provide us with a modicum of information on *vici* (villages) and *pagi* (country districts). A word of warning is requisite in using this evidence, however, because the Latin word *vicus* can also designate a subdivision of a city. Thus in the charter of Urso[31] the aediles are placed in charge of streets and *vici* (neighbourhoods), while at Corduba, inscriptions refer to a Vicus Hispanus (Spanish quarter) and Vicus Forensis (Roman quarter), reminding us of this city's origin as a joint Roman-indigenous settlement. However, most *vici* attested in the inscriptions seem to be rural villages. Though some may have originated as pre-Roman hill-forts, others sprang up along the Roman roads, and a few of these are named as *vici* in the Antonine Itinerary. Most *vici* are attested only once – not surprisingly, considering their humble status – and cannot be firmly identified, since the provenance of an inscription is not necessarily the site of the *vicus* mentioned on it. Nevertheless, the Vicus Spacorum named in the Antonine Itinerary can be pinpointed with reasonable certainty to the site of modern Vigo (named after it) in Pontevedra province. Excavation reveals that this was a *castro* occupied continuously from about 200 BC until the third century AD.[32] Another *vicus*, Vadinia, is attested both by an inscription from Cantabria and in Ptolemy's list of Cantabrian towns. Its inclusion in the latter source (which normally lists only cities) may be due to a shortage of major towns in this poorly urbanised region. Perhaps the most noteworthy features of the attested rural *vici* are that they all occur in the relatively unromanised zones of central, western and northwestern Iberia – none in Baetica or in eastern Spain – and that most of them bear non-Latin names. These facts strongly suggest indigenous settlements which may have existed since pre-Roman times. Though many of these *vici* were located in remote areas, at least one was in the domain of a larger town: 'Dercinoassedenses, vicani Cluniensium'.[33]

A very different type of rural community was the mining village. The population here consisted largely of slaves, whose living conditions would have been appalling, but there were also free entrepreneurs who worked abandoned diggings and who operated the concessions for various services, such as auctioneering, shoemaking, barbering, school-teaching and the baths. The village was administered by the procurator of the mine, who was a freedman of the emperor. At the Riotinto mine in Huelva province, the mining village occupied the entire hill of Cerro Salomon, about one kilometre. in diameter. The workers lived in multi-roomed houses built of unworked stones without mortar, similar to the shelters still used by local shepherds; clay was probably used to seal the chinks. The floors, paved in slate, could comprise several levels if the house was built on sloping ground. Only one room per house seems to have contained a hearth, and the large quantity of charred bones, teeth and boars' tusks found in one such hearth strongly suggests a kitchen.[34]

Pagi, on the other hand, are found almost exclusively in the highly romanised province of Baetica, whose massive olive oil exports imply an efficient organisation of the countryside. The two *pagi* attested outside Baetica are also in areas of regulated agrarian space: the colony of Emerita (bordering on Baetica) with its surveyed colonists' lots, and the Pagus Rivi Larensis on the east coast, whose inhabitants were apparently involved in a property dispute. Unlike the majority of *vici*, the *pagi* tend to bear Latin names like Augustus or Suburbanus; sometimes the name indicates the town to which the *pagus* was attributed, for example Pagus Carbulensis near Carbula. In some Spanish inscriptions, as well as in Roman law, the *pagus* designation is used to indicate the location of farms.[35] Another important purpose of the *pagus* organisation was undoubtedly to facilitate the census and tax-collection, as it did in Italy. But both *vici* and *pagi* probably had a commercial function as well. Villages and country districts must have been the scene of periodic rural markets where peasants could exchange or sell farm produce with their neighbours, and perhaps acquire basic manufactured goods like cloth and pottery. Though evidence from Spain is lacking, we know that provincial markets were often held every eight days, and that *ius nundinandi* (the right to hold such markets on a regular schedule) could be granted by Rome. In the north-west, where rural organisation was less advanced, each tribe had a *forum* (central market-place or trading centre) which bore the tribe's name, such as Forum Gigurrorum or Forum Limicorum.

RURAL ROMANISATION

Ancient literary sources place so much emphasis on urban life that it is sometimes difficult to remember that Roman society was essentially agrarian. Every town had a rural territory, and even in regions of advanced economic development, the rural population outnumbered the urban by a ratio of at least ten to one.[36] It is no accident that the most urbanised regions of Roman Spain, the southern and eastern coastal plains, were also the principal agricultural zones: cities depended on the surrounding countryside for the food that kept them alive and for the fleece, flax and leather that provided their clothing. Moreover, the urban elite owed their wealth primarily to the land and its products, and agrarian profits paid for the splendid public monuments erected by the local aristocracy, who maintained residences in both town and country. The peasants, too, were dependent on the towns, not only as markets for their produce but as centres for news, justice, festivals, medical treatment and schools, if they could afford them. The modern image of the 'consumer city' is apt to mislead us into thinking of ancient cities preying on the countryside, whereas the reality was not so much parasitic as symbiotic.

The Roman conquest had far-reaching effects on the rural economy. Not only was valuable manpower led off into slavery and precious lands and mines confiscated by the state, but the system of subsistence farming which had characterised pre-Roman Spain was challenged by Rome's imposition of taxes, rents and compulsory grain sales. Peasants had hitherto produced just enough food for their families, plus a small surplus to barter for pottery or other goods from craftsmen and merchants. The new Roman imposts meant that the peasant had to produce a much greater surplus in order to survive. Forest and scrubland had to be cleared and former pasture brought under cultivation. When periodic crises such as drought, flood, blight or locusts made payment impossible, farmers had to borrow money at interest from Roman financiers and risk foreclosure on their property, which would be sold to men with sufficient capital and sufficient diversity of holdings to withstand local crop failures. Moreover, the large estates with their greater production volume could afford to purchase slaves or hire extra labourers in season, and to experiment with new cash crops such as olives and grapes. This model accords well with Finley's proposal of an ancient trend for landholdings to increase in size.[37] However, it would be a mistake to assume a complete transformation from subsistence economy to villa economy in Roman Spain. Even in the rich agricultural zone of the lower Guadalquivir valley with its proliferation of magnificent villas manufacturing their own shipping amphoras and crushing their own olives, the intensive field surveys of Michel Ponsich have revealed a large number of small farms, particularly in areas where the soil is well adapted to cereal production. Similarly in Catalonia, the joint Anglo-Catalan field survey in the Comarca de Banyoles has discovered a mixture of large villas and smaller farms.[38] Thus, although economic conditions did favour the growth of large production units, rural settlement involved a hierarchy of sites rather than a homogeneous 'villa culture'.

Although small farmsteads are increasingly being documented, most of our evidence about rural settlement comes from villas. Well over a thousand certain or possible villas have been detected, often in the course of archaeological field surveys, and an increasing number of these are being excavated. However, we must distinguish between villa in the English sense (a country residence) and villa in the Roman sense, which could designate either an entire rural estate or the buildings situated at its centre. Moreover, these buildings can be subdivided into three types, the *villa urbana* or owner's residence, the *villa rustica* or farm-workers' lodgings, and the *villa fructuaria* or buildings for processing and storing the harvest. Barns and bunk-houses could be made of wood or mud-brick, so what usually survives is the 'urbane' villa, soundly constructed of stone, luxuriously decorated with mosaics, fresco and sculpture, and not infrequently equipped with private baths. It was, in fact, the rural counterpart of the owner's townhouse (*domus*), and provided with as many urban comforts as possible. If we add to the impressive archaeological remains (including fine ceramics and glassware for the table, and oil lamps to turn night into day) those materials which must have perished – furniture, curtains, cushions, all of exotic materials and richly ornamented; fine foods and wines; the flowers and ornamental trees in the peristyle court; the splendid view – we get some idea of what it was like to live here. The solid outer walls kept the villa cool in summer and shielded it from winter blasts, while a hypocaust system beneath the floor warmed the rooms with heat generated from a slave-operated furnace. Despite these amenities, it must not be forgotten that the villa was also a working farm, and while farm buildings rarely survive, the small finds show that villas were pressing their own olives and grapes and producing their own amphoras to ship the resulting oil and wine to market. The earliest villas appear in Late Republican times, chiefly in Catalonia but also in the Ebro and Guadalquivir valleys and in the vicinity of Carthago Nova. The number of villas in the Guadalquivir increases dramatically in the early first century AD, coinciding with a growth in oil and wine exports. By the end of the century, the villa system has spread into western, central and north-western Spain, and continues to flourish throughout the Early Empire. Although the evidence for the third century is sparse, the fourth sees the triumph of the grand villa: the *villa urbana* is more magnificent, and the estate much larger (to judge from the spacing of surviving villas) than in the preceding periods.[39] Although the immense size of these late farms invites comparison with the infamous *latifundia* or slave plantations of southern Italy and Sicily in the first century AD, their operation depended far less on servile labour than on tenant farmers (*coloni*) who provided the landlord with a portion of his harvest as rent, setting a precedent for the feudal system of the Middle Ages.

The system of land tenure in Roman Spain is inadequately documented and remains controversial. The second-century AD jurist Gaius claims that provincial land was the property of the State: individuals could enjoy possession or usufruct of the land, but not formal ownership (*dominium*). Moreover, unlike land in Italy, it could not be transferred by fictitious sale (*mancipatio*) nor acquired by long-term possession (*usucapio*). This artificial distinction between Italian and provincial land was unrealistic and has even been called 'a conveyancer's phantasy'. Indeed, an imperial rescript of AD 199, possibly modifying earlier rulings which do not survive, recognises private ownership of provincial land after ten years' residence or 20 years' absentee possession, and by the time of Justinian, ownership of provincial land thus acquired is actually called *dominium*.[40] The possibility of private ownership did not, however, prevent an irrevocable reshaping of the landscape by the Roman administration. In pre-Roman times land had been controlled by the indigenous tribes. After the conquest, Rome as absolute landlord confiscated huge tracts of terrain for colonies, for legionary *prata* (grazing lands), and for the emperor's estates. These latter, sometimes designated as *praedia Caesariana*, were managed by bailiffs or leased to contractors (*conductores*) who sublet the land to tenants. Moreover, the rural space not only of colonies but also of indigenous towns like Palantia and Salmantica was totally reorganised by Roman surveyors. The lines of the Roman centuriation can still be seen in aerial photographs of the territories of Ilici in Citerior, Carmo in Baetica, and most spectacularly Emerita in Lusitania, whose surveyed territory extended to the region of Turgalium, 70 km distant.[41] In addition to arable land (*ager*), the rugged Spanish landscape included vast stretches of upland pasture (*saltus*) suitable for grazing. Even cultivators had to find extensive pasturage, since their draught animals required more land for grazing than they could clear by ploughing,[42] though part of this need could be met by growing fodder or by grazing animals in fallow fields. For large-scale livestock owners, transhumance was the answer: lowland plains in winter, cool highlands in summer. Varro's farming manual records this practice in Italy, while Seneca complains about the immense herds of cattle feeding on entire provinces. The hilly Meseta and the dry plains of Extremadura were naturally suited to ranching and pastoral activity; shepherds are recorded here in Hannibal's day.[43] Unfortunately, excavators of rural sites have largely ignored the archaeozoological remains, whose examination could shed valuable light on the animal population and ranching activities.

7

PRODUCTION AND EXCHANGE

The rich agricultural and mineral resources of Roman Spain are well known from ancient literary sources and have often been catalogued,[1] but the peninsula's economic history can hardly be pieced together from mere inventories of commodities. We need to know who exploited these resources, with what manpower and facilities; where products were shipped, in what quantities and in what time period; whether goods were exported as tribute or for profit; who the traders were, what routes and conveyances they used; what impact trade had on the Spanish economy. Though these questions are not new, it is only quite recently that we have had enough evidence to tackle them. Well over a thousand confirmed or possible villas have been identified and a growing number have been excavated, revealing the pressing and storage rooms, the slave quarters, the brick and amphora kilns, the opulence and sometimes the name of the owner. Spanish amphoras carrying a variety of products are coming to light in increasing numbers, most dramatically through the exploration of underwater shipwrecks, which also provide information on the size and sailing routes of ships. Coin finds from Spanish sites are beginning to document monetary circulation, whose importance has been underlined by the recent demonstration that long-distance trade was stimulated by the need to pay taxes and rents in cash. Analysis of epigraphic evidence is revealing the extent of personal wealth and the motivations for conspicuous consumption.[2]

One of the biggest steps forward has come from the quantification of amphora evidence from both shipwrecks and villas. At last we are beginning to get answers to the question of how much of what was shipped where, and when. For instance, from 78 shipwrecks of Spanish origin in the period 50 BC to AD 250, the cargoes consisted of 66 per cent *garum* (fish paste), 26.5 per cent olive oil and 7.5 per cent metals; however, in the last century of this period, oil amphoras outnumbered those

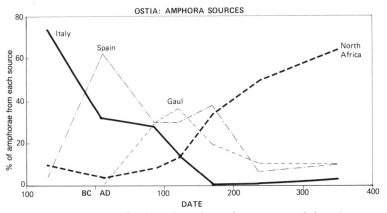

Figure 7.1 Quantification of amphoras from excavated deposits at Ostia. Source: Greene (1986). (Courtesy of B.T. Batsford Ltd.)

containing *garum*. The rise and fall of Spanish exports is dramatically illustrated in recent studies of the large quantities of amphoras found at Ostia (Rome's seaport) and at the villa of Settefinestre near Cosa in Etruria. Both sites reveal a similar pattern (Figure 7.1). During the Late Republic the number of amphoras carrying products from Spain is dwarfed by those from Italy. By the early first century AD, Spanish amphoras (representing wine, oil and fish products) have moved into the lead, accounting for 50–60 per cent of all amphoras. In the Flavian period, Spanish exports are competing with Gallic wine, which holds the upper hand (in terms of number of amphoras) in the reign of Trajan. By the mid-second century, however, Gallic trade declines and Spanish amphoras again dominate until the end of the century, when they are eclipsed by African exports.[3]

A further index of economic vitality is provided by the circulation of money within a community. Quantified data from coin finds are so far available for only a few sites, but these suffice to demonstrate the tremendous variations which could exist. Figure 7.2 shows the percentage of coins attributable to successive historical periods at three distant sites: Portus Ilicitanus on the east coast, Clunia in north-central Spain, and Conimbriga in the west. To a certain extent the data shown on this graph reflect changes in the number of coins circulating in the Roman world as a whole. For instance, the fact that all three sites show a relatively high percentage of coins in the 15 years from AD 260 to 275, compared with the preceding 67 years, is attributable to the well attested increase in the volume of debased coins minted during this troubled period. Other fluctuations, however, are not so easily explained. For instance, the Augustan and Flavian periods at Conimbriga, which see the construction of the forum, basilica and shops in the city centre, ought to be a time of economic growth, but there are few coins dating to these periods. This paucity cannot be due simply to the passing out of circulation of old coins, since the other two sites have a strong showing of first-century examples. On the other hand, whereas the majority of coins from Conimbriga and Portus date to the fourth century, this period accounts for only 8 per cent of coins from Clunia, despite an attested flurry of building activity on this site and a heavy influx of coinage into the peninsula until about 360. Moreover, while Clunia has a strong component of coins from the Antonine period (96–192), there are comparatively few at Conimbriga and Portus; this is particularly surprising at the latter site, a shipping centre which should have flourished during the heavy-volume commerce of the second century. It remains unclear whether these fluctuations represent regional economic differences or merely local ones; we urgently need quantified coin dates from other Spanish sites to complete the picture.

MANAGERS, MERCHANTS AND MANPOWER

Control of the means of production could reside in the hands of three agencies: the state and imperial treasuries (*aerarium, fiscus*), private individuals, and companies (*societates*). State control is most

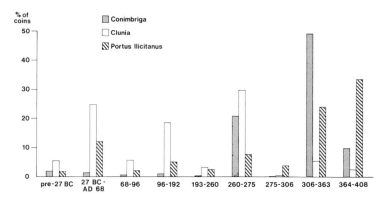

Figure 7.2 Comparison of coin finds, by period, from three Spanish sites. Source: Based on Pereira, Bost and Hiernard (1974), Gurt Esparraguera (1985) and Abascal (1989).

clearly attested in the mines, which were run by a procurator who was an imperial freedman, but the *aerarium* and *fiscus* must also have owned extensive tracts of agricultural land, either worked by slaves or leased to chief tenants (*conductores*) for subletting to tenant farmers (*coloni*).[4] Apart from colonists and peasants, who farmed lots of limited size, private ownership is represented by the villas, whose size and extravagance point to ownership by members of the elite, whether senatorial, equestrian or decurial. Only rarely do we have epigraphic evidence to identify the owners of these villas; for instance the villas of Els Munts and Els Viláns in Catalonia were owned by local magistrates, while that of Nossa Senhora da Tourega in Lusitania belonged to Q. Iulius Maximus, a Roman senator from nearby Ebora. We know too that the prominent *eques* and would-be senator Voconius Romanus of Saguntum had a seaside villa, not yet identified by archaeologists. The local elite were also involved in business dealings, for instance the exportation of lead ingots from the region of Carthago Nova by such families as the Aquini and Planii, to be discussed shortly. One of the *terra sigillata* manufactories at Tritium Magallum (Tricio) was owned by 'Mamilius P.', who may well be the local magistrate and provincial priest T. Mamilius Praesens attested in an inscription. Another member of this elite family, T. Mamilius Martialis of Tritium Magallum, is attested at Saguntum, where he may have played a role in commercialisation of this pottery.[5] Not all the owners were Spanish, however. Roman senators, who were prohibited from owning ships and therefore had to invest in land, preferred to diversify their holdings by buying property in various provinces, so that a drought or blight in one region would not wipe out all their assets. So pronounced was provincial investment that Trajan and Marcus Aurelius were obliged to order senators to put at least a fraction of their money into Italian land. How senators got their products to overseas markets without engaging in sordid commerce is a thorny problem. They could use their freedmen as overseas agents, but they would still need a middleman to transport the goods. Alternatively, they could sell their products to merchants, who had to find their own overseas customers. Merchants tended to be of low status, usually freedmen and foreigners. The association of Syrian and Asian merchants at Malaca, and the *negotiatores* of Spanish wine and salt fish in Italy, represent two links in the shipping chain. One *negotiator* from Citerior, a freedman, was clearly rich, being buried in Italy at the huge cost of 100,000 sesterces.[6] The third type of control, the *societas* or partnership, dealt with a specific commodity or resource. Such companies often handled government supply contracts, such as the Italian *societates* which provided grain, clothing and naval supplies to the Roman forces in Spain during the war with Hannibal, or the grain contractors dismissed by Cato in 195. Though the *socii* who produced *garum* were apparently a private company, the *societates* which operated mines in the late Republic were probably *publicani*, state contractors. Since the Senate had neither the experience nor the staff to run the mines, it had little choice but to farm them out to contractors, who provided the necessary capital and managerial staff. Though senators could own shares in these companies (at least in the first century BC), they could not actually be *socii*, so the partnerships were in the hands of *equites*. In the mining regulations from Vipasca (second century AD), entrepreneurs working diggings, slag heaps or quarries are permitted to have partners (*socii*), so long as they pay their share of the expenses. Those companies which were not under government contract could sell the commodity they controlled at a premium: Pliny notes that the *garum* of the *socii* fetched extravagant prices. The danger of monopolies creating artificial shortages and consequent higher prices is foreseen in chapter 75 of the Flavian municipal law, which forbids hoarding of commodities by *societates* or individuals.[7]

TRANSPORTATION AND TRADE ROUTES

The swiftest and least expensive means of transportation within the peninsula was by river, and nowhere is this principle better exemplified than on the Guadalquivir. Grain, olive oil and minerals from the Sierra Morena were loaded at Corduba and carried downstream by *scapharii* (boatmen), who had an association at Hispalis, where cargoes were transferred onto seagoing vessels. Further south, another Baetican river, the Guadalete (ancient Cilbus) emptied into the bay of Cádiz. At the mouth of this river a new harbour town was constructed in the first century BC, the Portus Gaditanus (Puerto de Santa María). Significant harbours were also established at Olisipo (Lisbon) at the mouth of the Tejo and Dertosa at the mouth of the Ebro. Although Emerita was at the highest navigable point of the Guadiana, it served only local river traffic because the 60 m waterfall at Pulo do Lobo ('wolf's leap') precluded access to the river mouth. On the lower Guadiana, the river port of Myrtilis was an export centre for minerals from southern Lusitania.

Not all of Spain is served by rivers, however, and since most of them flow away from the Mediterranean, their usefulness for trade was limited. Therefore land transport, though slow and expensive, was often obligatory. Thus we find a procurator of Baetica repairing, at his own expense, the road from Castulo to Sisapo, which had been washed out by rain but was necessary for transporting products to market. Since the roads tended to join towns, their course was far from straight, and had moreover to negotiate hilly and even mountainous terrain; medieval figures suggest that a cart could cover, at most, 25 miles a day in central Spain.[8] In Republican times, the main land route was the Via Heraclea, a coastal road running from Rome to Gades. This was later supplemented by a network of interior roads linking the major cities of Spain, with major hubs at Emerita, Asturica and Caesaraugusta. The amount of commercial traffic these roads would bear might vary from year to year, depending on local need; for instance, crop failure in one part of the peninsula might necessitate importation of food from neighbouring districts. Since long-range road transport was prohibitively expensive, the chief commercial use of the roads was to convey goods to the nearest seaport or river, whence they could continue by water. For instance, the *terra sigillata* pottery from Tricio in the Ebro valley, which is found throughout the northern Meseta, must have been transported by land across the Iberian Cordillera to the Duero and Tajo riverheads. Mules were not only the primary means of hauling wagons along the roads (though oxen were also used) but could also serve as pack animals, traversing mountain paths. Each mule could carry a 300 lb load, and the mules raised in rugged Celtiberia commanded a high price. Animal transport must have been particularly important in the olive-growing region east of Corduba, where field survey has recently revealed a complete absence of Dressel 20 oil amphoras, which are ubiquitous further downstream. Since the Guadalquivir is not navigable beyond Corduba and cargoes therefore could not be sent by river, these heavy, clumsy and breakable amphoras were clearly useless. Because wood for barrels is also scarce in this region, the oil must have been transported in animal skins by either wagon or mule train to Corduba, where it could be repackaged in amphoras or *dolia* and loaded onto barges.[9]

Overseas cargoes travelled on wooden merchant ships, steered by stern oars and powered by a large rectangular mainsail, with a capacity of 100–500 tonnes. One well-preserved vessel discovered off the south coast of France could have held between 5,800 and

7,800 amphoras, arranged in three or four layers. The distribution pattern of Spanish amphoras and other products outside of Spain suggests three major sea routes: along the coast of the Riviera to Rome, with numerous ports of call (including Massilia, from which products travelled up the Rhône); along the north coast of Africa from Morocco to the neighbourhood of Carthage; and up the Atlantic coast – past the famous lighthouse at Brigantium – to Britain and the mouth of the Rhine. But commodities destined for the Rhine could also travel, by river or road, up the Rhône and Saône valleys, and then continue overland to the Moselle. Perishable materials such as textiles, which have not survived, probably followed similar routes. Recorded trading voyages from Spain to the Red Sea (*via* an ancestor of the Suez Canal) and the Persian Gulf should be regarded as exceptional.[10]

MINERAL PRODUCTION

Pre-Roman mining in Spain mostly involved scratching the surface, though the Phoenicians and Massiliots were said to derive great profit from Iberian silver. There was also panning for gold in the rivers, especially the Tajo. Golden jewelry (diadems, bracelets, torques) and vessels were produced from the Bronze age to Roman times, and silver and bronze coinage was struck by numerous Iberian towns until the reign of Caligula. The elder Pliny, describing gold mining techniques in Spain, uses a number of native terms which lack Latin equivalents; this indigenous vocabulary perhaps points to development of these mining techniques in the pre-Roman period. While Pliny's claim that the whole of Spain abounds in gold, silver, lead, copper and iron is exaggerated, it is true that throughout the first centuries BC and AD Spain was the most important mineral supplier in the Roman world. But by AD 100 other provinces such as Britain and the Balkans were in competition, and Trajan's acquisition of the Dacian gold mines tipped the balance. At the same time, Spanish production was becoming more difficult and costly, as the easily accessible deposits became exhausted. After the second century AD, Spanish mining production was considerably reduced, though it did continue on a small scale into the Late Empire.[11]

Precious metals can take various forms: metallic ores, semi-processed ingots and processed products. The remains of all three provide evidence for Roman mining in Spain. Gold is of course the most glamorous of these metals, and Spain was the El Dorado of

the Roman world. This mineral occurs mostly in the north-west –
Galicia and Asturias – in veins of auriferous quartz in which the gold
is in more or less pure form, though often joined to sulfurs. Florus
notes that Augustus ordered the exploitation of the gold in Asturias,
while Pliny attests full-scale gold mining under Vespasian. He notes
– though the figures may be as early as Augustus – that the mines of
the north-west produced 20,000 lb of gold per annum, i.e. 90 million
sesterces, and adds that Spain provided 7,000 lbs of gold crowns for
Claudius' British triumph. Pliny was procurator of Citerior around
72–4 and appears to have seen these mines first-hand. The marked
concentration of mines in Asturias confirms Pliny's statement that
this region supplied the bulk of the gold. The alluvial terraces of
several river valleys were extensively mined. The most impressive
alluvial mine in the north-west is Las Médulas in León province.
Here Roman opencast workings penetrated almost vertical cliffs.
Aqueducts carried water to tanks with removable gates on top of
the mountain, and burrows were dug into the deposit, sufficiently
undermining the hill that part of it would collapse. When the water
was released from the tanks, the dislodged material was swept
into waiting ditches at the foot of the cliff, lined with wood
and scrub brush to trap the gold as the water rushed through.
Such is Pliny's description of the technique, and the Las Médulas
operation is the one most closely resembling it. Archaeologists have
discovered here the aqueducts, the huge tanks, the tunnels, and the
washed-out debris.[12] Another major gold-working district was the
upper valley of the river Duerna, south of Astorga, where numerous
man-made dams and reservoirs have been discovered. These were
almost certainly used for the mining techniques nowadays known
as 'hushing' (breaking up a mineral deposit by the sudden release of
a huge volume of water) and 'ground sluicing' (separating alluvium
from the mineral with a steady flow of water).[13]

The finest silver was said to come from Spain. The mine at Baebelo
dug by Hannibal yielded 300 lb per day, while the mines at Carthago
Nova in the second century BC were said to produce 25,000 denarii
a day for the Treasury, or about 36.5 million sesterces per year.
By Strabo's time the silver mines appear to have been in private
possession, but the early emperors seem gradually to have taken
them over. None the less, the accessible ore veins in the south-east
were already becoming depleted, and a recent study of miners' coins
suggests a migration of Celtiberian workers from Carthago Nova
and Castulo to the lucrative new mines in Galicia.[14] A focal point

for archaeological research has been the Riotinto district in Huelva province – possibly the site of the legendary Tartesos. These rich silver and copper mines were worked in a modest way from the seventh to fifth centuries BC and were reopened in the late Republic. Archaeological exploration of the Republican mining sites here has revealed that silver, not copper, was the Romans' goal, and that the mines reached their peak in the second century; production finally ceased in the mid-fifth century with the Visigothic invasion, as coin evidence suggests. The Roman mining town stood on the Cerro Salomon, where a thousand galleries removed the ore close to the surface. The veritable mountains of slag from these ancient workings amount to some 16 million tons, of which 15 million are silver and the rest copper. A smelting process separated silver from lead in white clay furnaces. Water from the mines was drained by means of eight pairs of gigantic wheels which raised the water nearly 30 metres, the wheels turning in opposite directions so that the water from both wheels would flow in the same direction in the launder. Estimated output was 2,400 gallons an hour. This system was obviously labour-intensive, and the ore deposits must have been quite rich to justify such measures. To navigate the cramped, dark galleries the mining slaves carried clay lamps, mostly with vertical handles and undecorated, though a few have simple mould designs.[15]

Copper mines occur elsewhere in the peninsula. The mine at Vipasca in Lusitania, from which come the famous mining regulations on a lengthy Hadrianic inscription, involved both silver and copper workings. This was a state-owned mine, controlled by a procurator who was an imperial freedman, and concessions were rented to various tradesmen. The best-known copper district, however, was the Sierra Morena north-east of Corduba, producer of the famous *aes Marianum*, used in minting Roman bronze coins. The mine, which also produced gold, was apparently owned by one Sextus Marius who was put to death on a trumped-up charge of incest by Tiberius, who wanted to confiscate the mine, according to Tacitus. Though Tacitus is well known as a hostile witness, a milestone recording the construction of a road leading to the mine one year before Tiberius had Marius hurled from the Tarpeian rock may suggest a premeditated plan. An imperial procurator of the *mons Marianus* is attested in the Flavian period.[16]

Lead, generally found with silver, is attested in the form of ingots; these have been recovered chiefly from shipwrecks off Carthago Nova and in the Bay of Cádiz, through which the products of

Figure 7.3   Lead ingots of the Roscii family, from Carthago Nova.
(Museo Arqueológico Nacional, Madrid.)

the Sierra Morena were shipped. Many of them belong to the Aquinus family, which flourished at Carthago Nova at the end of the Republic or beginning of the Empire. A C. Aquinus is also attested as a magistrate in this city and it may be that the Aquini were Italian immigrants who formed a prominent part of the local elite. Another family represented on these ingots, the Planii, who flourished in the second half of the first century BC, is also attested in a cargo at Marseille. A cache of some 30 ingots from Orihuela, north of Carthago Nova, bears the stamp of the Roscii, a senatorial family from Italy (Figure 7.3). Also in the vicinity of Carthago Nova was a *societas montis argentarii* ('Silver Mountain Company') near the town of Ilucro, one of whose lead ingots was recovered from the Tiber river at Rome; an actual stamp used for marking the Silver Mountain ingots is housed in the Archaeological Museum of Murcia.[17] Seventeen ingots from a shipwreck off Mallorca bear not only the mould mark of their manufacturer L. Manlius, but the imperial die stamp 'Vesp(asianus) Aug(ustus)'; they are therefore to be dated to the 70s and confirm that lead mines had passed into imperial hands in the first century AD.[18] The contemporary record of Pliny mentions that certain lead mines were under state control, though lead coins (negotiable only in the mining community) from El Centenillo near ancient Castulo, bearing the countermark 'SC' – possibly *societas Castulonensis* – raise the possibility of private or at least state-franchised companies operating in the interior. Lead ingots found at Rome are stamped *societas argentariarum*, suggesting a private corporation mining both silver and lead. Fifty-two lead smelting furnaces have been discovered on the Cape de Gata in Almería province.[19]

Another important Spanish mineral was cinnabar – red mercuric sulfide, also known as vermilion or, in Latin, *minium*. Used for red lettering in inscriptions and books, it was extracted from mercury-laden veins of quartzite. The cinnabar company of Sisapo produced 2,000 lb per year at 70 sesterces per lb, according to Pliny. Sisapo is traditionally associated with the rich mercury mines at Almadén in Ciudad Real province, whose name is the Arabic word for mines. Coins of Sisapo have been found at Almadén, where there are hand-dug cinnabar and lead mines containing Roman artifacts; one cinnabar gallery, 450 m long, was only 25 m below ground level.[20] However, there is no sign of a Roman town here, and a recently published inscription suggests that Sisapo was actually located at La Bienvenida, about 30 km to the south-east. Spanish cinnabar was exported far afield. An inscription from Capua records an apparent agent of the cinnabar company (*vilicus sociorum Sisaponensium*). Pausanias attests its use at Phigalia in Arcadia, apparently to colour a statue of Hercules. The red paint used on statuary and inscriptions is occasionally preserved, and its visual impact reveals why cinnabar was worth shipping to the far end of the Mediterranean. For red fresco pigment, however, the Romans preferred red ochre (earth coloured by iron oxide), of which the Balearic Islands produced a particularly splendid variety.[21]

MANUFACTURED GOODS

Pottery was another commodity for which Spain found a ready market abroad. Iberian painted ware, including the distinctive *sombrero de copa* or top-hat vase type produced in the Elx-Arxena region, was exported to numerous Italian sites during the last two centuries BC, and especially to the cities of Liguria and the Tyrrhenian coast. It is not yet clear whether the examples excavated on the Byrsa at Carthage belong to the Punic period, i.e. prior to 146, or to the supposed resettlement under Caesar. As for the wares reaching Italy, the point which may surprise is that these Iberian painted pots with their rather crudely executed figures were considered worth importing by Italians who had access to the latest Campanian products. In addition to the distinctive painted vases, the workshops of the east coast produced black-gloss wares from the fourth to second centuries BC, imitating Attic and Campanian pottery.[22] By the time of Augustus, Spain was importing *terra sigillata* from Italy, and in the first century AD from southern Gaul. But potters also followed the army, and the *figlinarius* of the Fourth Legion was producing *sigillata* at Herrera de Pisuerga prior to AD 40. By about AD 50 Spain was producing its own variety of it, the so-called *terra sigillata hispánica*, ranging in colour from rosy beige to bright red to light brown, and with some variants in shape and design from the standard Dragendorff series. A number of production sites are known, notably Tricio on a tributary of the Ebro, and Andújar in Granada, and several kilns have been excavated. This Spanish *sigillata* has long been regarded as inferior to the products of Arezzo, La Graufesenque and other classic production centres, and intended for domestic consumption only. Thirty years ago, the only known find-spots were in Spain and at two sites in northern Morocco. More recent work has shown, however, that Spanish *sigillata* was exported to southern France, Algeria, and even (in small quantities) Ostia. In view of this distribution network, we may need to reassess the relative merits of Spanish *sigillata vis-à-vis sigillata* produced elsewhere, in terms of aesthetic appeal and price. We may note too that the *parois fines* or thin-walled wares of southern Spain have been found at many sites in Narbonese Gaul, as well as in Italy, Germany and Britain.[23]

Spanish production of colourless glass, using a mixture of one part sand to three parts soda, is mentioned by Pliny, and some aspects of the Roman technique can still be detected in the glass of Islamic Spain. Although a few glass furnaces have been identified at Iluro and other sites on the east coast, the bulk of our evidence for Spanish glass manufacture comes from the south, where a wide range of distinctive jugs, flasks, drinking cups and cinerary urns in pale or colourless blown glass was produced in the first two centuries AD. The location of the production centre or centres for this early glass remains in doubt. At Emerita, excavations outside the Roman wall, in the vicinity of the modern bull-ring, revealed numerous fragments of green glass in association with pottery of the first two centuries AD, but found no proof that the glass was manufactured locally. On the other hand, there is clear evidence for glass production in this same neighbourhood in the Late Empire, since a deposit datable to the fourth century contained 31 glass moiles (residue from the glass-blowing process) as well as 13 long, narrow pieces of iron tubing which appear to be glass-blowing irons.[24]

Spain was also noted for its textile industry. Spanish linen is praised by the elder Pliny, who notes that the linen of Tarraco is very fine and has a special lustre due to the stream (the Río Francolí) in which it is dressed. The flax of Zoelae in Galicia, he notes, had recently been imported into Italy and was especially useful for nets used in hunting. The flax of Saetabis (Xátiva), while unsuitable for such nets, was reckoned the best in Europe and was very much in demand; in the twelfth century the Arabs used the linen of Xátiva to manufacture paper. Flax was also used for making sieves and grain-sifters, both of which were said to have been invented by Spaniards. The production of linen was an important industry, attested in inscriptions as well as by Strabo, who specifically cites the flax-workers at Emporiae on the east coast.[25] Wool-workers are also mentioned epigraphically. The most famous woollen cloth was that woven at Salacia in Lusitania, using fleece that produced an attractive chequered pattern. Garments of Baetican wool were considered a luxury fit for a Maecenas. Woollens from Asturia are mentioned in Diocletian's price edict of 301, suggesting trade with the eastern provinces.[26]

FISH AND FISH SAUCE

The coastal waters of Spain teemed with fish of many varieties, and those native to the Atlantic (such as tuna) were naturally a profitable export to Mediterranean lands. Fish were caught in rivers as well as on the sea, but the requirement to salt them for travel gave the export monopoly to the coastal regions. Off the Mediterranean coast of Baetica, two fishing capitals are attested: Sexi, where mackerel was caught, and Carteia, haunt of the trumpet fish and porphyry, both used in the purple-dyeing industry. Fish and fishermen are prominently displayed on the coins of Carteia under Augustus and Tiberius. From the Atlantic coast came oysters and mussels of great size, conger eels, lampreys and other edible species. The dory, caught at Gades, was numbered among the choicest of fish. But the prize catch was the tuna, a migratory species which can grow to five feet in length and weigh 600 lb; Strabo refers to 'large numbers of plump, fat tunafish' in this region. Off the coast of Gades, at the mouth of the river Barbate, are submerged, artificial structures of stone, 5–30 m below the surface, some carved out of the rock, others built of blocks. These structures are circular in form and appear to be fish corrals. In antiquity they would have been above sea level. Pliny indeed speaks of the *cetariae* or fish ponds of mackerel in Spain.[27]

The most profitable exports were salt fish and fish sauce. Even in pre-Roman times the Iberians salted their catches of tuna, mackerel and sturgeon in the waters off Gades, and the Phoenicians were reputed to have constructed actual fish-salting installations to conserve fish. Gaditanian salt fish was already known at Athens by the fifth century BC. The fish was gutted and cut into cubes or triangular chunks, with slits in the flesh to aid the penetration of salt; the pieces were placed together in rectangular vats (such as those excavated at Sexi, containing materials from Claudius to the fourth century) with an equal quantity of salt and allowed to steep for 20 days; they were then removed from the vats and sealed in amphoras. The salt used in fish-processing was undoubtedly obtained by evaporation in salt pans (*salinae*) and any surplus salt was presumably sold as a preservative for other foods.[28] Even more profitable was the fish sauce (*garum, liquamen*), made from the viscera and blood of fish that had been salted (notably tuna and mackerel) together with whole small fish, such as anchovies; this mixture was placed in a brine solution and left in the sun for two months, or in a heated room for less time. After several decantations emerged the black sauce which added great zest to bland dishes. Being versatile it was also costly: Pliny quotes 1,000 sesterces for about twelve pints.

Garum was produced chiefly on the coasts of Baetica and Lusitania. Garum factories have also been excavated, for example at Baelo and Carteia on the south coast. The Baelo installations date from the late first century BC if not earlier; the waterproofed concrete vats, when excavated, still contained tuna skeletons. The best-known garum operation in Lusitania was at Tróia, conveniently situated at the mouth of the river Sado, from which the product could easily be shipped.[29] On the east coast, garum operations have been discovered at Carthago Nova and Lucentum, while Ausonius praised the garum exported from Barcino. None of the excavated garum factories is demonstrably earlier than Augustus, though Greek texts attest Spanish garum as early as the fifth century BC. Salt fish and garum were exported throughout the Mediterranean as well as into the north-western provinces. A first or second century AD amphora from Alesia in Gaul bears the painted inscription 'cordyla arguta excellens' (prime, piquant fish sauce from baby tuna); another from the same site, as well as one from Amiens (ancient Samarobriva), reads 'cordyla Portus vetus' (aged fish sauce from baby tuna of Portus Gaditanus); and one from Vindolanda in Britain mentions prime mackerel sauce, presumably from Lusitania. Baetican fish amphoras also appear at Colchester, Verulamium and other British sites in the first two centuries AD, usually representing about 10 per cent of the total amphora population. In the Mediterranean region, fish products were extremely popular, accounting for about 60 per cent of Spanish amphoras from shipwrecks and from two quantified samples at Ostia.[30] The shippers are represented by painted inscriptions on the neck and shoulder of the amphora, and occasionally on stone inscriptions. One P. Clodius Athenius – a freedman, to judge by the name – was a *negotians salsarius* in first-century AD Rome, representing the fish salters of Malaca (*negotiantium Malacitanorum*), while at Malaca itself there is a group of Syrian and Asian merchants, who may have been trading for garum. Among various amphoras recovered from shipwrecks off the coast of Almería in south-eastern Spain is a Dressel 14 of the late first or second century, bearing on its neck the painted inscription 'liq(uamen) fl(os) excel(lens)' and the name of the exporter, L. Sert(orius) Licinyclens(?). The Saint-Gervais shipwreck at Fos-sur-Mer (France) included a Baetican Dressel 7–11 amphora with the painted inscription, 'scomb(ri) flos' and the shipper Junius Cilo '(e)x of(ficina) Augg(ustorum)', the last phrase indicating production at an imperial installation. Another of the Fos amphoras bears the names 'Sabinus et Avitus', perhaps a *societas*.[31]

The elder Pliny praises the *garum sociorum* ('fish sauce of the Associates') made of whole mackerel, the most popular kind in his day. Contemporary corroboration comes from Pompeii, in the form of a pot inscribed 'garum sociorum'; garum amphoras of Claudian date occur at Ostia, Castro Pretorio, Verona, Longarina and Nijmegen. Spanish garum merchants are attested at Puteoli, and *garum Hispanum* is named on amphoras at Augst (ancient Raurica) in Switzerland. Numerous shipwrecks off the coast of Spain, Narbonensis and Corsica have revealed fish sauce en route to Italy. Baetican fish sauce also reached Carthage and Berenice in North Africa.[32] Lusitanian garum amphoras from beyond the Straits of Gibraltar have been found at the eastern extremity of the Mediterranean, in Bulgaria and in Palestine. Garum exports continue through the second century, though they are overshadowed by the burgeoning oil exports, so that garum amphoras, which predominate in first-century Ostia, are hardly noticeable in the Monte Testaccio at Rome (though the Monte has not been fully excavated, and there were probably other amphora dumps elsewhere in the city). The trade breaks off in the third century, and is renewed only modestly in the fourth, having a chiefly local circulation. None the less, the fourth-century *Expositio* still names *liquamen* among Spanish exports, and the recent discovery of Almagro 50 and 51C amphoras in Sardinia suggests that Spanish garum was still finding overseas markets in the fourth and early fifth centuries.[33]

DRY CROPS

Wheat was the principal source of nourishment in the Mediterranean diet. Spanish wheat was particularly heavy: that from the Balearic Islands, at 35 lb per peck, outweighed all others, while that of Baetica, at 21 lb per peck, was heavier than all except the African and northern Italian varieties. During Gildo's revolt at the end of the fourth century, when the usurper had seized control of the African ports, Rome had to import grain from Spain; one gathers that this was the exception rather than the rule by this period. The harvested wheat was stored in underground silos (*putei*) whose bottoms were covered with straw to keep the grain dry; wheat stored in this manner was said to last 50 years. Archaeologists have recently uncovered several bell-shaped silos in the vicinity of ancient Ategua (Campiño de Córdoba). They range in capacity from 35 to 68 cubic m (allowing storage of 27,000–53,000 kg of wheat in each silo), and the walls of the larger ones are lined with Roman brick.[34]

Perhaps more important as an export was the broom plant – Latin *spartum*, modern Spanish *esparto* – which grew on the arid Campus Spartarius in the hinterland of Carthago Nova, which Pliny defines as an area less than a hundred Roman miles long by thirty wide. Shoes and cords made of esparto have been recovered from Stone and early Bronze age sites in Spain, and it is still used for ropes, sandals, canvas and torches. Esparto baskets and ropes have been excavated in the ancient mines near Carthago Nova, and Pliny adds that the rustics used it also for bedding, fuel, torches, footwear and shepherds' clothing; it could be soaked in sea water and pounded to produce a rough cloth. Cato used esparto as a cover for urns and amphoras in his vineyard; other authors cite its use in making shoes for cattle and oxen, nailed horseshoes being unknown in antiquity. Strabo notes that the dryness of the Campus Spartarius makes Spanish broom ideal for twisting into ropes and says it is exported to all regions and particularly to Italy. An inscription from Gades attests a *spartarius*, a maker and seller of rope; the seaport of Gades was a logical place to market ships' ropes. A sarcophagus relief from Ostia shows a cobbler's shop operated by two men, one of whom appears to be unwinding a coil of rope. It appears, then, that esparto was used to produce some sort of shoe, perhaps comparable to today's espadrilles.[35]

WINE

The origins of wine in Spain are lost in time. Viticulture was reputed to have been introduced by the Phoenicians who brought vines from the eastern Mediterranean in the sixth century BC. In 1972 a shipwreck of the fourth century BC was excavated off Palma de Mallorca in the Balearic Islands; on board were containers of olives, almonds, shoots of wild olive, and grape vines, sealed in amphoras and ready for planting. Since the ship also carried Red Figure pottery it was clearly heading west and therefore (the excavators concluded) probably en route to Spain. This may well be so, but it need not mean that vines were only just being introduced. Conclusive evidence came only in June 1984 with the discovery of twenty-two fossilised grape seeds, recovered by flotation and now radiocarbon dated to the first half of the third millennium BC on the Final Neolithic site of El Prado de Jumillo in Murcia province. Where there is fruit, there are people who will discover how to ferment it; and it may be that the Iberians discovered wine even before the Phoenicians.[36]

St Isidore, in his *De laude Spaniae*, calls Spain 'rich in grapes'; even today it ranks third in world wine production. Spanish wine was not considered as good as the best Italian wine, though it was an excellent *vin ordinaire*: Pliny calls it the best-rated of the inferior brands. Yet Ovid concedes only that it was good enough to drug a servant, and it is noteworthy that the wine list at Julius Caesar's triumphal banquet for his conquests in Spain in 60 BC included no Spanish brands. The *balisca* or *basilica* vine, known in pre-Roman Spain as the *coccolobis*, produced grapes which Columella considered 'by far closest to the very best; for their wine stands long keeping and attains excellence with age;' they were also hardy and resistant to storms. There were two types of *coccolobis*, one producing round grapes, the other oblong grapes; the latter type are depicted on coins of the

Baetican town of Acinipo during the late Republic. Pliny admits that *coccolobis* has a high yield, though he calls it 'unfriendly to the head' (*capiti inimica*).[37] Today Spanish grapes are grown by *secano* or dry cultivation. But Columella notes that vines will grow in every country, climate and soil, and it appears that the ancient Spaniards opted for wet farming. Pliny says the Spanish vines are planted in well watered soils and, indeed, that the Spanish vintagers pick the grapes when the ground is under water rather than draining it off. What did bother the vines were the south and south-east winds; for this reason, says Columella, Baetica is not the best area for grape-growing. Despite Columella's caution about viticulture in Baetica one of his own farms which produced wine was named Ceretanum. It was once supposed that this was at Caere in Etruria, but a more probable identification is the town of Ceret near Cádiz, Columella's native district. Ceret is also thought to be near Jérez de la Frontera, the centre par excellence of sherry production for centuries.[38] The development of a Spanish wine industry in the Late Republic – perhaps managed chiefly by Italian settlers – not only reduced the requirement to import wine but created a surplus. Strabo, in the time of Augustus, notes that large quantities of wine are exported from Baetica, while Columella, writing under Claudius, points out that as Italian viticulture declined, wines from Baetica and Gaul were being imported by Rome. Amphora evidence corroborates these claims, and the Port Vendres II shipwreck was loaded with Haltern 70 Baetican wine amphoras destined for either Narbonensis or Italy, in the reign of Claudius.[39]

Wine seems to have been produced on the east coast from an early date. In the fourth and third centuries BC, large quantities of Catalonian wine, perhaps carried by Greek merchants, were being exported to Africa, to judge by the amphora evidence from Carthage. Although temporarily eclipsed on the Mediterranean market by superior Italian products, Iberian wines gradually achieved a come-back, as illustrated by the Cap Béar III shipwreck (end of Republic or early Augustan), whose wine amphoras were five-sixths Italian and one-sixth Laietanian. Pliny, Florus, Martial and Silius Italicus praise the wine of Tarraco, and Pliny that of Lauro. Kilns for wine amphoras have been excavated at Tarraco and Barcelona, and Pliny observes that the wines of Laietania (the Barcelonan coastal strip) were famous for the quantity of their wine whereas the products of Tarraco and the Balearic Islands were noted for their quality.[40] This suggests that the Laietanian wines, which began production under the late Republic or Augustus, were not so good. Martial indeed refers to the *faex Laietana*, 'Laietanian dregs'; similarly in the Middle Ages the wine of Catalonia sufficed to meet the needs of the capital, Barcelona, but did not find much of an export market. The wines of Saguntum further south were also inferior: a scholiast on Juvenal calls Saguntum 'a city of Spain in whose territory bad wine is grown'! In Lusitania, Strabo mentions an island at the mouth of the Tagus (presumably one of the islands in the Lisbon estuary) which grew excellent vines. In the interior of the province, cupids are shown picking grapes on a sarcophagus from Vila Franca de Xira, while a third-century mosaic from Emerita (Figure 7.4) depicts grape treaders merrily producing wine. The Douro region further north is now the heartland of the port wine industry, for which there is no ancient evidence. Nonetheless, excavation of Bronze age cemeteries in the region has uncovered carbonised grape seeds and vine shoots.[41] The central plateau or Meseta of Spain was not a wine-producing region – the inhabitants of central and northern Spain, who were Celtic rather than Iberian, were reputed to drink beer instead – but the valley of the river Ebro (the only one of the peninsula's four major rivers to flow into the Mediterranean) was engaged in viticulture. A wine factory and warehouse located on a Roman villa at Funes in Navarra has been excavated (or at least 700 square metres of it); it is equipped with presses and vats and dates from the first to third centuries AD. Gold coins of Flavian and Hadrianic date perhaps reflect the profitability of this establishment.[42]

Where did the wine go? As Columella attests, Baetican wine went to Rome, a fact verified by fragments of Baetican wine jars in the Monte Testaccio. The wine arrived through Ostia in the first century – the new harbour built by Claudius must have greatly facilitated imports – as well as through the Trajanic Portus north of the Tiber in the second, where wine magazines (*cellae vinariae*) are attested epigraphically. East coast amphoras of Dressel 2–4 painted 'Lauronense' (wine from Lauro) are found at Ostia, together with inscriptions of *negotiantes vinarii* and a *negotiator ex Hispania citeriore* (possibly of wine).[43] An Ostian mosaic shows wine amphoras of Dressel 2–4 (types exported from Citerior) being reloaded onto a riverboat for the final leg to Rome. Strabo implies that Spanish wine goes to Ostia and Dicaearchia (Puteoli), and it is at Puteoli that Trimalchio's friend Habinnas is served Spanish wine poured over hot honey at a funeral banquet. At Pompeii in the

Figure 7.4 Grape treaders, on a mosaic from the house of the Amphitheatre Emerita. (Foto Barrera. Museo Nacional de Arte Romano, Mérida (Badajoz).)

first century we find Tarraconensian wine amphoras, again labelled 'vinum Lauronense'.[44] A fresco from the House of the Vettii shows cupids drinking wine from Dressel 2–4 amphoras.

Baetican Haltern 70 wine amphoras occur at Luni and at several sites in Gaul, as far north as Amiens, where a Haltern 70 has a painted inscription mentioning *sapa* or boiled-down wine. A combination of amphora and epigraphic evidence suggests a trade in Spanish wine up the Rhône to the Mosel valley by the second century AD (Spanish wine was already reaching Britain in the first). Wine from the east coast also reached northern Africa. At Carthage are found Dressel 2–4 amphoras from Tarraconensis and Pascual 1 amphoras from Laietania, all of the first centuries BC/AD, as well as Haltern 70s from Baetica. A wall of amphora sherds excavated on the Byrsa by Delattre around the turn of the century contained an example with the painted inscription 'Lauronense'. From the end of the first century AD Spanish wine imports decline at Carthage, which switches to Campanian wine.[45] Because Britain, Spain and Gaul supported Clodius Albinus against Septimius Severus in the 190s, Severus took harsh measures against these provinces. His confiscation of various enterprises resulted in a collapse of the central Gaulish *sigillata* industry and near collapse of the Spanish wine business. Amphora evidence indicates a major interruption of the wine trade; Spanish wine now reaches Gaul and Britain in only the tiniest quantities. Spanish wine is not mentioned in Diocletian's price edict, and the trade seems to have ceased altogether.

OLIVE OIL

Oil was Spain's premier export commodity. Pliny quotes Fenestella as saying that in 581 BC the olive was not found at all in Italy, Spain or Africa. Yet it was obviously in place and flourishing by the Late Republic, especially in Baetica where the olive was the largest of all trees and naturally adapted to the gentle slopes of that region. Around Emerita there were even sweet olives, sweeter than a raisin, which were otherwise found only in Africa.[46] Unlike the vine, olives required great investment of time and capital, and it is doubtful whether oil production reached surplus capacity before the beginning of the Principate. Ulia in Baetica is the only town to display the olive on its late Republican coinage. The earliest overseas amphoras, the Oberaden 83 (also known as Haltern 71), are of Augustan date. The main production zone was the Guadalquivir valley (Figure 7.5), especially around Arva, Axati and Ilipa on the middle Guadalquivir (now in Seville and Córdoba provinces). Field survey work in this region suggests the cultivation in antiquity of at least 5 million olive trees, and the number of olive presses could easily have exceeded 1,000. Stamps of numerous producers have been found on ancient estates, for instance the Aelii Optati, who were a family of oil magnates at El Judio between Arva and Axati in the second century.[47]

Dressel's excavations in the Monte Testaccio at Rome suggested that the zenith of Baetican oil exports occurred under Antoninus Pius, since a large proportion of the amphora stamps were datable to the years 146–54. However, more recent calculations for the Monte suggest that, of an estimated 45 million amphoras dating from Augustus to the end of the second century, more than 35 million are earlier than 146, 9 million date to 155–200, and less than half a million (or about 1 per cent of the total) to 146–54.[48] There is a probable reduction at the end of the second century, thanks to the Severan confiscations, but no sharp decline. Unlike wine, which suffered badly at this time, Spanish oil was in high demand at Rome for the emperor's public distributions. What does change is the ownership. Oil passes from private hands into the grasp of the *fiscus*, and the amphoras of the period 217–35 read, 'fisci rationis patrimoni provinciae Baeticae' and 'Augustorum nostrorum'.

Through most of the Early Empire, Baetican oil travelled in the globular amphoras known as Dressel 20, which held just

Figure 7.5 Olive harvesters, on a relief from Córdoba. Late 3rd or early 4th century AD. (Museo Arqueológico de Córdoba; courtesy of Junta de Andalucía).

under 77 litres of oil. The known kiln sites were located along the Guadalquivir river and its tributary the Genil, perhaps in regional centres rather than on individual farms, in order to bottle the oil for transport downstream. Overseas oil shipping was costly but essential. In the first century AD Baetican oil invades Rome, Ostia, Pompeii, Stabiae and other excavated sites. Aquitania and Narbonensis import it – Narbo being an important entrepot for Spanish oil – and it penetrates up the Rhone to the Rhine, occurring frequently on the German frontier and at several Swiss sites. Spanish traders also braved the rough waters of the Bay of Biscay to bring their wares to Bordeaux and north to Brittany, where at least twenty sites with Baetican oil amphoras are recorded. Britain was already receiving Baetican oil in small quantities in the age of Augustus, long before her conquest. Shortly before the Claudian invasion, Dressel 20 represents thirty per cent of the total amphora assemblage; at its peak in the second century the figure is seventy per cent, and some of the Severan amphoras with the 'fiscus' inscription also occur there. Oil also went to Mauretania, conveniently close to Baetica; but at Carthage there is very little evidence for Spanish oil importation at any time.[49]

It was long believed that Baetican oil was not shipped further east than Italy. But in 1973 news was announced of Baetican amphoras at Split in Yugoslavia, and numerous Yugoslavian sites are now known. It seems that, shipping costs notwithstanding, Baetican exporters in the early years of the empire rushed in to fill the vacuum left by the decline in Italian oil exports, and their energy knew no bounds. Baetican amphoras have now been recognised at Antioch, Knossos and Alexandria, where quantities are sufficient to suggest that Alexandria was the chief eastern market for Spanish oil. It also occurs at Corinth, Rhodes and even Athens, whose traditional symbol was the olive tree of Athena. It appears that the Greeks preferred the mellower taste of the Spanish olive oil, as do many people today. Moreover, the great variety of Dressel 20 amphora stamps in the eastern Mediterranean bespeaks fierce competition for the oil market among the various Spanish exporters.[50] In the end, conservatism in package design spelled the doom of the Baetican oil monopoly. African oil producers developed a cylindrical amphora which was lighter and more closely packable than the clumsy globulars. By the mid-third century Africa had supplanted Baetica as the main supplier of oil to Rome, and by the late third, she had also become the main supplier of Hispania Citerior.[51] Tripolitanian oil amphoras of the late third or early fourth century even occur in Baetica at three sites in the Cádiz peninsula, including Baelo. Baetican production never stopped, but exports were reduced to a trickle.

The large quantities of Dressel 20 amphoras discovered on military sites along the Rhine frontier have led to speculation that Baetica was subject to the *annona militaris*, a tax-in-kind to supply the army in Germany, during the Early Empire. Apart from the amphoras themselves, this hypothesis relies on inscriptions from the 160s AD, informing us that an assistant of the *praefectus annonae* (prefect of the grain supply) was in charge of appraising Spanish and African oil and paying the freighters.[52] There are at least two drawbacks to this hypothesis. One is that Baetican oil amphoras are also found in huge quantities in civilian towns along the Rhine (e.g. over 3,000 Baetican amphora fragments at the colony of Augusta Raurica from the Augustan period onward),[53] suggesting that a well-organised commercial network was in operation; thus the amphoras on military sites could have been purchased from merchants who were already plying the Rhine. Secondly, the *praefectus annonae* was in charge of the grain supply for the civilian populace at Rome, not for the army; the *annona militaris* was managed by the praetorian prefect. That the *praefectus annonae* regularly handled oil as well as grain for the urban populace may be deduced from inscriptions of the early second century, in which two such prefects are commemorated by oil merchants from Baetica and Africa.[54] Moreover, the fact that they are merchants (not freighters), and that they have cause to thank these officials, makes it clear that they were being paid handsomely for their oil. In short, there is no evidence that the Roman state was exacting oil from Baetica in this period, either as *annona militaris* or *annona civica*.

8

THE ROMANISATION
OF BELIEFS

GENERAL CONSIDERATIONS

Rome, it is said, had more gods than citizens, but Spain had more gods than Rome. Their profusion is attributable to several factors: the plurality of indigenous cultures (Iberian, Celtic, Basque), each with its own pantheon; the implantation of successive foreign cults (Phoenician, Greek, Roman, Oriental); and the polytheistic nature of ancient religious thought which allowed all these gods to co-exist without inherent contradiction. Since the Romans were usually tolerant of other people's beliefs, innumerable indigenous deities, of which new examples frequently come to light, continued to flourish throughout the imperial age. None the less, and particularly in the more romanised zones of the peninsula, there was a tendency to adopt Roman gods outright or to modify an indigenous cult to conform with a Roman one.

The evidence for religious practice in Roman Spain is copious, though never sufficient to give us a thorough comprehension of so complex a subject. While surviving temples are scarce, there are many remains of the columns, friezes and other sculptural elements which once adorned them. Statues in bronze, marble or terracotta reveal the visual conception of the gods worshipped in Spain. Another sculpted artifact, coins, portrays not only deities and temples but altars, ritual vessels and cult scenes. Literary sources, notably Strabo, contribute some otherwise unknown (though not necessarily reliable) details about pre-Roman worship. However, the most informative type of monument is the votive inscription, often in the form of a small altar dedicated to a god as recompense for the granting of a prayer: these invariably provide us with the name of the god or goddess and usually some information about the devotee. There are also inscriptions which commemorate the construction or repair of a temple or the dedication of a cult statue, usually by a local magistrate, priest or (in military camps) commander.[1] Though by no means complete, the surviving artifacts can probably be considered a representative sample of the cult objects of antiquity (apart from perishable items such as temple records on papyrus, or articles in precious metals which were later melted down), but even a complete collection would reveal two limitations: a preponderance of materials from sites in Andalusia and Catalonia (which were admittedly much more populous), and a tendency for monuments to be erected by members of the upper classes. These restrictions leave us with a feeble understanding of the religious beliefs of the inhabitants of other zones of the peninsula, and particularly the beliefs of the lower classes. It is true that the occasional monument is erected by a slave or freedman, but for the most part the urban pauper or rural peasant remains silent – unfortunately for us, since it is precisely these humbler folk whom one might expect to form an unromanised substratum, with more primitive beliefs and superstitions. Rural regions in particular are likely to have continued clinging to their traditional gods long after these had been supplanted by Roman deities in the towns.

Indigenous deities are attested chiefly in Galicia and Lusitania north of the Tejo, which were among the last regions to come under Roman dominion. In Baetica and on the east coast they were practically extinct by the imperial era. Given Roman tolerance towards foreign cults, why was there a widespread conversion to Roman deities? To some extent there may have been a perception that the gods of the conqueror were more potent or had stronger magic than those of the vanquished. Then too the exposure of eastern and southern Spain to Greek influence had acquainted those zones with the Olympian pantheon, which was readily assimilated with the Roman. But more importantly, the worship of Roman gods was an integral component of romanisation, a *sine qua non* of being accepted as a Roman. None the less, religion is among the most conservative of institutions, and one of the last to be surrendered. Therefore, what appears Roman may not be entirely sincere or deep-seated. Indeed, in much of the peninsula what we find is not so much a wholesale abandonment of the native gods but a reconciliation with the Roman pantheon through a process of conflation which Tacitus aptly termed *interpretatio Romana*. This syncretism is readily evident in theonyms, where the Roman name often masks a non-Roman deity. The god Mars, frequently worshipped in Lusitania and Galicia, is more likely the perpetuation of a Celtic war god than a representative of Rome, while the ubiquitous Iuppiter Optimus Maximus superficially conceals the native sky and weather god. Indigenous mother goddesses may lurk behind the worship of Juno, Diana and Venus, while the popular Silvanus is probably a native woodland spirit once removed. Clearer (and more honest) examples are afforded by the numerous 'Hispano-Roman' deities – Roman gods bearing an indigenous surname, epithet or toponym (for example Mars Tarbucelis) – which are patently just native gods in Roman guise.

Syncretism may also be detected in other kinds of monuments. A striking example is afforded by a silver plate from Tivissa (Tarragona), of Republican date, whose iconography exhibits a curious blend of Iberian and Greco-Roman concepts about the underworld. Another silver plate, from the province of Cáceres, portrays a goddess standing before an altar, wearing a mural crown and holding a cornucopia. The type is unmistakably Fortuna, but the legend around the rim reads, 'Band. Araugel.', signifying a local version of the well attested Lusitanian goddess Bandua.[2] A bronze statue of a young god from the Biscay port of Flaviobriga (Castro Urdiales) might pass as a crudely executed Apollo or Mercury, except that he supports a dolphin in his left hand and wears round his neck a gold collar, from which is suspended a crescent moon. The hand-held dolphin reappears in a statue of Neptune at Valencia, and in both works the right hand is raised to grip a (now lost) trident;[3] but the classical Neptune is typically a mature, bearded god. Here then we find syncretised with the Roman sea god his youthful indigenous counterpart, whose lunar attribute perhaps symbolises the nocturnal tides or simply divinity. Statues of Venus and Diana occurring in a town like Barcino or Italica need not surprise us, but their frequent appearance in backwoods regions may signal syncretism with a native fertility cult. In less remote areas of Spain we find conventional statuary renderings of the Greco-Roman gods, often imitating works by Praxiteles, Lysippus and various Hellenistic masters. These may attest romanisation (or at least hellenisation), but one may question whether the sculptor's primary concern in copying these famous pieces was religious rather than artistic. Surely décor, rather than worship, invited the numerous representations of deities and mythological characters found in Spanish mosaics (mostly from private homes), while scrappy remnants of fresco show that painted gods once adorned the interior walls.[4]

One important caveat must be borne in mind when considering the nature of indigenous deities, namely, that individual gods often exercised a variety of functions. Thus a prime defect of *interpretatio Romana* is that the powers of a pre-Roman god often overlap those of several Olympian gods, who tend to control specialised areas like love, war or wine. For instance, the god Lug is associated (in Gaul at least) with commerce and applied arts; however, his name means 'brilliant', as if a god of light, and in Irish legend he is a war god. The Lusitanian theonym Endovellicus is thought to mean 'very black', implying an infernal god, yet his memorials often read 'pro salute', appropriate to a god of healing. Either these gods had more extensive connotations than their classical counterparts, or their attributes varied from place to place.

INDIGENOUS CULTS

Well over 300 different Hispanic theonyms are attested in inscriptions (our chief source), but it is unclear whether these are all separate deities or whether the same god was worshipped in different places under different names or aspects. Every pre-Roman tribe had its own set of gods, which probably overlapped but did not necessarily coincide with the pantheon of its neighbours; and then there were local gods or spirits associated with a particular rock, spring, cave or the like. These *numina* or spirits can still be seen in northern Spain, for instance the Asturian *xanas* (female spirits similar to Diana) or the *lamias* and other genii of the Basques, whose names and functions often differ from village to village. A handful of deities attested in Spain appear to be pan-Celtic, found in Gaul and other Celtic areas: these include the horse patroness Epona, the stag god Cernunnos, the hammer-wielding Sucellus, and Lug(u), patron of trade and technology.[5]

Those deities whose functions can be surmised from the iconography or context of their monuments tend to fall into several general groups. Sky gods include sun, moon, stars and presumably a weather god. Funerary stelae in central and northern Spain often show moons, stars and a rosette or wheel motif in a circle, which is probably a solar symbol, for the Celts believed that the dead went to heaven, the abode of the gods, not to an underworld. But the moon

Figure 8.1 Coin from Obulco, showing a goddess(?)
wearing a double strand of pearls. Late 2nd century BC.
Diameter 30mm. (Royal Ontario Museum, Toronto).

appears in other contexts which are less clear. The lunar pendant of
the Flaviobrigan sea god has already been mentioned, and second
century BC coins from Obulco in Ulterior depict a crescent moon
beneath a female bust wearing a pearl necklace of one, two or three
strands, with her hair coiffured in parallel tresses. The lunar emblem
here may indicate a fertility goddess,[6] yet the same figure sometimes
appears without this attribute (Figure 8.1).

Animal cults included those of the bull (symbol of strength and
potency) and the horse (bearer of souls to heaven). Sertorius' albino
doe was believed to bring him messages from the gods. A number of
other animals are depicted in religious contexts, either as attributes
of gods or as allegories of fertility or immortality, without necessarily being objects of worship in themselves.[7] On an altar of
the Lusitanian god Endovellicus, a boar is prominently displayed;
this has prompted unwarranted speculation that Endovellicus is a
chthonic deity, since boars are supposedly funerary animals (though
the monument is not funerary). It seems likelier that this relief
is intended to illustrate the animal sacrifices customarily made at
altars. Endovellicus has been variously interpreted as a war god,
water god, medicine god or cupid; his true functions remain a
mystery.[8] Animals were not the only embodiments of fecundity.
Cults of human fertility are attested in southern and eastern Spain in
pre-Roman times by terracotta ex-voto statuettes of ithyphallic gods,
and goddesses breast-feeding their babies.[9] In inscriptions from several parts of Spain we find dedications to *Matres* (transparent Latin

camouflage for an indigenous mother-goddess cult) and the phallic garden god Priapus.

Among nature cults may be mentioned the mountain cults of northern Spain[10] (hill tops being frequently the site of rural sanctuaries), the woodland spirits or fauns (depicted in reliefs, and syncretised with Diana or Silvanus in epigraphy) and various nymphs (attested chiefly in Galicia and Lusitania). There can be no doubt that animism was widespread in Celtic Spain, especially in the countryside. Strabo's surprising comment that the Galicians were atheists is probably due to misunderstanding of their lack of Olympian gods, temples and theology. Half a century ago it was reported that nymphs and sirens still persisted in the folk tradition of all regions of Spain.[11] In the Roman age we find a wide variety of nymphs; many of these are associated with water, especially springs and medicinal waters. In Latin epigraphy they are worshipped as Nymphae, Fontes, Aquae or Salus, sometimes modified by a local epithet. The famous *Fontes Tamarici* of Cantabria, known to Pliny and since identified in Palencia province, were considered prophetic because of the irregular flow: for 10–20 days they would be dry, then would miraculously gush. A silver plate from Otañes near Flaviobriga, inscribed 'Salus Umeritana', depicts the reclining local nymph as well as activities utilising her healing waters.[12] A Galician deity of healing waters, Bormanicus, reappears in Gaul and Liguria as Bormanus.[13]

A large number of indigenous theonyms, many of them occurring only once, probably represent local genii rather than major gods. Many of these were worshipped as protective spirits, similar to the Roman Lar or Genius. In romanised areas of Spain there are a number of legitimate dedications to the *genius municipii, coloniae* or *conventus;* but when we encounter a Genius Tiauranceaicus, Genius Laquiniesis, Lar Pemaneiecus or Lares Tarmucenbaeci Ceceaeci, we are obviously dealing with native rather than Roman deities.[14] The Lares Viales who occur so frequently in the epigraphy of Galicia (and sporadically in Cantabria and Celtiberia) are clearly roadside deities of non-Roman origin, despite their latinised name. Perhaps gifts of food, which have left no trace, were made to these gods. More sinister was the infernal goddess Ataecina, worshipped either under her Celtic name or syncretised as Proserpina. An irate curse tablet from Emerita calls upon this goddess by both names to punish the unknown thief who has filched six shirts, two over-coats and underwear![15] And no doubt there were other pre-Roman spirits whose character would be as incomprehensible to a Roman as to us.

HISPANO-ROMAN CULTS

If the less romanised parts of the peninsula tend to contain the lion's share of indigenous theonyms, it follows that the majority of attestations of Roman gods occur in the romanised Mediterranean coastal belt. This, however, is also the area where Phoenicians and Greeks made their cultural impact on Iberian civilisation and in large measure drove out the native gods. Syncretism of Greek and Roman pantheons was easy enough, but there remain traces of Phoenicio-Punic influence.[16] Nowhere is this more evident than in the cult of Hercules, whose temple near Gades was one of the most famous shrines in the ancient world. Built by the Phoenicians for their god Melqart, this temple (or Heracleion as the Greeks called it) supposedly contained two bronze pillars with the cost of the temple inscribed on them, which some visitors mistook for the famed 'Pillars of Hercules'. On the doors were scenes of the 'labours of Hercules', but since these were only ten in number and included special labours unknown to Greek tradition, they probably originated as labours of Melqart.[17] The temple was visited by distinguished Romans, including Caesar (who allegedly was inspired here to conquer the world) and Varro (who stripped the temple of its riches during the civil war). However, the Baetican governor Caecilius Aemilianus was put to death by Caracalla for consulting Hercules' oracle. 'Herc(ules) Gadit(anus)' is represented on coins of the Spanish emperor Hadrian (perhaps on the occasion of his visit to Spain), and is still the symbol of Cádiz.[18]

Jupiter, head of the Roman pantheon, is frequently commemorated in romanised areas, yet appears even more often in the north-west (usually in the form 'Iuppiter Optimus Maximus' or Iuppiter with indigenous epithet), where he probably succeeds a native supergod. This is a likelier explanation of the popularity of the Jupiter cult than the antiquated hypothesis that it was spread by the Roman army. Jupiter is also commonly attested in central Spain and was perhaps a suitable *interpretatio Romana* for the nameless god of the Celtiberi reported by Strabo.[19] The god who does have a military flavour is Mars, readily syncretised with indigenous war gods, occasionally in Hispano-Roman form, for example Mars Cariociecus.[20] At Saguntum we find a college of Salii, dancing priests of Mars familiar to students of religion at Rome. In a curious notice, Macrobius (c. AD 400) records that 'the Accitani, a Spanish people, worship with greatest devotion an image of Mars adorned with rays, calling it Neton'. A god Neton is indeed attested in inscriptions from Turgalium and Conimbriga (both in Lusitania), but it is highly improbable that this Celtic deity would be worshipped at Acci (Guadix) in the south-east corner of Spain. Either the name Accitani is an error, or (as I suspect) there was another Acci in Lusitania. This would not be surprising, since many towns are known from a single source, and hitherto unknown *municipia* have come to light in recent years. Not far from Turgalium we find an inscription mentioning M. Aeminius Acitanus (meaning native of Acci?).[21] The Lusitanian gentilics Acceiqum and Acceiniqum also contain this *acc-* element.

Numerous other Roman deities are attested in Spain; space permits mention of only a few interesting examples. One of them, Vulcan, is cited by Cicero as having had an indigenous predecessor in Spain. The household gods (Lares) are seldom attested in houses; an exception is the recent discovery of a *lararium* in the Late Roman villa at Vilauba (Girona), containing bronze statuettes of Lar, Fortuna and Mercury.[22] The oldest epigraphic attestation of a deity is a third-century BC dedication to Minerva from Tarraco, located beside a relief of this goddess incorporated in the so-called Tower of Minerva. Minerva is indeed attested more often in Spain than Juno, wife of Jupiter and fellow member of the Capitoline Triad.[23] However, there are several attestations of Caelestis, Juno's African counterpart, who probably represents the survival in Spain of the Punic goddess Tanit. Finally, a temple of the love goddess Venus is attested in the Montes Alberes, where the Pyrenees touch the Mediterranean; here, as at Corinth, love was apparently worth climbing for. The identity and location of this popular temple were still remembered in the fourteenth century, being mentioned by the Arab geographer Abulfeda.[24]

THE IMPERIAL CULT

The imperial cult, though based on the supposed divinity of certain emperors, had the essentially political purpose of strengthening the loyalty of the provinces and their inhabitants to the current ruler or dynasty. In Spain, however, the religious aspects of the cult seem to have been not only genuine, but easily reconcilable with Iberian tradition. The cult of the leader was an established phenomenon in pre-Roman Spain, where *devotio Iberica* entailed not only respecting, but worshipping and, if necessary, dying for him. When Indibilis, chief of the Ilergetes, was mortally wounded in battle, his bodyguard remained with him until they all perished in a rain of missiles.[25] Once the indigenous tribes had accepted Roman leadership, it was natural for them to treat an outstanding general like Scipio Africanus or Sertorius as a god. Sertorius' opponent Metellus not only insisted on being worshipped while in Spain, but was treated as a god at Rome when he triumphed.[26] Julius Caesar, who had amassed an extensive clientele in Spain, was deified at Rome after his death. Under the Empire, Spaniards worshipped the Roman emperors as they had worshipped previous leaders. Indeed, Spain was at the forefront of emperor worship in the Roman West. While Augustus was at Tarraco in 26–25 BC, a delegation arrived from the Greek city of Mytilene to bestow divine honours upon him.[27] Not to be outdone, the people of Tarraco built an altar to Augustus, and on one occasion eagerly informed the emperor that a palm tree had miraculously sprung out of it. Augustus replied sarcastically that they obviously didn't light fires on the altar very often; none the less, several coins of Tarraco proudly depict the tree growing on this altar.[28] There was also an altar of Augustus in Asturias, which served as the focal point of the *conventus Arae Augustae* (subsequently renamed *conventus Asturum*).[29] When Augustus died, the Tarraconenses successfully sought permission to build him a temple; but they surely acted without authority in designating him *deus* ('god') instead of *divus* ('deified') on coins depicting the new temple and cult statue. Ten years later, a request by the province of Baetica to build a temple to the living emperor Tiberius and his mother was refused, although permission had already been granted to the cities of Asia.[30] Clearly the emperor was embarrassed to be treated as a living god in the Latin provinces.

The imperial cult revered not only the deified Augustus and those of his successors who merited divinity, but also the emperor's protective spirit (Genius Augusti) and household gods (Lares Augustales). This tendency expanded until a large number of gods and goddesses were inducted into the Augustan pantheon, becoming in effect the emperor's own gods: Apollo Augustus, Hercules Augustus, Venus Augusta, Nemesis Augusta.[31] Also worshipped was the goddess Roma, often together with the emperor as 'Roma et (divus) Augustus', a formula attested as early as Tiberius' reign. The imperial cult began in the cities, as the example of Tarraco illustrates, but we subsequently find *conventus* cults and provincial cults as well. In Baetica, a senatorial province, the provincial cult is not attested until the reign of Vespasian, though the unsuccessful petition to Tiberius suggests earlier willingness to found one; the municipal cult here does begin under Tiberius.

MYSTERY CULTS

The imperial cult, like the traditional pantheon, was better suited to formal worship than to personal fulfilment. The official gods were too austere and lofty for the daily spiritual needs of the individual or to console his fears of mortality. 'Mystery' cults of Greek or eastern origin became increasingly popular in the imperial age, enticing devotees with their promises of purification, communion with the god and a joyous eternity. The exclusiveness of membership, the secrets divulged only to initiates, the pseudo-intellectual explanations of the universe, and the unwonted sensations aroused by fasting, flagellation, frantic music, intimacy with animals, even self-mutilation, provided an exciting, anthropocentric alternative to the old religion. The Greek wine god Dionysus (known to the Romans as Liber Pater) appears frequently in sculpture, mosaics and inscriptions, while the grain goddess Demeter (Ceres) is the subject of a smaller number of statues and dedications, including one offered by the Baetican city of Munigua. The 'Emesa triad' of Syrian deities introduced at Rome by the third-century emperor Heliogabalus is attested at Corduba by a curious altar with a Greek inscription naming Helios (Baal), Kypris (Astarte) and Athena Al-Lat ('mother of the gods').[32] However, the oriental gods most frequently encountered in Spain are Cybele, Mithras and Isis. Cybele or Magna Mater was a Phrygian fertility deity whose most spectacular rite was the *taurobolium*, a baptism in bull's blood. Alternatively one might perform a *crinobolium*, substituting a ram. Both types of blood-bath are attested several times in Spanish epigraphy, as are priests (*sacerdotes*) and an *archigallus* or high priest. Entry to this priesthood required self-castration, as if in emulation of Cybele's consort Attis, who died from the experience but was resurrected by the goddess. Altars of the cult occur both in Roman towns (e.g. the colonies of Corduba, Emerita, Metellinum and Pax Iulia) and in more remote areas. Shrines of Cybele are epigraphically attested at Mago (Mahón) in the Balearic Islands and on Monte Cildá (Palencia), the latter undoubtedly an outdoor sanctuary rather than a temple proper.[33]

The Egyptian goddess Isis seems to have been the most popular mystery deity in Spain, perhaps because of her versatility: Apuleius (second century AD), who wrote a novel describing the initiation into her cult, notes that Isis is syncretised with Mater Deorum, Minerva, Venus, Diana, Proserpina, Juno, Ceres and Hecate. Our earliest attestation seems to be at Emerita, where the marble head of an elderly priestess has been dated to the first century AD. Isis was a women's cult par excellence (though not confined to females) and her worshippers included slaves and freedmen.[34] She is often depicted nursing her son Horus (Harpocrates), sometimes accompanied by the jackal god Anubis or the ibis Thoth. Isis' consort Osiris/Serapis had his own following, and two *Serapea* (temples of Serapis) are attested archaeologically: one at Emporiae, which (despite the discovery of two inscribed Serapic flagstones) resembles in plan the Isis temple at Pompeii and may therefore be a joint temple of the Egyptian couple; the other at Panóias (Villa-Real in northern Portugal), a sanctuary built on slightly worked rock. Cavities carved into the floor may be the sacred *lacus* attested in inscriptions.[35]

In Spain there are relatively few monuments of Mithras, not so much because of Spain's distance from the eastern Mediterranean (which did not impede other mystery cults) as because of the limited presence of soldiers, who were the chief propagators of this male-oriented cult based on loyalty and discipline. More remarkably, not a single dedication to Mithras has been discovered at León, home of the Seventh Legion. However, one of the inscriptions from Emerita records the erection of a Mithraic altar by a *frumentarius* of this legion in AD 155. Some of the monuments describe Mithras as unconquerable (*invictus*); others, dedicated simply to *deo invicto*, are not necessarily Mithraic, since the sun god Sol also uses this title. The mythical scene of Mithras slaying the bull (whose death produces life) is portrayed in a free-standing marble statue from Igabrum (Cabra) as well as reliefs from Italica and Tróia, the latter including Mithras' assistant Cautopates and, in a separate panel, the banquet of Mithras and the sun god. Another character associated with Mithras is Chronos (time), strikingly illustrated at Emerita by two statues (one lion-headed) of the god bound by a serpent. The mysteries of Mithras were celebrated in underground temples symbolising the cave where Mithras slew the bull; remains of two of these have been excavated, at Emerita and Igabrum.[36]

REGIONAL WORSHIP

In general terms, the 'divine geography' (distribution of Roman and native gods) of Spain conforms to the overall pattern of romanisation, with the zones of Phoenician and Greek colonisation being the quickest to adopt the Roman pantheon, while northern and western Spain lagged far behind. From the epigraphic material it appears that Baetica and the east coast had completely cast off any indigenous deities long before the Julio-Claudian period, though some of the 'Roman' gods may be syncretisms of Phoenician and Greek deities introduced centuries earlier. The Iberian and Turdetanian gods attested in protohistoric art were no longer worshipped, unless secretly or in the countryside, for none are named in inscriptions or portrayed in sculpture (except possibly in the Tivissa treasure of the third century BC). Residents of towns along the Ebro river dutifully worshipped the Roman pantheon. However, in ascending the hills which flank this valley, one finds a mixture of Roman and indigenous deities, and the 'Roman' ones are often nature spirits such as Silvanus and the seemingly ubiquitous Nymphae, or thinly disguised survivals of sun and moon cults, such as Luna Augusta at the Roman town of Aeso (Isona) or a joint dedication to Jupiter and Sol at Argote (Alava).[37] On the northern tributaries of the Ebro, in what is now Navarra, we encounter such strange deities as Losa, Lacubegis and Selatsa, while sculptural evidence suggests the perpetuation of a pre-Roman bull cult, symbolic of male fertility.[38] Such deities as Suttunius and Sandaquinnus, Varna and Vurovius were worshipped in the upper Ebro basin, while the frugal epigraphy of Cantabria yields Cabuniaeginus and Erudinus, the latter attested as late as the reign of Honorius.[39]

For Central Spain we are fortunate in having two relevant documents in the Celtiberian language. One, on a bronze tablet from Contrebia Belaisca (Botorrita), mentions the gods Tokoitei (probably identical with Togoti, attested at Talavera de la Reina), Neito (the Celtic war god Neton again) and Sarnikio. The other, carved into the living rock at Peñalba de Villastar (Teruel) and datable to the first century BC, records the presence of a sanctuary of Lug(u), familiar from Gallic sources as the Celtic god of crafts and commerce, often syncretised with Mercury. Beneath the inscription is painted Lug's stock attribute, the raven. The Lugoves named on an altar from Uxama are possibly a pluralised form of this deity.[40] The Latin epigraphy of the region reveals numerous other indigenous deities, some of them unparalleled. A statistical analysis of these votive texts reveals that among the northernmost tribes (Vaccaei and Turmogi) indigenous and Roman gods are roughly equal in number, while the southernmost tribes (Arevaci, Celtiberi, Carpetani) show an overwhelming preference for Roman deities. In the middle are the Pelendones (located between Turmogi and Arevaci), with half as many native as Roman gods.[41]

Unquestionably the strongest survival of indigenous deities appears in the two westernmost regions, Lusitania and Galicia. Lusitania south of the Tejo offers only a handful of different indigenous theonyms, but this feeble variety is deceptive because there are 84 dedications to Endovellicus alone, while the total number of votive inscriptions to native deities (95) represents more than thirty per cent of those in the entire peninsula.[42] In eastern Lusitania, among the Vettones, indigenous deities (by my count) outnumber Roman ones by a ratio of about 5:2. At El Raso de Candeleda (Avila) a sanctuary of pre-Roman origin contains numerous dedications to the god Vaelicus or Velicus (no relation, apparently, to Endovellicus).[43] Vettonia is also the heartland of the *verracos* – monolithic statues of pigs, boars, sometimes bulls – whose significance, though problematic, is probably religious or funerary; some of these zoomorphic sculptures were reused as tombstones in Roman times. In Galicia, calculating from the tables compiled by Tranoy for indigenous and Roman deities (excluding imperial cult and oriental religions), proportions narrow as we move westward: in the eastern part of the region (*conventus Asturum*), 68 Roman to 25 indigenous deities (nearly 3:1); in northern Portugal (*conventus Bracaraugustanus*), 104 Roman to 86 indigenous (about 5:4); in the extreme north-west of the Peninsula (*conventus Lucensis*), 52 Roman to 48 indigenous (virtually 1:1, a poor score for romanisation).[44]

PRIESTS AND TEMPLES

It was traditional in both Iberian and Roman society that the priests belonged to the wealthy upper class. At Rome the major priesthoods were exercised by members of the Senate, and inevitably contributed to the holder's political prestige and career advancement. In other towns, both in Italy and the provinces, religious offices were discharged by members of the local aristocracy, who by their personal example, authority and social position played an important role in converting the community to Roman religion. In Spain, however, mentions of priesthoods, other than those of the imperial cult, are rare. The numerous inscribed altars to classical and indigenous gods were mostly erected by private individuals, often *ex voto* (to fulfil a vow) or occasionally *ex visu* (after a 'vision'). Sometimes the worshipper is identified as a soldier or official; usually, we are given only the dedicant's name, from which it is often difficult to distinguish his (or her) social status or ethnic origin. We do know that the Salii (priests of Mars at Saguntum) were local aristocrats and that their chief (the *magister Saliorum*) was normally an ex-duovir. But our chief source of information is the colonial law of Urso (antedating the imperial cult), which provides that the colleges of pontiffs and augurs are to be elected annually in the same manner as magistrates; that they may wear a purple-bordered toga; that they and their sons are exempt from military service; and (less informatively) that they are subject to the same conditions and privileges as pontiffs and augurs in every colony. The augurs are furthermore given authority in all matters concerning auspices (observation of flights of birds and similar signs). In fact there may be more pontiffs and augurs attested in honorific inscriptions than is sometimes thought, for the abbreviation 'pont. aug.', often interpreted as 'pontifex Augusti', may in some cases be 'pontifex, augur'.[45] Signs from the gods were also read by diviners (*haruspices*), who examined the entrails of sacrificial animals and interpreted heavenly phenomena such as lightning and eclipses. These men, attested already in pre-Roman Galicia and Lusitania, were not priests elected from the local elite but rather skilled tradesmen who made their living either by selling omens to private inquirers (e.g. the anxious soldiers besieging Numantia in 134 BC) or as salaried attendants of local magistrates (as at Urso, where each duovir was allowed to hire a *haruspex*). Though profiting from the delivery of the gods' messages, diviners were a necessary evil in every town, whose superstitious inhabitants preferred to consult the omens before undertaking major ventures. Even before a town was founded, a *haruspex* would be needed to determine by liver divination whether the proposed site was favourable.[46]

Priests of the imperial cult proudly display their titles in inscriptions, allowing us considerable acquaintance with their status. Since offices are usually listed in chronological order, it is possible to determine that these priesthoods were usually held after a civil magistracy, often after the duovirate, sometimes also after holding an equestrian post in the army or imperial bureaucracy. The alacrity of the local elite to accept these Roman priesthoods (which admittedly conferred privileges and prestige on the holder) must have contributed greatly to the success of the cult in every town. In the emperor's provinces (Citerior and Lusitania) the priest regularly bore the distinctive title, *flamen*; in the senatorial province of Baetica, the traditional priestly designation *pontifex* was often conserved. Those who had already held the local magistracies and priesthoods might be eligible for election by the provincial assembly to the prestigious provincial priesthood. (Citerior, the largest of the three provinces, also had *conventus* priesthoods.) Only a handful of the provincial priests of Baetica and Lusitania have left records. On the other hand, some 70 *flamines* as well as a dozen *flaminicae* (who were frequently but not invariably the *flamines'* wives) of the province of Citerior are attested, dating from Vespasian through the Antonines. Beginning in the Flavian period, these priests were *equites* who had already held equestrian military posts and often local magistracies as well. In the second century we find some provincial priests who lacked these military qualifications but had been adlected by the emperor as *iudices* at Rome. A final group, dating mostly to the period 120–80, were not equestrian at all but had all held honours in their home town. While not all the inscriptions can be closely dated, the general trend reflects the declining number of Spaniards being admitted into the equestrian order by either the military or civil route. The term of office was one year – there are no examples at the provincial level of a 'perpetual' priest as is sometimes found in towns – although it could be renewed if the incumbent was willing.[47] Another group of officials associated with the imperial cult was the *seviri Augustales* (sometimes abbreviated to *seviri* or *Augustales*) who were nearly exclusively ex-slaves. Appointed by the decurions, the *seviri* were originally (as the name implies) a college of six, though in the late second century some towns appointed more. An inscription from Barcino mentions freedwomen attaining the sevirate, but this seems to have been rare.[48]

Priests, whether serving the gods or the imperial cult, discharged their duties in a temple, an imposing edifice perched on a high podium and usually boasting a colonnaded porch and elaborate friezes. Unlike a modern church, the temple did not house the congregation but rather the deity, represented by a large, standing or seated statue within. While individuals might make vows to the deity in the *cella* or cult room, public prayers and sacrifices were normally performed outdoors, over an altar located upon or at the foot of the temple steps. Every town had its temples, and in rural areas there were often sanctuaries (less formal architecturally but no less revered) associated with sacred groves, springs or mountains. Several local temples are depicted (accurately or fancifully) on coins, and numerous others are mentioned in inscriptions, some of them recording that the construction or repair of the temple was paid for by a local official or private benefactor. A few such texts provide us with the cost of these buildings, ranging from a mere 6,000 sesterces for a temple of Hercules at Osqua (Archidona) to 200,000 for a temple of Apollo and Diana at Arucci (Aroche). We know from North African evidence that a really large temple could cost 600,000.[49] These costs presumably included not only the structure but the decorative reliefs, wall paintings, and perhaps the cult statue.

A variety of different temple styles is attested. Among those not surviving are a tetrastyle temple of Juno at Ilici, and three temples of the deified Augustus: tetrastyle at Emerita, hexastyle at Caesaraugusta, and octastyle at Tarraco, if the coin evidence may be trusted.[50] The only materially intact example is the diminutive (5.8 × 4.1 m.) temple of the imperial cult at Alcántara. This has a simple *in antis* plan, and is perhaps comparable in size and simplicity with the inexpensive Osquan shrine already cited. An inscription above the entrance, no longer extant, recorded the dedication of this temple by C. Iulius Lacer, the Trajanic architect of the adjacent Alcántara bridge. Several other temples are partially preserved (Figure 8.2). Those at Barcino, Corduba, Ebora and Emerita are all hexastyle peripteral, and some of them probably belong to the imperial cult, though identity is problematic. Temple chronology based on architectural style can only be approximate, but the Barcino temple seems to date to Augustus or slightly later, the Emerita temple is first century, while those at Corduba and Ebora are end of first or beginning of second.[51] A small (12.1 × 10.1 m) hexastyle prostyle temple at Ausa (Vic) is also of imperial date. At the north end of the Flavian forum at Conimbriga stood a tetrastyle pseudo-peripteral temple, whose dominant position suggests once again the imperial cult. Two tetrastyle temples – one identified as Republican, the other Antonine – were boasted by Augustobriga

(Talavera la Vieja) in eastern Lusitania. Above the architrave in the later example is an arch linking the two central columns, echoing the arched façade of the Temple of Hadrian at Ephesus.[52] Two types of Capitolium are represented in Baetica. A Republican example at Italica consists of a single building with three adjacent *cellae*, whereas at Baelo in the first century AD we find three separate temples side by side, all tetrastyle pseudo-peripteral, sharing a common altar.[53]

RITUAL AND RELIGIOSITY

When a pagan apologist in the late fourth century AD observed that 'everyone has his own gods and his own rites',[54] it may be doubted whether he was thinking of anything quite so peculiar or antiquated as the child sacrifices of Punic Carthage and Sardinia, or the Gallic *tête coupée* ritual. Though less famous than these examples, human sacrifices and other strange rituals are recorded in early Spain, attesting a barbarity which even the battle-hardened Romans found repugnant. In pre-Roman Andalusia we find such sacrifices being made at El Acebuchal (Carmona) and Baelo (Bolonia), presumably under Phoenician or Punic influence.[55] The notorious governor Galba claimed that he massacred the Lusitani in 150 BC because they had sacrificed a horse and a man according to their custom. This sacrifice of man and horse together has archaeological parallels in Gaul, and in several Iberian tombs in Andalusia and the north-east. Strabo notes that all the mountain dwellers sacrifice both horses and human prisoners, adding that the Lusitani use their prisoners' viscera for divination and offer their severed right hands to the gods.[56] Plutarch preserves a story that the Romans forbade the Bletones to sacrifice humans; these Bletones seem linguistically connected with the epigraphically attested town of Bletisama, modern Ledesma, in Vettonian country (not that the two were necessarily collocated), and the ban is usually associated with P. Licinius Crassus (governor of Ulterior in 96–93), under whose consulship the Senate outlawed human sacrifice.[57] Our sources fail to tell us in what sort of sacrifice the people of Segobriga were so thoroughly engrossed (*maxime occupatos*) that they did not notice Viriathus launching a surprise attack on their town, or whether the 'many sacrifices' offered at his funeral included human and equine victims. And when Julius Caesar is credited with 'removing the ancient barbarity from the customs and doctrine of the Gaditanians', could this be a reference to human sacrifice?[58]

AUGUSTOBRIGA

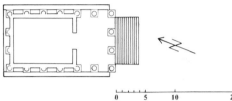

CONIMBRIGA

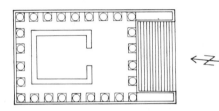

EBORA

CORDUBA

BARCINO

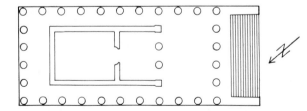

Figure 8.2 Comparison of Spanish temple plans.
Source: Based on Alarcão and Étienne (1977), García
y Bellido (1956–60 and 1970) and Hauschild (1982).

171

Roman sacrifices, while tamer, were still a necessary element of worship. A marble relief from Tarraco, of which nearly half has been lost since its discovery in 1827, depicts a bull sacrifice in which a bearded, bare-chested priest (perhaps of the imperial cult) holds the bull's reins in his left hand and in the other a small hatchet with which to slit his throat, while an attendant carries a bucket and a long-handled axe.[59] Not all Spanish sacrifices were so romanised. Another relief, unearthed in the 1790s at Duratón (Segovia) and now lost, represented a sacrifice in which one man, larger than the other (so presumably the priest) stood waiting while the smaller man (the assistant) placed upon the altar between them a boar – an animal more common in Celtic than Roman sacrifice.[60] An inscription from Cabeço das Fráguas (Guarda) in Lusitanian language and Latin letters, describes the equivalent of a Roman *suovetaurilia* (sacrifice of a bull, a pig and a lamb) – except that the honoured deities sport barbaric names like Reva and Trebopala.[61] Another inscription, from Marecos near Penafiel, records offerings of a cow, an ox, three lambs, a calf and a goat to Jupiter and several indigenous deities. However, the first-named deity is a local nymph, 'the excellent virgin protectress Nabia Corona', who receives the cow and ox; poor Jupiter is listed third and seems to be included as a token concession to Romanity by the presiding officials (*curatores*), who nevertheless have Roman names. The inscription also bears the consular date 9 April AD 147, suggesting the perpetuation of a pre-Roman annual spring fertility festival.[62] In addition to sacrifices, liturgical equipment is sometimes pictured. A bronze altar from Ercavica (Castro de Santaver) of the first century AD, reminiscent of the architrave frieze of the Temple of Vespasian at Rome, shows an *aspergilum* (sprinkler of sacred water), *apex flaminis* (priest's mitre), *simpulum* (ladle), *patera* (offering dish), *oinochoe* (wine decanter) and *bucranium* (head of sacrificial bull). Some of these ritual implements can also be seen in the coinage of Carthago Nova, Corduba, Ebora, Gades and Iulia Traducta.[63] A number of ritual vessels in silver or bronze have been identified at various sites; most spectacularly, a *simpulum* with its two-handled jar and a clay *thymiaterion* (censer) with appliquéd heads, were found abandoned in the temple of the first-century BC legionary camp at Cáceres el Viejo, which was probably destroyed in an attack by Sertorius.[64]

Religious festivals were traditionally occasions when work would be suspended in favour of worship and entertainments. The Flavian *Lex Irnitana* confirms that business will not be conducted during festivals of the imperial cult either.[65] Drama owed its origin to religious festivities, theatres sometimes formed part of the temple complex, and circus games were preceded by a religious parade (*pompa circensis*). The charter of Urso orders the duovirs to sponsor four games of *ludi scaenici* (dramatic presentations) or gladiatorial shows for the Capitoline Triad (Jupiter, Juno, Minerva), mostly at their own expense, while the aediles must present three days of similar entertainment for the Triad and one day of games in the circus or forum for Venus (ancestor of the colony's founder, Caesar). A fragment of a redware bowl depicting acorns and oak leaves, with the legend *felices fructus*, was probably a gift exchanged with friends on special occasions such as the New Year's festival.[66] The colourful *fiestas* celebrated in every Spanish town today, with religious processions, entertainments and general gaiety, undoubtedly owe their ultimate origin to these pagan festivals; the images of the gods carted through the streets in Roman times have been replaced by carved figures of Christ, the Virgin and the saints, mounted on floats.

While these city festivals attracted popular participation, the individual had his own religious occupations. The official gods were awesome and aloof; for day-to-day assistance the Roman worshipped his household gods, the Lares and Penates. To what extent these deities found sincere acceptance in the private worship of the indigenes is impossible to gauge, though syncretism with pre-Roman domestic spirits may have helped. Outside of the home, we know from inscriptions that individuals sought the aid of propitious abstract deities – again, with Roman names but possibly pre-Roman antecedents – such as Fortuna (luck), Salus (health), Tutela (protection) or Bonus Eventus (success). An obsession with fertility is also evident in the epigraphic and pictorial representations of Diana, Matres, Isis, Priapus and so on.[67] Curse tablets and apotropaic charms allowed the individual to divert evil from himself and onto his enemies. For instance, a recently published lead plaque found in the temple of Isis at Baelo implores the goddess to punish the thief who stole all the worshipper's bedding.[68]

CHRISTIANITY: REVELATION OR REVOLUTION?

How long did Christianity take to reach the western Mediterranean? St Paul's express intention (probably never realised) to preach in Spain presupposes the existence of an incipient Christian community to receive him. Where did it come from? Christianity was initially propagated among the Jews, and its spread into Spain, Gaul and North Africa may have been facilitated by Jewish settlers in those provinces. Judaean coins of the early first century AD have been found at Emporiae and Iluro (Mataró), and Jewish inscriptions are known from Tarraco, Emerita and elsewhere, though none of these is very early.[69] Another possible Christianising agency was the Greeks, long established on the east coast and to a lesser extent inland. Christianity had spread comparatively rapidly in the Greek-speaking cities of Asia, and it should be remembered that until the late second century AD, the Bible and other theological works used by the Church of Rome were written in Greek, not Latin.[70] The dearth of early references to Christianity in Spain may be attributed partly to the 'underground' nature of the outlawed faith in the first three centuries AD, which made advertisement perilous, and partly to the informality of its diffusion, which depended more on personal contacts with friends, neighbours and fellow workers than on bishops and clergy (who, given the illegality of the new religion, preached mostly to the converted in secret meeting rooms).[71] Even so, it is questionable whether the Christian community in Spain was very large before the third century. Our first explicit reference, dating to the 180s, occurs in the writings of St Irenaeus, bishop of Lyon, who would no doubt have had some idea of the Church's progress in neighbouring provinces. He vouches not merely for a Christian presence but for 'the established churches among the Germans, among the Iberians, among the Celts'.[72] Unless we assume rhetorical exaggeration, Christianity in Spain had already reached organised proportions by the late second century.

Spanish troops serving in North Africa in the second and third centuries, as attested by several inscriptions and by brick stamps of *legio VII Gemina* at Lambaesis, may have brought Christianity back with them, though their impact should not be exaggerated. If at Lambaesis Christian artifacts are remarkable for their scarcity, at León they still await discovery.[73] St Marcellus the centurion is now believed to have been martyred at Tangier, not León, and there is no evidence that he was Spanish. The martyrs' church excavated at Marialba near León was not built before the mid-fourth century when Christianity was legal, and the identity of the martyrs remains obscure.[74] However, a letter of St Cyprian in AD 254, addressed to the priest Felix and the people of Legio and Asturica, and to the deacon Aelius and the people of Emerita, demonstrates the existence of a Christian community here in the mid-third century (though it does not prove that Christianity was introduced by soldiers returning from Africa).[75]

By the end of the third century there were 'innumerable Christians' in Spain,[76] some of whom were martyred, though Spain seems to have escaped the mass persecutions recorded in some provinces. St Fructuosus, bishop of Tarraco, was martyred in 259, St Justa and St Rufina of Seville in 287, and several others c. 304, including St Felix of Girona, St Vincent of Zaragoza and St Eulalia of Mérida, who is also claimed by Barcelona. An earlier victim, St Lawrence (martyred 258) is sometimes claimed as Spanish because Prudentius wrote a poem about him (without, however, calling him Spanish); he died at Rome, and the legend of his passion on the gridiron belongs instead to St Vincent. There were also numerous local martyrs whose memory and alleged remains are often invoked in Christian inscriptions of the Visigothic age.

To the early fourth century – the exact date is still disputed – belongs the Council of Elvira, the most remarkable of the early Church synods.[77] The 81 regulations enacted by this council prescribe excommunication or penance for a wide variety of sins, including black magic, abortion, dice-playing, prostituting your own children and missing church three Sundays in a row. Christians are forbidden to marry Jews, and a widower cannot marry his wife's sister. Many provisions deal with the clergy: priests are forbidden to marry, to fornicate, to lend money at interest or to trade outside their own province. Contamination with the pagan community is avoided: magistrates cannot enter church during their year of municipal office (which perforce involved pagan ceremonies), and freedmen with pagan patrons are ineligible for the priesthood. Hardly less fascinating is the Council of Zaragoza in 380, which only a dozen bishops attended. The council had to deal with some novel problems: women who attended prayer meetings with strange men; communicants who received the bread and wine without swallowing them; virgins wearing veils before the age of forty; parishioners abstaining from church as their Lenten sacrifice; Christians who prayed barefoot or who hid in the mountains. The last problem was real enough, and there is ample attestation of troglodytic Christians in Late Roman and Visigothic times, particularly in north-eastern Spain, and there were even cave churches in the mountains of Cantabria.[78]

Although Christianity had been legalised by Constantine, there was some opposition to the new religion, particularly among the senatorial class. It was difficult for the Church of Rome to persuade provincials that Christianity was the one true religion, when their governors were overt pagans like Sextilius Aedesius, governor of Spain who underwent a *taurobolium* initiation in 376. Though some Christians were radicals, necessitating an edict in 399 by the Spanish governor Macrobius against the destruction of pagan temples and art works, others were only 'nominal Christians', who kept one foot in the pagan door. Examples of Christian-pagan confusion may be seen in a Christian epitaph from Tarraco which combines the chi-rho monogram with the pagan formula 'D(is) M(anibus)', and in the syncretism of St Justa and St Rufina with the cult of Adonis.[79] Christianity, which had begun late in Spain, took an incredibly long time to predominate: as late as 589, the Third Council of Toledo declared that 'the sacrilege of idolatry is rooted in nearly all of Gaul and Spain'. None the less, Christianity had made serious progress by the end of the fourth century, even in the north-west. The cleric and historian Orosius was born at Bracara in the 380s, and there are remains of a Paleochristian church near Quiroga (Lugo), including a round, marble top for an offering table, dating to about 400 or shortly after (Figure 8.3). In addition to a chi-rho emblem, this monument bears an inscription warning the reader to cast off all gold and silver – a suitable Christian admonition in a region famed for its precious metals.[80]

Spanish bishops were in all periods an obstinate and independent lot who sometimes caused more problems than they solved. Consider Martial, a third-century bishop who subsequently apostatised, joined a pagan *collegium* and participated in 'shameful and filthy Gentile banquets'; or Ossius of Córdoba, who took it upon himself to write the emperor Constantius II in 356, warning him to keep his nose out of church business, and quoting Matthew 22:21 ('Render unto Caesar . . .'); or Paul, bishop of Mérida at the end of the sixth century, a skilled obstetrician who was launching an urban building programme to rival that of Augustus, until the Visigothic king intervened.[81] Perhaps these are extreme examples, but they pale in comparison with the trouble posed by the heretics, most notably Priscillian, bishop of Avila, eventually beheaded at Trier in 385. Priscillian's teachings were associated by his critics with Manichaeism, a heresy denounced less for its theological doctrine than for the alleged participation of its adherents in sorcery and immoral behaviour. St Jerome accuses the Priscillianists of holding orgies and seducing women while reciting verses on divine copulation from Vergil's *Georgics*.[82] Despite such infamous (and inflated) charges, Priscillian had numerous supporters, including several bishops and the governor of Lusitania, Volventius. Priscillianism was discussed at the Council of Zaragoza in 380 but apparently without concrete results, since it is not prohibited in the canons; it was finally declared a heresy at Toledo in 400. A report sent to St Augustine *c*. 420 makes it clear that Priscillianism was still rife in Catalonia, where an informant who denounced a heretical priest at Tarragona was threatened with stoning by the populace. There were witch-hunts for Manichees in the fifth century, and Priscillianism was rooted out, though pockets of these heretics could still be found in Galicia in the sixth century.[83]

Figure 8.3 Offering table from Quiroga with chi-rho symbol; early 5th century. (Deutsches Archäologisches Institut, Madrid; photo R. Friedrich).

9

'RESISTANCE' TO ROMANISATION

Spain has long been considered the most thoroughly romanised province of the Roman West. Of the Celts, Iberians and similar groups the great provincial historian Haverfield remarked, 'It was possible, it was easy, to romanise these western peoples.'[1] But the romanisation of Spain was neither thorough nor simple. Admittedly the southern province (Baetica) and the eastern coastal strip enjoyed a high level of romanisation, but in large parts of the Iberian Peninsula there was opposition, active or passive, to the Roman presence.

ARMED RESISTANCE

The epitomist Florus, writing in the second century AD, sagely observed that it is more difficult to retain provinces than to create them, and the Spanish provinces were no exception. The general revolts headed by Viriathus and Sertorius in the Republican period are early examples of popular resistance which made effective use of guerrilla tactics. But violence continued into Imperial times. The praetorian *iuridicus* L. Calpurnius Piso was assassinated by a peasant of Termes in AD 25, and an attempt was made to assassinate the emperor Hadrian during his visit to Tarraco in the winter of 122–3. On a larger scale, there were repeated violations of the *pax Augusta*, even within Augustus' own lifetime. An inscription from the forum at Rome records the erection of a golden statue to Augustus by the province of Baetica, because he had pacified the province. This inscription (which cannot be earlier than 2 BC because Augustus bears the title *pater patriae* conferred upon him that year) apparently alludes to the quelling of an insurrection, long after the supposed cessation of hostilities in Spain in 19 BC. That Baetica, characterised by Strabo as the most romanised of the Spanish provinces, still needed to be pacified by Augustus around the turn of the Christian era, casts serious doubts on the effectiveness of romanisation up to this point.[2] We can readily believe that Augustus inherited a less than peaceful Baetica (or Hispania Ulterior as it was then called), since the charter of the Caesarian colony of Urso in 44 BC empowers the duovirs to place the inhabitants under arms to defend the colony. Another disturbance, also involving Baetica, occurred in AD 21, when all of Gaul was in revolt, with the aid of Germans, and the Spanish provinces were said to be wavering. This allegation of Spanish dissidence finds possible corroboration in the conviction of Vibius Serenus on a charge of treason in AD 24, for having sent agents to incite the Gauls to revolt. At the time of the Gallic uprising Vibius Serenus had been governor of Baetica – a post he forfeited in 23 when convicted of unlawful use of force – and the agents he sent to persuade the Gauls to rebel may well have been Spaniards.[3]

An uprising in northern Spain in the late 50s, unattested in the literary sources, is mentioned in an inscription commemorating a procurator of Lusitania under Nero, who at an earlier stage of his career, as a centurion in *legio VI Victrix*, had been decorated for his actions in a campaign against the Astures. This was less likely a full-fledged revolt than a protest against taxation or conscription, but required a military force to suppress it. At the end of Nero's reign the governor of Citerior, Sulpicius Galba, declared himself emperor and was successfully supported in this treason (admittedly against an unpopular emperor) by the people of his province, who not only endorsed his bid for power but took up arms to enforce it. Galba apparently found support also among the leading men of Baetica, some of whom hoped to secure speedy advancement in this way.[4] Another uprising by a governor of Citerior occurred in 145; the culprit, Cornelius Priscianus (possibly a Spaniard himself) was apprehended and condemned by the Senate, but committed suicide. In 197 the governor of Citerior, Claudius Candidus, was also 'commander in that [province], by land and sea, against the rebels, public enemies' – by which are meant the supporters of Clodius Albinus. And in 280, the pretender Bonosus allegedly had the support of the Spanish, Gallic and British provinces.[5]

The barbarian invasions of the fifth century provide an interesting perspective into the attitude of the Spaniards to their conquerors. One might logically expect the more romanised parts of Spain –

Baetica and the east coast – to fight to the end for the preservation of Romanity, while the recalcitrant inhabitants of the north
might welcome the opportunity to throw off the Roman yoke.
Instead, the opposite occurs: it is precisely the Vaccaei, Callaeci
and Astures, distrustful of any overlord, who fight off the waves
of Suevi and Visigoths. The Basques resisted vigorously, and indeed
aggressively, making incursions into the Ebro valley and even to the
Mediterranean coast in the sixth and seventh centuries. Neither they
nor the Cantabri were ever brought under Gothic rule; indeed, King
Roderic was still fighting the Basques when the Arabs invaded in
711. But in 'romanised' Spain there was little effort to impede the
invaders. Most towns were betrayed from within or, at best, deceived
by enemy stratagems.[6] The fleet assembled by the emperor Majorian
at Alicante on the east coast for use against the Vandals, was set on
fire with the help of Spanish traitors. Moreover, a large proportion
of the Spanish populace defected to the barbarians in the early fifth
century in order to evade the oppressive Roman taxes, and many
former 'Romans' were to be found in the enemy's ranks. A rare
exception to this apathy or collusion was a futile 'last stand' by the
aristocracy of Tarraconensis against the Visigoths around 472.[7]

I have left to the end of this section a special category of insurgents, known as Bacaudae – a generic term for dispossessed peasants,
runaway slaves and army deserters. They ravaged Gaul and Spain on
repeated occasions, beginning in the 180s, and by the middle of the
fifth century the Bacaudae of Tarraconensis were a serious threat
to what would nowadays be called national security. From small
bands of oppressed and discontented yokels, the Bacaudae swelled
into armies which overran the peninsula in armed insurrection. It is
a measure of the fear inspired by the Bacaudae among the writers of
the propertied class that they do not give us more information on
the Bacaudae, and a measure of the seriousness of the problem that
we hear about them at all.[8]

CULTURAL RESISTANCE

But armed resistance was only the visible and dramatic extremity
of a much more profound problem. The bulk of the opposition to
Rome was exercised on a cultural plane. I think it legitimate to call
this process 'cultural resistance'; those who spurn employment of
the last word in any but a bellicose sense may prefer to think in
terms of 'persistence of pre-Roman institutions and beliefs'. The net

result is the same: a failure of romanisation to penetrate the roots of provincial society. To what extent this process was due to deliberate hostility or stubbornness on the part of the indigenes, and to what extent they were unconsciously carrying on old traditions because Rome had failed to re-educate them, remains a contestable point.

Cultural resistance comprises numerous facets – social, religious, artistic, linguistic, and so on. Among social factors we may first note the survival of the pre-Roman clan and tribal structures throughout the Roman period, especially in northern and north-western Spain. The names of these clans (*gentes, gentilitates*) end in *-um* or *-on*, and well over 300 of them are preserved in inscriptions. The *gentilitas* seems to be a subdivision of the larger *gens:* an inscription from Astorga records the *gentilitas Desoncorum* and *gentilitas Tridiavorum* as both belonging to the *gens Zoelarum* in AD 27. These gentilic designations form part of indigenous nomenclature, either following or (especially among the Vettones) preceding the person's filiation, for example 'Segontius Talavi f[ilius] Talabonicum' or 'Dobiterus Caburoniqum Equaesi f[ilius]'. The pre-Roman tribal structure also continued, and the names of Iberian tribes that figure in accounts of the wars of the Republican period are still used as current nomenclature by Pliny in the first century AD and Ptolemy in the second. Pliny also refers to the 'barbaric' names of the peoples of the *conventus Lucensis* and *conventus Bracaraugustanus* in north-western Spain, which he declines to name for fear of trying his readers' patience. Another strange social survival is the pre-Roman system of hospitality. In the inscription from Astorga already cited, the two *gentilitates* renew an old guest-host agreement (*hospitium*) and receive each other and their descendants into *fides* and *clientela.* As Robert Broughton has remarked, this reciprocal pledge in which *both* parties become mutual and hereditary clients is quite foreign to Roman practice.[9] Another hospitality agreement, between the towns of Consabura (near Toledo) and Maggavia in AD 14, not only lists local magistrates with non-Roman names, but is written on either side of a bronze boar, in the best pre-Roman tradition. Another and more barbaric social custom was the eating of human flesh in times of famine. This is chiefly attested in the Republican period; but in AD 408, when food supplies were plundered or burnt by the barbarians, the starving Spaniards again resorted to cannibalism, and mothers devoured their children.[10]

Settlement patterns also reveal survivals. The rescript of Vespasian to the magistrates of Sabora in AD 77, giving them permission to move down into the plain, demonstrates that some tribes in 'romanised' Baetica were still inhabiting Iron age hill-forts in the Flavian period. In north-western Spain these hill-forts (*castros, citânias*) remained in use even longer. The celebrated Citânia de Briteiros continued to about AD 400 (with primitive stone architecture and funerary chambers), while Castro de Mohias in Oviedo province contains occupation material up to the sixth and possibly ninth centuries AD. The permanence of settlement patterns is perhaps most strikingly illustrated by the situation following the Christian Reconquest: pre-Roman population centres were reoccupied so faithfully that the limits of the ancient tribal regions were reproduced with almost mathematical precision.[11]

Religion tended to be one of the most conservative and entrenched elements in Roman provincial society, and it is precisely in this aspect that we encounter some of the strongest opposition to romanisation. Romanised regions such as Baetica and the east coast have left very few traces of their pre-Roman religious beliefs, but in the west and north of the peninsula – Lusitania, Galicia, Cantabria – we find a high proportion of indigenous deities represented in votive inscriptions of the Roman period. The Lusitanian god Endovellicus and the goddess Ataecina are found in numerous inscriptions over an extensive geographical area, while the sanctuary of Candeleda in Avila province contains a series of dedications to the god Vaelicus. In the north-west we often find Bandua and Cosus, as well as various nature gods; and across the north of Spain, mountains were apparently worshipped as deities. In all, about 300 different indigenous deities appear in inscriptions of imperial date, of which approximately half occur only once. In chapter 8 I have attempted to quantify the relative proportions of indigenous and Roman deities in various tribes.

The worship of indigenous deities was not confined to rural districts or to the humbler classes of society. At Aeso in north-eastern Spain, a local magistrate dedicates to the Moon, and at Olisipo (Lisbon) the governor of Lusitania dedicates to the Sun and Moon, while elsewhere in that province a Roman knight dedicates to the indigenous god Endovellicus.[12] These examples illustrate the failure of romanisation to penetrate completely at the religious level, even among the elite. Nor are these religious survivals confined to the Early Empire. An altar from the modern province of Santander, bearing a consular date of AD 399, contains a dedication to an otherwise unknown god Erudinus, who had evidently survived the imposition not only of Roman paganism but also of Christianity. Even in the late sixth century the Christian Church in Spain was having to deal with widespread idolatry, while in the Basque country, indigenous deities and demons were still being worshipped in the seventh and eighth centuries.[13] Within Christianity itself there was the Priscillianist movement, which began in the late fourth century as a heretical sect but soon, like the Circumcellions in Africa, became a vehicle or 'front' for resistance to the established order, chiefly among the rural population.[14]

Architecture is another field in which romanisation failed to capture the hearts or imagination of the inhabitants in certain regions. In the north-west especially, the populace had always dwelt in *castros* and had no understanding of, or use for, sophisticated public edifices. Additionally, there were very few human agglomerations of sufficient density to be called cities. Thus we find an almost total lack of public buildings in Galicia, and certainly nothing as advanced as a theatre, temple or circus. The stone huts of circular or oval plan from this region continue from pre-Roman times into the early Middle Ages (as occurs also in Celtic Gaul), and prehistorians have even used modern derivatives of these huts to reconstruct their ancestors.[15] In Central Spain we encounter a more developed sense of urbanism and hence of architectural display, but in the two north-western tribes of this region (the Vaccaei and Turmogi) there is hardly any trace of public works other than a few essential bridges. Even on the south and east coasts there is ample evidence of indigenous influence on the architecture of the Roman period.[16] Town plans changed very little. At Numantia, the streets of the Roman period, though somewhat straighter than their indigenous predecessors, largely overlap them. Here, as also in the Iberian towns in the Valencia region, Roman private houses, though made of new materials, continue the pre-Roman plan and structure.[17] Finally, we should remark the reoccupation, in the fourth and fifth centuries AD, of prehistoric caves in the Rioja and Basque country.[18]

In terms of fine art we again find deviation from Roman canons. In some cases this consists of 'provincial' adaptations of forms imported from Rome, and hence a modified species of romanisation. But there are other cases in which indigenous art continues without apparent interruption or influence from Rome. This phenomenon does not necessarily imply a deliberate display of opposition on the part of the indigenes: ancient taste is difficult to assess objectively in retrospect, and it may well be that Spaniards simply considered that their own art forms had more aesthetic merits than those proffered by the conqueror. But however valid their reasons or innocent their intentions, the net result is a cultural resistance, conscious or otherwise. Thus in central Spain and Lusitania we find art in a Celtic style reminiscent of Gallia Comata, while on the south and east coasts, hellenised Iberian art apparently continues into the reign of Augustus. In north-western Spain, the golden torques, rings and other jewelry which are the hallmark of the pre-Roman elite, continue to be produced and used into the Roman period; and at the end of the Empire, amidst the migrations of Suevi and Visigoths, suppressed pre-Roman art forms suddenly re-emerge.[19]

The medium in which indigenous art is best preserved is stone, and this is especially evident in the decoration of funerary stelae. Decorated tomb monuments were not unknown at Rome, but the motifs occurring in parts of Spain are definitely of pre-Roman character. Such stelae are found frequently in northern and eastern Lusitania, and in the modern provinces of León, Burgos, Lleida and Navarra (Figure 9.1). They date chiefly to the second and third centuries AD and sometimes the fourth, though earlier ones engraved with Iberian characters are also known. They scarcely ever occur in Baetica or on the east coast, though they occasionally make an appearance in the southern Meseta and in the Pyrenees. A wide variety of decoration is featured on these stelae: the sun (in the form of a solar disc, a spoked wheel or a rosette, usually six-petalled), the moon (symbolising the abode of the dead), arches and architraves (representing the gateway to the next world), funeral banquets, human figures (usually in combination with one of the two preceding motifs), animals (e.g. the bull, possibly intended to give strength to the deceased in the next world, and birds, representing the departed soul in flight), botanical elements (ivy or acanthus symbolising immortality, and laurel symbolising victory over death), armed horsemen (of debated significance), and swastikas (possibly of magical value).[20] Interestingly enough, similar tombstones bearing these same symbols and Celtiberian names have been found in Dacia and Pannonia, although the apparent connection with Spain has yet to be explained. Within Spain, this indigenous symbolism survives the pagan period, for several of the motifs appear on a Christian epitaph of AD 354, from Cantabria.[21] A specialised form peculiar to northern Spain is the discoid stela, comprising a decorated, sometimes inscribed disc and a sloping base to support it, all carved from a single piece of stone. These stelae begin in the pre-Roman

Figure 9.1 Funerary stela of Antonia Buturra, from Gastiain (Navarra), with solar disc and other symbols. (Museo de Navarra, Pamplona.)

185

period, often displaying a horseman and an inscription in Iberian characters, and continue through the Roman period (with a variety of indigenous motifs) into Christian times (with a stylised cross in the disc) and even into the twentieth century. Discoid stelae with 'eyes' are found in pre-Roman, Roman and medieval contexts.[22]

Ceramic evidence also reveals resistance to cultural takeover. The indigenous Iberian pottery, which was theoretically superseded by Roman *terra sigillata*, in fact continues alongside it into the first century AD and even later. Indeed, some of the ceramic motifs used in Spanish *sigillata*, such as bands containing a series of circles (often concentric or enclosing other decorative elements) are peculiar to Spain and clearly derived from Iberian painted ware. What is more surprising is the abuse or misunderstanding of Roman *sigillata* styles by the natives. At Numantia and Villalazán in the interior of the peninsula we find Spanish *sigillata* on the surface of which have been painted barbotine designs; the Numantia excavations have also yielded pieces of thin-walled ware (first century AD) with concentric semicircles painted over them in the Celtiberian manner. A misguided attempt to copy part of the Roman *sigillata* technique while still clinging to indigenous tradition is to be seen in the products of the Azailan potter Protemus, whose name appears sometimes in Latin, sometimes in Iberian script, *in planta pedis* in the Roman tradition, but on *mortaria* of indigenous tradition.[23] Among non-*sigillata* ceramics, we may mention the fine grey wares of the Conimbriga region in northern Portugal, which continue from the Iron age into the early Imperial period with no detectable change (either visually or by neutron activation analysis) in composition or technique, and with such continuity in form that specimens are often difficult to date to one period or the other.[24] At Castulo in the south-east we find painted pottery in the fourth century AD which recalls the wares of the pre-Roman period. In the Basque country, the coarse wares in black or brown maintain the indigenous tradition so staunchly that it is often difficult to tell Iron Age pottery from Roman, while in Galicia the techniques, forms and decorations of indigenous pottery continue into the Middle Ages.[25] Lastly, a terracotta *tessera* from Uxama, with a Latin inscription, depicts a running rabbit, a peculiarly Spanish motif which also occurs not only on indigenous painted pottery of the Roman period at the same city, but also on fifteenth-century plates and tiles.[26]

Spaniards were no less resistant to technological innovation. L. Iunius Moderatus Columella, a native of Gades who spent most of his life in Rome, wrote a treatise on scientific methods of agriculture, but it seems to have had little effect in his homeland, where pre-Roman methods have continued into recent times. The primitive toothed plough and yoke depicted on Iberian coinage and miniature iron models are practically identical with those in use in Andalusia and the Balearic Islands until quite recently, and adzes similar to those of the fourth to third centuries BC were still being used in Catalonia in the first half of the twentieth century. In the 1970s, Reynolds saw a Spanish farmer clearing the earth from the point of his ard with a stick, while another man swept the flies from the oxen's faces with a leafy twig – a scene identical to that depicted in Bronze age rock carvings! The modern harrow was known to the Romans, but was apparently absent from Spain in the Middle Ages, because the twelfth-century agronomist Ibn al-Awam of Seville, relying on an earlier writer named Cassius, gives his readers a detailed description of how to construct this unfamiliar contraption.[27] Pre-Roman mining techniques continued in use throughout the Roman period. These ore-extraction methods were so primitive and inadequate that several Roman mines in the Sierra Morena were reopened in modern times and profitably reworked, because deep mineral veins had been left unexploited by the Romans. Metal weaponry also resisted change. Daggers found at fourth-century AD sites in north-central Spain continue the pre-Roman Celtic tradition. *Faláricas* (javelins) of Celtiberian type were still in use in the thirteenth century; and it is reported that in the early days of bullfighting, the participants were mounted gentlemen equipped with the *rejon*, the same short spear used by the ancient Spaniards.[28]

The final attestation of resistance concerns the sphere of linguistics. This phenomenon is perhaps most strikingly illustrated by the persistence of pre-Roman toponyms and personal names. Toponyms tend to be very conservative, and many continued not only into the Roman period but far beyond. Names of Phoenician or Punic origin include Gades, Malaca, Mago and Carthago Nova, which survive practically unchanged today as Cádiz, Málaga, Mahón and Cartagena. The names of the Greek colonies Emporion (Latin Emporiae) and Rhode (Latin Rhoda) survive today as Empúries and Roses. There has been much debate as to whether the indigenous toponymic endings '-berri' and '-gorri' are ultimately of Basque origin, but in any event they continue through the Roman period in such names as Iliberri(s) and Calagurri(s), and are still attested today in north-eastern Spain.[29] Toponyms containing the element '-nt-' are pre-Celtic and occur chiefly in the north (Palantia, Salmantica, Numantia) but also on the east coast (Saguntum, Lucentum). The perpetuation of Iberian and Celtic toponyms into Roman and later times was very widespread, and has formed the subject of numerous regional studies. Of those elements occurring frequently and over an extensive area may be mentioned the Iberian prefix 'Il-' (Ilurco, Ilici, Ilerda, etc.), found throughout southern and eastern Spain; the suffix '-ci' or '-gi' (Acci, Tucci, Astigi, Murgi, etc.), frequent in Andalusia; and the Celtic ending '-briga' ('hill-fort') which occurs in all of the peninsula except the north-east. A few pre-Roman toponyms such as Saguntum and Titulcia have actually been revived in modern times by Spanish communities proud of their ancestry.

The preservation of pre-Roman toponyms in Roman times does not necessarily prove continuing resistance to romanisation. Half the states of the United States have names of North American Indian origin, though the native peoples are now largely Americanised. Toponyms tend to become fossilised. Personal names, on the other hand, change from generation to generation, and in many parts of Spain and other Roman provinces we can see proof in the inscriptions that succeeding generations adopt more romanised names than their parents. But this is not everywhere the case, and studies of the nomenclature of various regions indicate local trends. In central Spain, for instance, despite a considerable occurrence of the Latin *nomen gentilicium*, we find a high incidence of single name (*cognomen*) alone. An analysis of all the *cognomina* from this region shows that in the three northernmost tribes, fewer than half the *cognomina* are Latin (Pelendones 43 per cent, Turmogi 41 per cent, Vaccaei 36 per cent, as against Arevaci 64 per cent, Celtiberi 64 per cent, Carpetani 71 per cent). In Galicia, although only 20 per cent of names contain no Latin element whatever, Tranoy found 287 types of indigenous names, with a total of 478 occurrences. And figures for the Tras-os-Montes region of northern Portugal reveal that 54 per cent of the names in Roman inscriptions are indigenous.[30] The nomenclature patterns also reflect differentiation in social status. At Conimbriga in northern Lusitania, only 33 per cent of persons named on stone inscriptions have indigenous *cognomina*, but among those whose names appear on pottery, the figure is 75 per cent. Attention has also been drawn to the fact that the Spanish amphora stamps in the Monte Testaccio at Rome, which are mostly of Imperial date, contain some barbarous names.[31] Another index of lack of progress in romanisation of nomenclature is the type of filiation used in inscriptions. Roman filiation comprises the father's *praenomen* in the genitive case (but usually abbreviated to one or two letters), followed by 'f.' (for 'filius'). Indigenous nomenclature consists of the father's non-Latin *cognomen* in the genitive, with or without 'f.' A variant of the latter pattern, in which the filiating *cognomen* is Latin, marks an intermediate stage in romanisation. Statistics published for north-western Spain show that 67 per cent of the filiations in inscriptions are of the purely indigenous type, a further 22 per cent are of the intermediate type, and only 11 per cent are of the true Roman type. In the most north-western district of all, the *conventus Lucensis*, 76 per cent of the filiations are indigenous, 20 per cent intermediate, and only 4 per cent Roman. Of course, even if the father has an indigenous name, we can claim romanisation if the child's name is Latin. Thus in the northern province of Alava, out of 78 families attested in inscriptions, only 30 have completely Latin names, but in another 19 instances the father has an indigenous name and the son Roman. If we count both categories as romanised, they thus outnumber the 29 families in which both fathers' and sons' names are indigenous. The author of this study concludes on this basis that Alava was one of the most romanised areas of the north. However, the absence from the epigraphy of any attestation of a local magistrate or priest emphasises the lack of urbanism in Alava province and the danger of arguing from nomenclature alone.[32]

There is also considerable evidence for the continuing use of pre-Roman languages in the Roman Imperial period. When the Spanish peasant who assassinated the juridical legate of Citerior in AD 25 was being tortured, he cried out in his native tongue that he would never confess. Spanish words for various creatures and objects are sometimes mentioned by Latin writers under the Empire, for instance *tardae* for a type of goose, *coccolobis* for the basilica vine, *dureta* for a wooden bathtub.[33] Numerous words of pre-Latin formation still survive in modern Catalan, Portuguese and Galician. Latin inscriptions from Spain occasionally contain non-Latin words, like *paramus* for a plateau and *lausia* for a flagstone, while the Hispano-Roman writer St Isidore uses such indigenous terms as *cama* and *sarna*. The inscriptions of Peñalba de Villastar in Teruel province, though written in crude Latin characters, are all in the Celtic language, except for one quotation from Vergil's *Aeneid*. Conversely, Latin names are written in Iberian script on inscriptions and coins from Emporiae, on Campanian pottery from two sites near

Barcelona, and in an inscription from Italica.[34] In Lusitania and the north-west, inscriptions in indigenous language continue into the Imperial period. There are also bilingual inscriptions in both Latin and Iberian script, including one at Saguntum on the east coast, and another at present-day Siruela near the border between Baetica and Citerior. In the Ebro valley, we find graffiti in Iberian characters on Roman pottery.[35] And although there are many thousands of Latin inscriptions in the peninsula, a great many of them contain peculiar forms of spelling and grammar. Although some of these are archaisms or features of Italic dialects, testifying to the presence and influence of soldiers in Republican Spain, the majority are plain errors caused by unfamiliarity with Latin. Mistakes in declension, conjugation and syntax reflect the semi-literate state of the inhabitants, while the wide range of wrong letters (both consonants and vowels) suggests popular mispronunciation of the language under influence of indigenous phonetics. An analysis of this phenomenon in the Latin inscriptions of Spain, published some eighty years ago, runs to nearly 300 pages, and the number of examples could probably be doubled today.[36]

CONCLUSIONS

Part of the problem in dealing with romanisation and resistance is that what appears to be non-romanisation is sometimes just slow romanisation; and while some regions became assimilated more quickly than others, the process was nowhere completed overnight. Strabo in the early first century AD boasts that the inhabitants of Further Spain were completely romanised: but it must be remembered that Further Spain had been a Roman province for well over 200 years. Also Strabo's remark, while applicable to the cities, was probably not true for the countryside. As for the bulk of the Iberians, Strabo dismisses them as wild barbarians, an opinion shared by Cicero and Valerius Maximus.[37] And although the conquest of Spain was officially considered complete in 19 BC, it had still taken two centuries, whereas Caesar had conquered Gaul in less than a decade. Therefore, in those instances where we are able to see romanisation at work, we find it a slow and gradual process. Punic and Iberian coin legends, for instance, continue for some time under the Roman regime before being replaced by Latin ones. The same applies to the coin designs, as witness their gradual romanisation at Abdera for instance.[38] Romanisation took hold most rapidly in the political, social and economic spheres; in religion, language and art, the old ways died hard. In regions isolated by mountains, distance from the sea, or lower cultural levels, romanisation fought an uphill battle.

The reasons for the incomplete success of romanisation are not easily defined; as this chapter has demonstrated, it is far easier to describe resistance than to explain it. Should we attribute this apparent conflict of cultures to 'nationalism' (in the sense of concerted and deliberate opposition to Roman control), or rather to the failure, or at least, disinclination, of Rome to enforce assimilation? Indeed, is our current concept of romanisation, as an attempt at total assimilation, valid? I would suggest that Rome was *not* committed to imposing her culture on the provincials in any thorough or systematic manner. Official policy was aimed chiefly at pacification, justice and tax collection. In terms of religion, the polytheistic Romans were tolerant of other cults, except where these posed a political threat (Christianity, for example); the Spanish pantheon offered no such danger. In terms of material culture, Roman goods were introduced not by official policy but by free enterprise, as their distribution patterns make clear; Roman imports found few markets in the interior with its limited economic networks. In terms of onomastics, the adoption of Roman nomenclature reflects the Spaniards' own desire to appear romanised, either for career advancement or increased social prestige; Rome did not force anyone to become a citizen, and her grants of *ius Latii* to provincial communities were received as a favour rather than an imposition. Architecture was not uniformly implanted but rather reflects local needs: in the already urbanised areas of southern and eastern Spain, Roman construction techniques were often adopted, whereas in Galicia and Cantabria, which lacked real cities, there was little requirement for monumental buildings. The failure of romanisation in the north-west can be attributed in part to the lack of colonies and immigration, but this in itself suggests that Rome was not intent on assimilating these regions.

This chapter presents just one side of the story. No one would deny that romanisation made serious inroads in Spain, as we have seen in the preceding chapters. Moreover, apparent survivals of pre-Roman elements do not necessarily imply continuity of their pre-Roman functions. Nonetheless, romanisation failed in three essential areas: first, in dispersion, because despite a high grade of romanisation in the south and east, the western and north-western regions were only partly assimilated, and the Cantabrians and

Basques were never romanised; second, in depth, because in much of the peninsula romanisation was but a superficial veneer, barely masking the indigenous subculture; third, in durability, because in the Late Empire the northern, western and central regions became de-romanised, and pre-Roman cultures re-emerged. In short, romanisation was not a homogeneous or consistent process, but varied greatly from region to region. To document this process, new approaches are needed. There are plenty of books and articles (including a few in English) on Roman Spain, written mostly by classicists or classical archaeologists. There are also plenty of books and articles (hardly any in English) on the pre-Roman Iron age in Spain, written mostly by prehistoric archaeologists. The classicist, on the one hand, confines his attention to the Roman period, searching the literary and material records for evidence that Spain was indeed romanised; the prehistorian, on the other hand, understandably sees the Roman conquest as the *terminus ante quem* for his studies. But if we accept the premise that romanisation is a transition, it is necessary to study *both* sides of the time-line – a proposition which runs counter both to the chronological compartments into which we automatically parcel history, and to the specialised training of classicists on one side and prehistorians on the other. We shall have no understanding of the romanising process until either classicists master Iron age archaeology or prehistorians master classics – or until they learn to work with each other, freely exchanging information and ideas. This means discarding traditional disciplinary boundaries and rivalries, and engaging in productive dialogue and diachronic study of sites and regions. Archaeology in the twentieth century has uncovered a huge quantity of evidence about both the Iron age and the Roman period. Let us hope that the twenty-first century will see an effective synthesis of how the one culture adapted to and became assimilated with the other.[39]

NOTES

INTRODUCTION

1 *AE* 1969–70, 254.
2 L. Pericot, *Cerámica ibérica* (Barcelona, 1977), figs 126, 172, 175; Catullus, 37, 39; Strabo, 3.3.7, 3.4.16–17; Martial, 10.65.
3 Strabo, 3.5.7, 10.
4 L.A. Curchin, 'Jobs in Roman Spain', *Florilegium*, vol. 4 (1982b), pp. 36–40.
5 Pliny, *NH*, 25.85 (potion); Strabo, 3.3.7.
6 A. Fernández de Avilés, 'Carrito de juguete, en terracota, procedente de Elche' in *Homenaje al profesor Cayetano de Mergelina* (Murcia, 1961–2), pp. 311–17. Dolls: J.L. Díaz Moreno *et al*, *Atlas de Castilla-La Mancha* (Madrid, 1986), p. 97.
7 J. Aparicio Pérez, 'Sobre la casa ibérica' in *Homenaje a D. Pío Beltrán* (Madrid, 1974), pp. 15–20.

1 THE PENINSULA AND ITS INHABITANTS

1 Pliny, *NH*, 3.1.3–4; Gellius, 10.26.6.
2 Pindar, *Olymp.*, 3.44.5, anticipating the mediaeval motto, 'ne plus ultra'.
3 C. Delano Smith, *Western Mediterranean Europe* (London, 1979), pp. 330–2, 372–3.
4 Strabo, 3.4.7; Livy, 26.19.11.
5 Delano Smith, *Western Mediterranean Europe*, p. 314.
6 R. Way, *A geography of Spain and Portugal* (London, 1962), pp. 60–3; J.M. Houston, *The western Mediterranean world* (London, 1964), pp. 202–5.
7 Polyb., 34.8.5; Pliny, *NH*, 37.203; cf. A.F.G. Bell, 'Some Spanish flower names', *Bulletin of Spanish Studies*, vol. 3 (1925), pp. 12–15.
8 F.J. Lomas, 'Origen y desarrollo de la cultura de los campos de urnas' in J.M. Blázquez *et al*, *Historia de España antigua*, (Madrid, 1980), vol. 1, pp. 13–28. The classic study of the dual wave theory is P. Bosch Gimpera, 'Two Celtic waves in Spain', *Proceedings of the British Academy*, vol. 26 (1940), pp. 25–148.

9 H.N. Savory, *Spain and Portugal* (London, 1968), p. 246.
10 W. Schüle, *Die Meseta-Kulturen der Iberischen Halbinsel* (Berlin, 1969); R. Martín Valls, 'Segunda edad del hierro' in G. Delibes *et al, Historia de Castilla y León* (Madrid, 1985), vol. 1, pp. 105–31.
11 Livy, 28.1.4
12 R.J. Harrison, *Spain at the dawn of history* (London, 1988), pp. 30–5.
13 Dionysius, *Periegesis*, 337.
14 J.M. Blázquez, 'Panorama general de la presencia fenicia y púnica en España' in *Atti del I congresso internazionale di studi fenici e punici* (Rome, 1983), vol. 2, p. 314.
15 Strabo, 3.1.6.
16 Ps.–Aristotle, *De mirab. ausc.*, 135; Diod. Sic., 5.35.4.
17 Pausanias, 6.19.2–4; A. Blanco and J.M. Luzón, 'Pre-Roman silver miners at Riotinto', *Antiquity*, vol. 43 (1969), pp. 124–31.
18 A. Arribas, *The Iberians* (London, 1963), pp. 52–3.
19 Diod. Sic., 17.113.2; Oros., 3.20.8; M.L.Z. Munn, 'Corinthian trade with the West in the classical period' 1983, unpublished Ph.D thesis, Bryn Mawr College.
20 Livy, 23.26.
21 Justin, 44.5.2–3; P.A. Barceló, *Karthago und die Iberische Halbinsel vor den Barkiden* (Bonn, 1988), pp. 61, 82–4.
22 T. Chapa Brunet, *Influjos griegos en la escultura zoomorfa ibérica* (Madrid, 1986), pp. 237–9, dates Phoenician influence to the seventh through fifth centuries, with Greek beginning in the sixth and Punic in the third.

2 FROM FRONTIER TO PROVINCE

1 A. Schulten, 'Forschungen in Spanien', *Archäologischer Anzeiger*, 1927, col. 233, and 1933, col. 525.
2 Livy, 23.29.
3 Livy, 25.33–6.
4 Jordanes, *Romana*, 198; H.H. Scullard, *Scipio Africanus, soldier and politician* (London, 1970), pp. 52–8, on Scipio's tactics and historical parallels for the effects of wind on shallow waters; cf. Vitruvius, 1.4.11 and A. and M. Lillo, 'On Polybius X 10, 12 f.', *Historia*, vol. 37 (1988), pp. 477–80 on the likelihood of sluices controlling the water level.
5 Polyb., 11.20.1; App., *Iber.*, 25; cf. J. Millán León, 'La batalla de Ilipa', *Habis*, vol. 17 (1986), pp. 283–303.
6 L.J.F. Keppie, *The making of the Roman army* (London, 1984), pp. 30 and 235, n. 10.
7 Oros., 7.2.
8 Livy, 32.28.11; Caes., *Bell. civ.*, 1.38.1. The early date of division has been challenged, on unconvincing grounds, by G.V. Sumner, 'Proconsuls and *provinciae* in Spain, 218/7–196/5 BC', *Arethusa*, vol. 3 (1970), pp. 85–102, and 'Notes on *provinciae* in Spain (197–133 BC)', *Classical Philology*, vol. 72 (1977), pp. 126–30.
9 Livy, 33.21.6, 33.25.9, 34.10.5.

10 Livy, 34.14–15. On the identity of the tribe, R.C. Knapp, 'Cato in Spain, 195/194 BC' in C. Deroux (ed.), *Studies in Latin literature and Roman history*, (Brussels, 1980), vol. 2, p. 33.
11 Plut., *Cato maior*, 10.3.
12 Livy, 34.19.1–2; Knapp, 'Cato in Spain', pp. 38–40, 47–54.
13 But plausibly identified with the Iacetani by G. Fatás, 'Hispania entre Catón y Graco', *Hispania Antiqua*, vol. 5 (1975), pp. 271–7.
14 Livy, 34.21.7.
15 D. Baatz, 'Recent finds of ancient artillery', *Britannia*, vol. 9 (1978), p. 1.
16 J.M. Nolla and F.J. Nieto, 'Alguns aspectes de la Romanització al nord-est de Catalunya' in *Els pobles pre-romans del Pirineu* (Puigcerdà, 1978), p. 240.
17 J. Martínez Gázquez, *La campaña de Catón en Hispania* (Barcelona, 1974), pp. 161–2, 168; M. Tarradell, 'Un fortí roma a Tentellatge' in *Els pobles pre-romans del Pirineu*, pp. 245–50.
18 J.S. Richardson, *Hispaniae: Spain and the development of Roman imperialism 218–82 BC*, (Cambridge, 1986), pp. 97–8.
19 Polyb., 32.8; Livy, 37.46.7.
20 *Bell. Hisp.*, 8; Strabo, 3.4.13; Pliny, *NH*, 3.1.15; *ILS*, 15.
21 Livy, 39.21, 39.31.
22 Livy, 40.39–40; Oros., 4.20.16; *Inscriptiones Italiae*, XIII/2 (Rome, 1963), pp. 16 (text), 495 (commentary); J. Champeaux, *Fortuna: Recherches sur le culte de la Fortune à Rome* (Rome, 1987), vol. 2, p. 150.
23 Livy, 40.50, 41.7, *Per.*, 41.
24 Livy, *Per.*, 41; Festus, ed. Lindsay, 86; *ILER*, 1287; cf. R. Wiegels, 'Iliturgi und der "deductor" Ti. Sempronius Gracchus', *Madrider Mitteilungen*, vol. 23 (1982), pp. 152–211.
25 P.A. Brunt, *Italian manpower, 225 BC–AD 14* (Oxford, 1971), pp. 661–3; Richardson, *Hispaniae*, p. 105.
26 Livy, 41.26; *Per.*, 43, 46; App., *Iber.*, 43.
27 Polyb., 35.1.1.
28 App., *Iber.*, 56–7.
29 Livy, *Per*, 47. Probably also because the calendar had fallen behind the seasons: P. Brind'Amour, *Le calendrier romain* (Ottawa, 1983), pp. 130–2.
30 Richardson, *Hispaniae*, pp. 134–6.
31 App., *Iber.*, 45–6; A. Schulten, *Geschichte von Numantia* (Munich, 1933), pp. 41–8 and plate V.
32 Polyb., 35.2–3; App., *Iber.*, 49–50; R.W. Bane, 'The development of Roman imperial attitudes and the Iberian wars', *Emerita*, vol. 44 (1976), p. 415; Richardson, *Hispaniae*, pp. 141–4.
33 App., *Iber.*, 51–5; L. de Castro García and R. Blanco Ordas, 'El castro de Tariego de Cerrato (Palencia)', *Publicaciones de la institución 'Tello Téllez de Meneses'*, vol. 35 (1975), pp. 55–138.
34 App., *Iber.*, 56–60; Livy,*Per.*,49; Suet.,*Galba*,3; Val. Max., 9.6.2; Oros., 4.21.10; H. Simon, *Roms Kriege in Spanien 154–133 v. Chr.* (Frankfurt, 1962), pp. 60–7.
35 App., *Iber.*, 61–6.

36 App., *Iber.*, 76–80; Livy *Per.*, 54–55; Cic., *De oratore*, 1.40.181; Oros., 5.4.20.
37 App., *Iber.*, 70, 74; Diod. Sic., 33.21; Dio, fr. 75; Florus, 1.33.17.
38 Livy, *Per.*, 54–5; App., *Iber.*, 71–2; Strabo, 3.3.1; Florus, 1.33.12; Oros., 5.5.12; Plut., *Quaest. rom.*, 34; P. Kalb and M. Hock, 'Moron – historisch und archäologisch', *Madrider Mitteilungen*, vol. 25 (1984), pp. 92–102; C.F.C. Hawkes, 'North-western castros: Excavation, archaeology and history', *Actas do II Congresso nacional de arqueologia* (Coimbra, 1971), pp. 283–6.
39 Eutrop., 4.19; Festus, *Brev.*, 5; Jordanes, *Rom.*, 212; T.R.S. Broughton, *The magistrates of the Roman Republic* (Cleveland, 1950), vol. 2, p. 437.
40 App., *Iber.*, 81–3; Obsequens, 26; Livy, *Per.*, 56.
41 App., *Iber.*, 85–92; Val. Max., 2.7.1; J.M. Blázquez, 'Luftbilder römischer Lager aus republikanischer Zeit in Spanien' in *Studien zu den Militärgrenzen Roms III* (Stuttgart, 1986), pp. 681–8.
42 App., *Iber.*, 96–8; Livy, *Per.*, 59; Florus, 1.34; A.E. Astin, *Scipio Aemilianus* (Oxford, 1967), pp. 153–5.
43 H.G. Gundel, 'Probleme der römischen Kampfführung gegen Viriatus' in *Legio VII Gemina* (León, 1970), p. 120.

3 TO THE BOUNDARY OF OCEAN

1 M.G. Morgan, 'The Roman conquest of the Balearic islands', *California Studies in Classical Antiquity*, vol. 2 (1969), pp. 217–231; cf. B. Leroy, *L'Espagne au Moyen Age* (Paris, 1988), p. 43.
2 Livy, *Per.*, 60; Strabo, 3.5.1; Florus, 1.43; Oros., 5.13; Plut., *C. Gracchus*, 6.2.
3 Plut., *Marius*, 6.1 On his praetorship, T.R.S. Broughton, *The magistrates of the Roman Republic*, (Cleveland, 1950), vol. 1, p. 532.
4 Cic., *Verr.*, 2.4.56; App., *Iber.*, 99 (Piso); Val. Max., 6.9.13; Eutrop., 4.27.5; *Fasti Triumph., an.* 107 (Caepio); *ILS*, 5812–13; Val. Max., 6.3.3.
5 Obsequens, 42; *AE* 1984, 495.
6 Obsequens, 44a; App., *Iber.*, 100.
7 Dolabella: *Fasti Triumph., an.* 98. Didius: App., *Iber.*, 99–100; Frontin., *Strat.*, 2.10.1.
8 D. Vaquerizo Gil, 'Serie de 39 denarios romano-republicanos, conservados en Orellana de la Sierra (Badajoz)', in *XVIII Congreso nacional de arqueología* (Zaragoza, 1987), pp. 873–93.
9 Crassus: Plut., *Crassus*, 1.1; *Fasti Triumph., an.* 93. Flaccus: App., *Iber.*, 100; Granius Licinianus, ed. M. Flemisch, 31–2.
10 Vegetius 1.7; J. Harmand, *L'Armée et le soldat à Rome de 107 à 50 avant notre ère* (Paris, 1967), 460–1.
11 Val. Max., 9.1.5; Plut., *Sert.*, 12.4–13.1.
12 Sall., *Hist.*, 1.112.
13 P.O. Spann, 'Lagobriga expunged: Renaissance forgeries and the Sertorian War', *Transactions of the American Philological Association*, vol. 111 (1981), pp. 229–35.

14 Oros., 5.23.4; Caes., *Bell. Gall.*, 3.20.1.

15 Frontin., *Strat.*, 2.5.31; Oros., 5.23.10.

16 A. Schulten, *Sertorius* (Leipzig, 1926), p. 111; P.O. Spann, *Quintus Sertorius and the legacy of Sulla* (Fayetteville, 1987), p. 111.

17 Cic., *Pro Balbo*, 2.5; Plut., *Pomp.*, 19.2–3; *Sert.*, 19.4.

18 Sall., *Hist.*, 2.98.1; App., *Bell. civ.*, 1.110; Plut., *Sert.*, 21.1; cf. P.O. Spann, 'Saguntum vs. Segontia', *Historia*, vol. 33 (1984), pp. 116–19. Some scholars refer to this as the battle of the Turia, though that river does not flow within 20 km of Saguntum.

19 Cic., *Pro Font.*, 6.13. Many of the coins of 74 BC have been found in Spain: M.H. Crawford, *Coinage and money under the Roman Republic* (Berkeley and Los Angeles, 1985), pp. 211–13.

20 App., *Bell. civ.*, 1.112; Strabo, 3.4.10. On the date, see W.H. Bennett, 'The death of Sertorius and the coin', *Historia*, vol. 10 (1961), p. 459–72.

21 Cannibalism at Calagurris: Val. Max. 7.6, ext. 3.

22 Sall., *Hist.*, 2.98.9.

23 App., *Iber.*, 101; cf. C.F. Konrad, 'Afranius imperator', *Hispania Antiqua*, vol. 8 (1978), pp. 67–76.

24 Suet., *Jul.*, 18, 54; Dio 37.52–3; Plut., *Caes.*, 11–12.

25 Caes., *Bell. civ.*, 1.85. Vaccaei: Dio 39.54.

26 Suet., *Jul.*, 34.

27 Caes., *Bell. civ.*, 1.37–55 and 59–87. On the strategy, J.F.C. Fuller, *Julius Caesar: Man, soldier, tyrant* (London, 1965), pp. 195–206; J. Harmand, 'César et l'Espagne durant le second "Bellum civile"' in *Legio VII Gemina* (León, 1970), pp. 186–94. On the topography, F. Lara Peinado, *Lérida romana* (Lleida, 1973), pp. 22–28.

28 Caes., *Bell. civ.*, 2.19–21; C. Castillo, 'Miscelánea epigráfica hispano-romana', *Studia et Documenta Historiae et Iuris*, vol. 52 (1986), pp. 376–81.

29 *Bell. Alex.*, 48–64.

30 *Bell. Hisp.*, 1–2; Dio 43.29–30.

31 *Bell. Hisp.*, 4–6; Dio 33.2. R. Corzo, 'Die Belagerung von Ategua durch Julius Caesar (45 v. Chr.)' in C. Unz (ed.), *Studien zu den Militärgrenzen Roms III* (Stuttgart, 1986), pp. 689–91.

32 The site of Munda is much debated: see A. Caruz Arenas, 'La última campaña de César en la Bética: Munda', in J.F. Rodríguez Neila (ed.), *Actas del I Congreso de historia de Andalucía: Fuentes y metodología, Andalucía en la Antigüedad* (Córdoba, 1978), pp. 143–57.

33 Utrera: *CIL* II, 4965. Osuna: A. Engel and P. Paris, 'Une forteresse ibérique à Osuna (fouilles de 1903)', *Nouvelles Archives des Missions Scientifiques et Littéraires*, vol. 13 (1906), pp. 458–66.

34 Cic., *Att.*, 15.20, 16.4; Dio, 45.10.6; App., *Bell. civ.*, 3.4; cf. M. Hadas, *Sextus Pompey* (New York, 1930), pp. 52–5.

35 Dio, 48.1.3.

36 Dio, 48.10.1; App., *Bell. civ.*, 5.20.

37 Dio, 48.42.1–6; *ILS*, 42.

38 C. Norbanus Flaccus, L. Marcius Philippus, Ap. Claudius Pulcher, C. Calvisius Sabinus, Sex. Apuleius.

39 T. Statilius Taurus (29–28 B.C.): Dio, 51.20.5; *CIL* II, 3556.
40 Dio, 48.45.1–3 (Bogud), 51.6.3, 51.8.5, 51.10.4; *ILS*, 2672.
41 Dio, 51.20.5; Plut., *Moralia*, 322 C; Florus, 2.33.47.
42 K. Raddatz, *Die Schatzfunde der Iberischen Halbinsel vom Ende des dritten bis zur Mitte des ersten Jahrhunderts vor Chr.* (Berlin, 1969), pp. 172–97; R. Martín Valls and G. Delibes de Castro, 'Hallazgos arqueológicos en la provincia de Zamora', *Boletín del Seminario de Estudios de Arte y Arqueología*, vol. 47 (1981), pp. 153–5.
43 See R. Syme, 'The conquest of north-west Spain' in *Legio VII Gemina*, pp. 79–107; A. Rodríguez Colmenero, *Augusto e Hispania* (Bilbao, 1979), pp. 52–130.
44 Strabo, 3.4.18
45 Florus, 2.33; Suet., *Aug.*, 20–1; Dio, 53.25.5–8; Oros., 6.21.
46 Suet., *Aug.*, 29; Dio, 54.4.2.
47 Dio, 53.29.1–2, 54.5.1–3, 54.11.2–5, 54.20.3.
48 *Res Gestae*, 12; Pliny, *NH*, 4.118; *ILS*, 103.
49 Livy, 28.12.12.
50 A.M. Eckstein, *Senate and general: Individual decision making and Roman foreign relations 264–194 BC* (Berkeley, Los Angeles and London, 1987), pp. 187–231 (on the Hannibalic war); J.S. Richardson, *Hispaniae* (Cambridge, 1986).
51 J.M. Blázquez, 'El impacto de la conquista de la Hispania en Roma (154–83 a.C.)', *Klio*, vol. 41 (1963), p. 175.
52 P. Le Roux, *L'Armée romaine et l'organisation des provinces ibériques* (Paris, 1982), p. 34.

4 THE MACHINERY OF CONTROL

1 Suet., *Jul.*, 7; Caes., *Bell. civ.*, 2.19.3.
2 *AE* 1984, 553.
3 G. Alföldy, *Fasti Hispanienses* (Wiesbaden, 1969), pp. 13–15 (on Arruntius), 275–9 (on Baetica).
4 Strabo, 3.4.20; *AE* 1952, 122 and 1979, 377; *RIT*, 143.
5 Suet., *Galba*, 9.
6 Oros., 5.1; App., *Iber.*, 44; Livy, 43.2.12.
7 M.H. Crawford, *Coinage and money under the Roman Republic* (Berkeley and Los Angeles, 1985), p. 95.
8 Cic., *II Verr.*, 3.6.12; C. González Román, *Imperialismo y romanización en la provincia Hispania Ulterior* (Granada, 1981), pp. 74–7 (on soldiers' pay); A.H.M. Jones, *Studies in Roman government and law* (Oxford, 1960), pp. 101–3.
9 Livy, 43.2.12; Plut., *C. Gracchus*, 6.2.
10 Dio, 60.24.5; Pliny, *Pan.*, 29.
11 Plut., *Galba*, 5.6.
12 *HA Hadr.*, 12.4; *ILS*, 318; R. Syme, 'Hadrian and Italica', *JRS*, vol. 54 (1964), pp. 142–9.
13 Tac., *Hist.*, 1.78; *HA Hadr.*, 19.9.
14 Sen., *Apocol.*, 3.3; *ILS*, 1978 (Claudius); Strabo, 3.2.15; Tac., *Hist.*, 3.55; Pliny, *NH*, 3.30.

15 R. Etienne, 'Les sénateurs espagnols sous Trajan et Hadrien' in *Les Empereurs romains d'Espagne* (Paris, 1966), pp. 55–82.
16 Pliny, *NH*, 8.218; *Collatio*, 11.7.
17 *ILS*, 6092.
18 *AE* 1962, 288; cf. Tac., *Ann.*, 14.28.
19 *ILS*, 287 (Alcántara), 256 (Munigua), 7223 (Hispalis); cf. Pliny, *Ep.*, 10.34.
20 Patrons: *CIL* II, 1525 (Augustus), 1529 (Tiberius), 5930 (Nero); duovirs, on coins: L.A. Curchin, *The local magistrates of Roman Spain* (Toronto, 1990), p. 63; oath: *ILS*, 190.
21 Curchin, *Local magistrates*, pp. 22–4.
22 On quaestors and quattuorvirs see Curchin, *Local magistrates*, pp. 29–35.
23 On magistrates' duties see Curchin, *Local magistrates*, pp. 60–3.
24 Fines in connection with *vectigalia: ILS*, 6087, ch. 65.
25 Curchin, *Local magistrates*, pp. 35–6.
26 *ILS*, 2648.
27 P. Le Roux, *L'Armée romaine et l'organisation des provinces ibériques* (Paris, 1982), pp. 84–5.
28 Le Roux, *L'Armée*, pp. 127–40.
29 Spaniard in Sixth: *CIL* II, 1442. Galbiana: Tac., *Hist.*, 2.86, 3.7, 3.10, 3.21. Hispana: Tac., *Hist.*, 1.6.2; *AE* 1972, 203. Vascones: Tac., *Hist.*, 4.33.6; cf. Le Roux, *L'Armée*, p. 132. Sulpicia: *CIL* XVI, 23.
30 Tac., *Hist.*, 2.11, 2.86, 3.22.
31 Tac., *Hist.*, 2.58, 2.67; P. Le Roux, 'Une inscription fragmentaire d'Augusta Emerita de Lusitanie à la lumière des "Histoires" de Tacite', *Chiron*, vol. 7 (1977), pp. 283–9. Withdrawn: Tac., *Hist.*, 4.69, 4.76, 5.19.
32 Pliny, *Paneg.*, 14; Josephus, *Bell. Jud.*, 3.5; B. Dobson, 'The "Rangordnung" of the Roman army' in D.M. Pippidi (ed.), *Actes du VII Congrès international d'épigraphie grecque et latine* (Bucharest and Paris, 1979), p. 194.
33 According to G. Forni, *Il reclutamento delle legioni da Augusto a Diocleziano* (Milan and Rome, 1953), Appendix B, the army was about 65 per cent Italian from Augustus to Gaius and 49 per cent under Claudius and Nero.
34 A.N. Sherwin White, *The Roman citizenship*, 2nd edn (Oxford, 1973), p. 321, n. 3; J.C. Mann, *Legionary recruitment and veteran settlement during the* Principate (London, 1983), p. 49.
35 Le Roux, *L'Armée*, pp. 255–7; Mann, *Legionary recruitment*, pp. 21–3.
36 *ILS*, 2693, 2707.
37 *ILS*, 6102; Le Roux, *L'Armée*, p. 91.
38 *HAE*, 1035–42, 1869.
39 *AE* 1928, 165; Tac., *Ann.*, 4.46; Suet., *Galba*, 10.2.
40 J. Arce, '*Notitia Dignitatum Occ.* XLII y el ejército de la Hispania tardorromana' in A. del Castillo (ed.), *Ejército y sociedad* (León, 1986), pp. 51–61.
41 *Not. Dign. Occ.*, 42.26–32. Relevant inscriptions analysed by Le Roux, *L'Armée*, pp. 144–51. Cf. also N. Santos Yanguas, 'La *cohors*

I Celtiberorum equitata civium Romanorum', *Celtiberia*, vol. 29 (1979), pp. 239–51.

42 A. Schulten, 'Forschungen in Spanien', *Archäologischer Anzeiger*, 1927, col. 201–3; R. Martín Valls and G. Delibes de Castro, 'El campamento de Rosinos de Vidriales', *Studia Archaeologica*, vol. 36 (1975), pp. 3–7; Le Roux, *L'Armée*, p. 104 and plate I.

43 Britain: G. Webster, *The Roman imperial army*, 2nd edn (London, 1979), p. 205. Germany and Raetia: D. Baatz, *Der römische Limes*, 2nd edn (Berlin, 1975). The larger camps for *alae quingenariae* include Pförring at 3.9 ha, Kosching at *c.* 4 and Welzheim at 4.2 ha (Baatz pp. 204, 273).

44 M. Gómez-Moreno, *Catálogo monumental de España: provincia de Zamora* (Madrid, 1927), p. 48.

45 *AE* 1937, 166; *ILER*, 2069.

46 Le Roux, *L'Armée*, fig. 4; Baatz, *Römische Limes*, pp. 140, 290. Schulten had measured the small camp at *c.* 240 × 180 m.

47 Anonymous, 'Herrera de Pisuerga' in *Arqueología 83* (Madrid, 1984), p. 135; C. Fernández Ibáñez and E. Illarregui Gómez, 'Herrera de Pisuerga (Palencia): Segunda campaña de excavaciones', *Revista de Arqueología*, no. 52 (Aug. 1985), p. 61.

48 *CIL* II, 2666; cf. Le Roux, *L'Armée*, p. 106.

49 A. García y Bellido, 'Estudios sobre la *legio VII Gemina* y su campamento en León' in *Legio VII Gemina* (León, 1970a), pp. 571–2.

50 *CIL* II, 5676; *AE* 1974, 390.

51 M. Risco, *Historia de la ciudad y corte de León y de sus reyes* (Madrid, 1792), plan reproduced in P. Lavedan and J. Huguenay, *Histoire de l'urbanisme (antiquité)*, 2nd edn (Paris, 1966), p. 422.

52 García y Bellido, 'Estudios sobre la *legio VII Gemina* . . .', pp. 571–5; Le Roux, *L'Armée*, pp. 391–2.

53 J.E. Bogaers, 'Die Besatzungstruppen des Legionslagers von Nijmegen im 2. Jahrhundert nach Christus' in *Studien zu den Militärgrenzen Roms* (Köln and Graz, 1967), p. 59.

54 I.A. Richmond, 'Five town-walls in Hispania Citerior', *JRS*, vol. 21 (1931), pp. 91–3.

55 H. von Petrikovits, *Die Innenbauten römischer Legionslager während der Prinzipatszeit* (Opladen, 1975).

56 Petrikovits, *Innenbauten*, p. 102 and fig. 28.

5 SOCIAL STATUS AND SOCIAL RELATIONS

1 M.I. Rostovtzeff, *Social and economic history of the Roman Empire*, 2nd edn (Oxford, 1957), pp. 211–13.

2 R. Etienne, 'Sénateurs originaires de la province de Lusitanie', *Tituli*, vol. 5 (1982), pp. 521–9.

3 C. Castillo, 'Los senadores béticos', *Tituli*, vol. 5 (1982), pp. 465–519; P. Le Roux, 'Les Sénateurs originaires de la province d'Hispania Citerior au Haut-Empire romain', *ibid.*, pp. 439–64.

4 L.A. Curchin, *The local magistrates of Roman Spain* (Toronto, 1990), no. 975.

5 Strabo, 3.5.3; A. Stein, *Der römischen Ritterstand* (Munich, 1927), pp. 162, 248, 389, 391.
6 On the Annaeus family, see L.A. Curchin, 'The creation of a romanized elite in Spain', unpublished Ph.D thesis, University of Ottawa, pp. 400–15.
7 Pliny, *NH*, 22.120; G. Alföldy, 'Drei städtische Eliten im römischen Hispanien', *Gerión*, vol. 2 (1984), pp. 204–12.
8 L.A. Curchin, 'Personal wealth in Roman Spain', *Historia*, vol. 32 (1983), pp. 237–44.
9 Alföldy, 'Drei städtische Eliten', pp. 212–18.
10 Curchin, *Local magistrates*, pp. 21–27.
11 R. MacMullen, *Roman social relations 50 BC to AD 284* (New Haven and London, 1974), p. 93; M.R. Weisser, *The peasants of the Montes* (Chicago, 1976), p. 97. *Insulae: CIL* II, 3428.
12 App., *Iber.*, 43; Plut., *Caes.*, 12.3; *Collatio*, 1.11.1–4; Mart., 3.14.
13 J. Mangas, *Esclavos y libertos en la España romana* (Salamanca, 1971), pp. 187–230 (slaves), 388–485 (freedmen); L.A. Curchin, 'Social relations in central Spain: Patrons, freedmen and slaves in the life of a Roman provincial hinterland', *Ancient Society*, vol. 18 (1987b), p. 76, and 'Demography and romanization at Tarraco', *Archivo Español de Arqueología*, vol. 60 (1987a), p. 161.
14 *CIL* II, 4524, 6014; Paul., *Sent.*, 2.19.9
15 Suet., *De gram.*, 20 (Hyginus); J.M. Serrano Delgado, *Status y promoción social de los libertos en Hispania romana* (Seville, 1988), pp. 25–73.
16 Livy, 21.43.8; Strabo, 3.3.5; App., *Iber.*, 59.
17 MacMullen, *Roman social relations*, pp. 28–32; L.A. Curchin, 'Non-slave labour in Roman Spain', *Gerión*, vol. 4 (1986b), pp. 178–81.
18 Strabo, 3.3.7, 3.5.4; Columella, 7.2.1.
19 Mangas, *Esclavos y libertos*, pp. 130–1.
20 *Lex Irnitana*, chs 28, 72, 79.
21 Strabo, 3.4.17; Sil. Ital., 3.352–5; M.L. Albertos, 'La mujer hispanorromana a través de la epigrafía', *Revista de la Universidad de Madrid*, no. 109 (1977), pp. 179–98.
22 *ILS*, 5496 (statue); Curchin, 'Non-slave labour', pp. 182–5.
23 L.A. Curchin, 'Familial epithets in the epigraphy of Roman Spain' in *Mélanges Etienne Gareau-Cahiers des Etudes Anciennes*, vol. 14 (Ottawa, 1982a), pp. 179–82. Mines: J.C. Edmondson, *Two industries in Roman Lusitania: Mining and garum production* (Oxford, 1987), p. 68.
24 Mart., 2.18; Tac., *Agr.*, 12.1.
25 Diod. Sic., 5.34.1; Val. Max., 3.23.21.
26 J.M. Blázquez, *La romanización* (Madrid, 1975b), vol. 2, p. 75; R. Etienne, P. Le Roux and A. Tranoy, 'La tessera hospitalis, instrument de sociabilité et de romanisation dans la Péninsule Ibérique' in *Sociabilité, pouvoirs et société: Actes du colloque de Rouen* (Rouen, 1987), pp. 323–36.
27 *HAE*, 547; *AE* 1983, 530; H.S. Sivan, 'An unedited letter of the emperor Honorius to the Spanish soldiers', *Zeitschrift für Papyrologie und Epigraphik*, vol. 61 (1985), pp. 273–87, line 17.

28 Mart., 12.18, 12.68; *Dig.*, 9.3.5.1; Conc. Elvira, canon 40; *Lex Irnitana*, chs 23, 97.

29 Inscriptions conveniently collected by Mangas, *Esclavos y libertos*, pp. 388–486, with analytical tables pp. 285–387. Sura: S. Mariner Bigorra, *Inscripciones romanas de Barcino* (Barcelona, 1973), no. 82–100.

30 Magistrates: *CIL* II, 1648, 4270, 6014 (wife), 6056; *HAE*, 552. Priests: *CIL* II, 3231, 3584, 4212; *Ephemeris Epigraphica* VIII, 83. Soldiers: *AE* 1971, 207 (tribune); *CIL* II, 4151, 4463; *HAE*, 809 (centurions); *CIL* II, 490, 2639, 4144, 4154–5, 5212 (wife); *HAE*, 868 (heir). Freedmen's freedmen: *CIL* II, 1479, 1733, 4292, 4297; *HAE*, 876 (all sevirs); *CIL* II, 485 (archivist), 3872 (teacher).

31 *CIL* II 491, 733, 2281; *Ephemeris Epigraphica* IX, 258; *HAE*, 1461.

32 *CIL* II, 60, 5614; *AE* 1933, 24; *AE* 1976, 284; Curchin, 'Familial epithets', pp. 179–82.

33 *CIL* II, 4033, 4390, 4534, 4627; *Ephemeris Epigraphica* IX, 258 (freeborn); *ILER*, 4974; cf. S. Treggiari, *Roman freedmen during the Late Republic* (Oxford, 1969), pp. 215–16.

34 F. Arias Vilas, P. Le Roux and A. Tranoy, *Inscriptions romaines de la province de Lugo* (Paris, 1979), no. 73.

35 Cic., *Div. in Caec.*, 20.66; Suet., *Jul.*, 28, 48; *CIL* II, 1525–7, 1529; O. Gil Farrés, *La moneda hispánica en la edad antigua* (Madrid, 1966), p. 353.

36 J.-N. Bonneville, 'Les patrons du municipe d'Emporiae' in *Hommage à Robert Etienne* (Paris, 1988), pp. 181–200. Governors: *CIL* II, 2820, 3414; *AE* 1957, 317; L.A. Curchin, 'Vergil's "Messiah": A new governor of Spain?' *The Ancient History Bulletin*, vol. 2 (1988), pp. 143–4.

37 Dio, 56.25.6 (proclamation); *AE* 1952, 116; *CIL* II, 3741; *RIT*, 132, 151.

38 *AE* 1962, 71 and 287; *CIL* V, 6987; *ILS*, 1016, 6109.

39 *CIL* II, 1121, 2015; H.-G. Pflaum, *Les carrières procuratoriennes équestres sous le Haut-Empire romain* (Paris, 1960), pp. 585–90.

40 *ILS*, 1353 (procurator), 6121 (Canusium); *CIL* II, 1054; cf. J.F. Rodríguez Neila, *Sociedad y administración local en la Bética romana* (Córdoba, 1981), ch. 8.

41 *RIT*, 427 (benefactions); *CIL* II, 1182, 2211; *Inscriptiones Graecae* XIV, 2540; *ILS*, 1340 (commercial patrons); *CIL* II, 5812; cf. J.H. Oliver, 'A Spanish corporation and its patrons', *Eos*, vol. 48 (1957), pp. 447–54.

42 Plut., *Sert.*, 3.4, 6.4; Strabo, 3.5.9.

43 *RIT*, 162–6 (coast guard), 140, cf. 135; P. Le Roux, *L'Armée romaine et l'organisation des provinces ibériques* (Paris, 1982), pp. 268–70.

44 *ILS*, 6957; Curchin, *Local magistrates*, ch. 7 (benefactions); *HA Hadr.*, 2 (Italica). Coastal units: *ILS*, 2672; cf. *AE* 1978, 335 (Octavian); *AE* 1948, 3 (Galba); Vegetius 4.31 (fleet); Le Roux, *L'Armée*, pp. 153–7.

45 Livy, 29.3.5, 34.9.12; Caes., *Bell. civ.*, 1.40; App., *Bell. civ.*, 1.109; Plut., *Sert.*, 13.3, 13.6, 21.1.

46 S. Piggott, 'Native economies and the Roman occupation of north Britain' in I.A. Richmond (ed.), *Roman and native in north Britain* (Edinburgh, 1958), p. 23; R. MacMullen, *Soldier and civilian in the later Roman Empire* (Cambridge, Mass., 1963), p. 4.

47 Dio Cass., 60.24.5; cf. G. Alföldy, *Fasti Hispanienses* (Wiesbaden, 1969), pp. 153–4.

48 App., *Iber.*, 54, 85; Pliny, *NH*, 14.91; B. Jones, 'The north-western interface' in P.J. Fowler (ed.), *Recent work in rural archaeology* (Bradford, 1975), p. 102; R. MacMullen, 'Rural romanization', *Phoenix*, vol. 22 (1968), p. 341.

49 K. Greene, 'Invasion and response: Pottery and the Roman army' in B.C. Burnham and H.B. Johnson (eds), *Invasion and response* (Oxford, 1979), pp. 99–106; V.G. Childe, 'Rotary querns on the Continent and in the Mediterranean basin', *Antiquity*, vol. 17 (1943), p. 25.

50 G. Ulbert, *Cáceres el Viejo, ein spätrepublikanisches Legionslager in Spanisch-Extremadura* (Mainz, 1984), pp. 61–9, 176–7.

51 *Arqueología 83* (Madrid, 1984), p. 135; A. Balil, 'Terra sigillata hispánica: A propósito de un libro reciente', *Boletín del Seminario de Estudios de Arte y Arqueología*, vol. 52 (1986), pp. 249–50.

52 M.G. Pereira Maia, 'Notas sobre a "terra sigillata" do Manuel Galo (Mértola)' in *Actas das II jornadas arqueológicas* (Lisbon, 1984), pp. 157–66 (outposts); F. Mayet, *Les céramiques sigillées hispaniques* (Paris, 1984), p. 238; A. García y Bellido, 'Estudios sobre la *legio VII Gemina* y su campamento en León' in *Legio VII Gemina* (León, 1970a), figs. 36.4, 44.3, 44.5 (pottery) and pp. 588–97 (tiles).

53 J.-G. Gorges, *Les Villas hispano-romaines* (Paris, 1979), pp. 275–6; C. García Merino, 'Nueva necrópolis tardorromana en la provincia de Valladolid', *Boletín del Seminario de Estudios de Arte y Arqueología*, vol. 41 (1975), p. 531; MacMullen, *Soldier and civilian*, pp. 29–30.

54 *HAE*, 1035–43 (*cohors IV*), 1470–7 (Iuliobriga); *ILS*, 2455 (Segisamo); MacMullen, *Soldier and civilian*, pp. 8–10; Le Roux, *L'Armée*, pp. 116–18.

55 Jones, 'The north-western interface', p. 100 and plate 6(g) (terraces); *Dig.*, 49.16.9, 13; MacMullen, *Soldier and civilian*, ch. 1.

56 *ILS* 6891, lines 23–4; Edmondson, *Two industries*, pp. 68–9; A. Alonso Sánchez, *Fortificaciones romanas en Extremadura* (Salamanca, 1988).

57 *CIL* II, 3272; F.J. Sánchez-Palencia, 'El campamento romano de Valdemeda, Manzaneda (León)', *Numantia*, vol. 1 (1986), pp. 227–34; Le Roux, *L'Armée*, pp. 270–4; Edmondson, *Two industries*, p. 69.

58 W.S. Hanson, 'The organisation of Roman military timber-supply', *Britannia*, vol. 9 (1978), pp. 293–305; Vegetius, 1.7, 2.11.

59 C. Castillo, J. Gómez-Pantoja and M. Dolores Mauleón, *Inscripciones romanas del Museo de Navarra* (Pamplona, 1981), no. 1–2; *ILS*, 254; I.A. Richmond, 'Five town-walls in Hispania Citerior', *JRS*, vol. 21 (1931), pp. 98–9.

60 Curchin, 'Personal wealth', pp. 227–42; Le Roux, *L'Armée*, p. 289.

61 Caes., *Bell. civ.*, 1.44, 1.86; *Bell. Alex.*, 53.

62 Le Roux, *L'Armée*, pp. 218–33; J.S. Richardson, *Hispaniae: Spain and the development of Roman Imperialism 218–82 BC* (Cambridge, 1986), p. 172, with references.

63 F. Vittinghoff, 'Die Entstehung von städtischen Gemeinwesen in der Nachbarschaft römischer Legionslager' in *Legio VII Gemina*, p. 342; MacMullen, 'Rural romanization', p. 338.

64 App., *Iber.*, 85; Livy, *Per.*, *57; Frontin.*, *Strat.*, 4.1.1; F. Braudel, *The Mediterranean and the Mediterranean world in the age of Phillip II* (New York, 1972), p. 1051 (prostitutes); *CIL* XVI, 48, 56, 166; A.N. Sherwin White, *The Roman citizenship*, 2nd edn (Oxford, 1973), p. 268.

65 *RIT*, 198 (*coniunx*); Livy, 43.3.2–4 (Carteia); Sherwin White, *The Roman citizenship*, pp. 248, 273–4.

66 Curchin, 'Familial epithets', pp. 179–82; Le Roux, *L'Armée*, pp. 194–216, 228–38.

67 O. Doppelfeld (ed.), *Römer am Rhein* (Köln, 1967), pl. 46.

68 Tac., *Ann.*, 3.40; Veget., 1.1; Diod. Sic., 5.33.2.

69 Herodotus, 7.165; Diod. Sic., 11.1.5; Polyaenus, 1.28 (Himera); Thuc., 6.90, cf. 6.30, 7.26; A. García y Bellido, 'Otros testimonios más de la presencia de mercenarios españoles en el Mediterráneo' in *Simposio internacional de colonizaciones* (Barcelona, 1974), pp. 201–3.

70 Diod. Sic., 14.75.9, 15.70.1; Polyb., 1.17, 3.56; Livy, 27.14.

71 G. Webster, *The Roman imperial army*, 2nd edn (London, 1979), p. 36; J. Harmand, *L'Armée et le soldat à Rome de 107 à 50 avant notre ère* (Paris, 1950), pp. 460–1.

72 *ILS*, 8888; cf. N. Crinite, *L'epigrafe di Asculum di Gn. Pompeio Strabone* (Milan, 1970), pp. 193–5. 'Salduvia' is the reading of most MSS of Pliny, 3.3.24; the alternative 'Salduba', which occurs in no MS but is an early editors' compromise between 'Salduva' and 'Saldubia' (which are surely variants of Salduvia) in two codices, should be abandoned.

73 Caes., *Bell. Gall.*, 2.7; Lucan, 3.710; *ILS*, 2487, cf. Arrian, *Tact.*, 40.

74 *AE* 1930, 57 and 1933, 95.

75 *CIL* V, 3365; VI, 9677; XII, 3167; XIII, 612, 621; XIV, 397 (merchants); L.A. Curchin, 'Jobs in Roman Spain', *Florilegium*, vol 4 (1982b), p. 43 (dancers); *ILS*, 5087, 9343 (gladiators), 5287 (Diocles).

76 H. de la Ville de Mirmont, 'Les déclamateurs espagnols au temps d'Auguste et de Tibère', *Bulletin Hispanique*, vols 12 (1910), pp. 1–22; 14 (1912), pp. 11–29; 15 (1913), pp. 154–69; Mart., 1.61, 4.55, 10.37. Tourists: Tac., *Dial.*, 10.2; Pliny, *Ep.*, 2.3.8.

6 TOWN AND COUNTRY

1 Strabo, 3.4.6, 13; Livy, 21.7, 21.14–15; Sil. Ital., 1.288–90.

2 *ILS*, 6087, ch. 103; Strabo, 3.2.1.

3 Pliny, *NH*, 3.7, 3.30.

4 J.M. Roldán Hervás 'Las querras de Lusitania (155–138) y Celtiberia (153–133)' in R. Menéndez Pidal (ed.) *Historia de España*, 2nd edn, vol. II/1 (Madrid, 1982), p. 115.

5 Strabo, 3.4.20.

6 Pliny, *NH*, 34.17; Ael. Arist., *Or.*, 26.97.

7 P. Paris, 'Antiquités pré-romaines de Mérida', *Comptes Rendus de l'Académie des Inscriptions et Belles-Lettres*, 1914, pp. 127–31; J.M. Blázquez, 'Bronces de la Mérida prerromana' in *Augusta Emerita: Actas del simposio internacional 1975* (Madrid, 1976a), pp. 11–17.

NOTES

8 J.M. Alvarez Martínez, 'El foro de Augusta Emerita' in J. Arce
(ed.), *Homenaje a Sáenz de Buruaga* (Badajoz, 1982), pp. 53–68;
idem, 'Excavaciones en Augusta Emerita' in M. Martín-Bueno (ed.),
Arqueología de las ciudades modernas superpuestas a las antiguas
(Madrid, 1985), pp. 35–53.
9 Strabo, 3.2.1; R.C. Knapp, *Roman Córdoba* (Berkeley, Los Angeles and
London, 1983), pp. 9–14.
10 Aqua Nova: A.U. Stylow, 'Apuntes sobre epigrafía de época flavia
en Hispania', *Gerión*, 4 (1986), p. 286. Forum: D. Vaquerizo Gil,
'Excavaciones en el foro romano de Córdoba', *Revista de Arqueología*,
no. 64 (Aug. 1986), p. 63.
11 J.F. Rodríguez Neila, *Historia de Córdoba* (Córdoba, 1988), vol. 1,
pp. 481–502.
12 *RIT*, 369; Mela, 2.90.
13 T. Hauschild, *Arquitectura romana de Tarragona* (Tarragona, 1983),
pp. 87–129.
14 R. Mar Medina and J. Ruiz de Arbulo Bayona, *La basílica de la colonia
Tarraco* (Tarragona, 1986); cf. Vitruvius, 5.1.7.
15 R. Cortes and R. Gabriel, 'Sobre el aforo del anfiteatro, teatro y circo de
Tarragona' in *XVI Congreso nacional de arqueología* (Zaragoza, 1983),
pp. 955–62.
16 J. Hernández Díaz *et al*, *Catálogo arqueológico y artístico de la provincia
de Sevilla*, vol. 3 (Sevilla, 1951), pp. 66–77.
17 Pliny, *NH*, 3.28; T. Mañanes, *Astorga romana y su entorno* (Valladolid
and Astorga, 1983), pp. 11–52.
18 Pliny, *NH*, 4.112; Auson., *Urb.*, 13; J. de Alarcão, *Roman Portugal*,
vol. 2 (Warminster, 1988), pp. 10–12.
19 Mela, 2.88; *HAE*, 2189.
20 A. Beltrán Martínez, 'Caesaraugusta' in *Symposion de ciudades
augusteas*, vol. 1 (Zaragoza, 1976), pp. 219–61 (with plans); M.
Beltrán Lloris, 'La arqueología urbana en Zaragoza' in M. Martín-
Bueno (ed.), *Arqueología de las ciudades modernas superpuestas a las
antiguas*, pp. 55–116 (with catalogue of finds).
21 Livy, 26.48.3; Polybius, 10.11; *CIL* II, 3426.
22 J.R. García del Toro, *Cartagena: Guía arqueológica* (Cartagena, 1982).
23 Suet., *Galba*, 9.2; P. de Palol, *Guía de Clunia*, 2nd edn (Burgos, 1969).
24 M.P. García-Bellido, 'Colonia Augusta Gaditana?', *Archivo Español de
Arqueología*, vol. 61 (1988), pp. 324–35.
25 Strabo, 3.5.3; J.A. Fierro Cubiella, 'El acueducto romano de Cádiz',
Revista de Arqueología, no. 95 (Mar. 1989), pp. 18–24.
26 African beasts: Columella, 7.2.4. Theatre: Cic., *Ad Fam.*, 10.32. On
Gaditanian topography see A. Tovar, *Iberische Landeskunde: Die Völker
und die Städte des antiken Hispanien*, II/1 (Baden-Baden, 1976), pp. 37–48.
27 Caes., *Bell. civ.*, 2.18.1; Isid., *Etym.*, 15.1.71; Strabo, 3.2.1; Sil.
Ital., 3.392.
28 J. Campos and J. González, 'Los foros de Hispalis colonia Romula',
Archivo Español de Arqueología, vol. 60 (1987), pp. 123–58.
29 Strabo, 3.2.15; J. de Alarcão, *Roman Portugal*, vol. 2, pp. 197–8 cf.
Ficheiro Epigráfico, no. 131 (1988).

30 A.M. Dias Diogo, 'O material romano da primeira campanha de escavações na Alcáçova de Santarém', *Conimbriga*, vol. 23 (1984), pp. 111–41.

31 *ILS*, 6087, ch. 19.

32 *Itin. Ant.*, 424.1; J.M. Hidalgo Cuñarro, 'El castro de Vigo: Nueva campaña de excavaciones', *Revista de Arqueología*, no. 64 (Aug. 1986), pp. 59–61.

33 *ILER*, 3492; Ptol., 2.6.50 (Vadinia); *AE*, 1953, 267; catalogue of *vici* in L.A. Curchin, '*Vici* and *pagi* in Roman Spain', *Revue des Etudes Anciennes*, vol. 87 (1985b), pp. 330–2.

34 *ILS*, 6891; A. Blanco, J.M. Luzón and D. Ruiz, *Excavaciones arqueológicas en el Cerro Salomon* (Seville, 1970), pp. 10–11, 22.

35 *RIT*, 143; *Dig.*, 50.15.1.4, Ulp.; catalogue in Curchin, '*Vici* and *pagi*', pp. 338–40.

36 L. White, Jr., 'The expansion of technology 500–1500' in C.M. Cipolla (ed.), *The Fontana economic history of Europe*, vol. 1 (London, 1972), pp. 144–5.

37 K. Hopkins, 'Taxes and trade in the Roman Empire', *JRS*, vol. 70 (1980), pp. 101–25; M.I. Finley, *The ancient economy* (Berkeley and Los Angeles, 1973), p. 102.

38 M. Ponsich, *Implantation rurale antique sur le Bas-Guadalquivir* (Paris, 1974), vol. 1, pp. 16–17; R.F.J. Jones *et al*, 'The Late Roman villa of Vilauba and its context', *Antiquaries Journal*, 1982, p. 258.

39 J.-G. Gorges, *Les Villas hispano-romaines* (Paris, 1979), pp. 23–57.

40 Gaius, *Inst.*, 2.7, 31, 46; A.H.M. Jones, *Studies in Roman government and law* (Oxford, 1960), p. 143; *FIRA*, 1² 84–5; Just., *Inst.*, 2.6 pr.

41 Frontin., *Agr. qual.*, 4.4; Hyg., *Const.*, 171; J.-G. Gorges, 'Remarques sur la détection de cadastres antiques en Péninsule Ibérique' in M. Clavel-Lévêque (ed.), *Cadastres et espace rural* (Paris, 1983), pp. 199–206.

42 R.J. Bradley, 'Economic change in the growth of early hill-forts' in M. Jesson and D. Hill (eds), *The Iron Age and its hill-forts* (Southampton, 1971), p. 79.

43 Varro, *RR*, 2.2.9–11; Sen., *Ben.*, 7.10.5; Livy, 21.43.8.

7 PRODUCTION AND EXCHANGE

1 J.J. Van Nostrand, 'Roman Spain' in Tenney Frank (ed.), *An economic survey of ancient Rome*, vol. 3 (Baltimore, 1937), pp. 119–224; L.C. West, *Imperial Roman Spain: The objects of trade* (Oxford, 1929); J.M. Blázquez, *Economía de la Hispania romana* (Bilbao, 1978a) and *Historia económica de la Hispania romana* (Madrid, 1978b).

2 K. Hopkins, 'Taxes and trade in the Roman Empire', *JRS*, vol. 70 (1980), pp. 101–25; L.A. Curchin, 'Personal wealth in Roman Spain', *Historia*, vol. 32 (1983), pp. 227–44 and *The local magistrates of Roman Spain* (Toronto, 1990), pp. 103–14

3 J. Edmondson, *Two industries in Roman Lusitania: Mining and garum production* (Oxford, 1987), p. 103; A. Carandini and S. Settis, *Schiavi*

e padroni nell'Etruria romana (Bari, 1979), plate 39; K. Greene, *The archaeology of the Roman economy* (London, 1986), p. 15.

4 P. Le Roux, 'Procurateur affranchi *in Hispania*: Saturninus et l'activité minière', *Madrider Mitteilungen*, vol. 26 (1985), pp. 218–33.

5 Curchin, *Local magistrates*, pp. 104–5; *CIL* II, 112; *PIR²*, L 210; E.W. Haley, 'Roman elite involvement in commerce', *Archivo Español de Arqueología*, vol. 61 (1988), pp. 141–56.

6 *Inscriptiones Graecae*, XIV, 2540; *CIL* VI, 29722; *AE* 1955, 165; *CIL* XIV, 397.

7 Livy, 23.29.1, 34.9.12; Pliny, *NH*, 31.94; E. Badian, *Publicans and sinners* (Ithaca, 1972), pp. 32–3, 128 n. 45.

8 *CIL* II, 3270; J.N. Hillgarth, *The Spanish kingdoms 1250–1516* (Oxford, 1976), vol. 1, p. 41.

9 Varro, *RR*, 2.8.5; Pliny, 8.170; M. Ponsich, *Implantation rurale sur le Bas-Guadalquivir* (Madrid, 1987), vol. 3, pp. 12–16.

10 Greene, *Archaeology of Roman economy*, pp. 25–6; Pliny, 2.169 ('commerci gratia').

11 Ps.- Aristotle, *De mirab. ausc.*, 87, 135; J.C. Edmondson, 'Mining in the later Roman Empire and beyond', *JRS*, vol. 79 (1989), pp. 88–91.

12 Florus, 2.33.60; Pliny, *NH*, 3.54, 78; P.R. Lewis and G.D.B. Jones, 'Roman gold-mining in north-west Spain', *JRS*, vol. 60 (1970), pp. 169–85; D.G. Bird, 'Pliny and the gold mines of the north-west of the Iberian Peninsula' in T.F.C. Blagg *et al* (eds), *Papers in Iberian archaeology* (Oxford, 1984), pp. 341–68.

13 R.F.J. Jones and D.G. Bird, 'Roman gold-mining in north-west Spain, II', *JRS*, vol. 62 (1972), pp. 59–74; C. Domergue and G. Hérail, *Mines d'or romaines d'Espagne: Le district de la Valduerna* (León) (Toulouse, 1978).

14 Strabo, 3.2.10; Pliny, *NH*, 33.96–7; M.P. García-Bellido, 'Nuevos documentos sobre minería y agricultura romana en Hispania', *Archivo Español de Arqueología*, vol. 59 (1986), pp. 13–46.

15 G.D.B. Jones, 'The Roman mines at Riotinto', *JRS*, vol. 70 (1980), pp. 146–165; B. Rothenberg and A. Blanco Freijeiro, *Studies in ancient mining and metallurgy in south-west Spain* (London, 1981); J.A. Pérez *et al*, 'Minería romana en Río Tinto (Huelva)', *Revista de Arqueología*, no. 56 (Dec. 1985), pp. 24–31.

16 *ILS*, 6891; *AE* 1908, 233 (Vipasca); Pliny, *NH*, 34.2–4; Tac., *Ann.*, 4.36; *CIL* II, 4935; *ILS*, 1591, cf. 3527.

17 *ILS*, 8706; *CIL*, XV, 7916.12; *AE*, 1907, 135; M. Jorge Aragoneses (ed.), *Museo arqueológico de Murcia* (Madrid, 1956), p. 57.

18 Aquini: J. D'Arms, *Commerce and social standing in ancient Rome* (Cambridge, Mass., 1981), p. 65. Planii: C. Domergue, 'Les Planii et leur activité industrielle en Espagne sous la République', *Mélanges de la Casa de Velázquez*, vol. 1 (1965), p. 9–25. Manlius: A.J. Parker, 'Lead ingots from a Roman ship at Ses Salinas, Majorca', *International Journal of Nautical Archaeology*, vol. 3 (1974), p. 147–50.

19 Pliny, *NH*, 34.165; García-Bellido, 'Nuevos documentos', p. 34; L.C. West, *Imperial Roman Spain: The objects of trade* (Oxford, 1929), p. 45.

20 Pliny, *NH*, 33.118; Vitruv., 7.9.4; F. Saupis, *La Géologie du gisement de mercure d'Almadén* (Nancy, 1973), pp. 28, 234.

21 *ILS*, 1875; Paus., 8.39.6; Vitruv., 7.7.2.

22 C. Bencivenga Trillmich, 'Observaciones sobre la difusión de la cerámica ibérica en Italia' in *XVII Congreso nacional de arqueología* (Zaragoza, 1985), pp. 551–6; J.-P. Morel, *Céramique campanienne: Les formes* (Rome, 1981), pp. 478–9.

23 M.A. Mezquíriz de Catalán, *Terra sigillata hispánica* (Valencia, 1961), 2 vols; F. Mayet, *Les céramiques sigillées hispaniques* (Paris, 1984) and *Les céramiques à parois fines dans la Péninsule Ibérique* (Paris, 1975).

24 J. Price, 'Some Roman glass from Spain', *Annales du 6e congrès international d'étude historique du verre* (Liège, 1974), pp. 65–84; 'Glass vessel production in southern Iberia in the first and second centuries AD', *Journal of Glass Studies*, vol. 29 (1987), pp. 30–9; J. Lang and J. Price, 'Iron tubes from a Late Roman glassmaking site at Mérida', *Journal of Archaeological Science*, vol. 2 (1975), pp. 289–96; M.P. Caldera de Castro and A. Velázquez Jiménez, *Augusta Emerita I* (Madrid, 1983), pp. 65–70.

25 Pliny, *NH*, 18.108, 19.9–10; Grattius, *Cyneg.*, 41; Strabo, 3.4.9.; *Lintearii*: *AE* 1965, 79; *RIT*, 9. Cf. L.A. Curchin, 'Men of the cloth: Reflections on the Roman linen trade', *Liverpool Classical Monthly*, vol. 10 (1985a), pp. 34–5.

26 Strabo, 3.2.6; Pliny, *NH*, 8.191; Juv., 12.42; Mart., 5.37; *Edict. Diocl.*, 25. The supposed mention of Spanish garments in an Egyptian papyrus is due to misinterpretation: see J. Arce, *'Spania, spanos-spane-spanon* on papyri', *Zeitschrift für Papyrologie und Epigraphik*, vol. 61 (1985), p. 31.

27 Strabo, 3.2.7; Pliny, *NH, 9.49;* A. Moreno Páramo and L. Abad Casal, 'Aportaciones al estudio de la pesca en la Antigüedad', *Habis*, vol. 2 (1971), pp. 209–21.

28 Eupolis, fr. 186; Edmondson, *Two industries*, pp. 114–15.

29 Edmondson, *Two industries*, pp. 122–34.

30 Auson., *Ep.*, 25; R. Lequément, 'Deux inscriptions peintes sur amphores de Bétique à Alesia', *Revue Archéologique de l'Est et du Centre-Est*, vol. 31 (1980), p. 256; D. Bayard and J.-L. Massy, *Amiens romain* (Amiens, 1983), p. 156; Edmondson, *Two industries*, pp. 103–4.

31 *ILS*, 7278; *Inscriptiones Graecae* XIV, 2540; B. Liou and R. Marichal, 'Les inscriptions peintes sur amphores de l'anse Saint-Gervais à Fos-sur-Mer', *Archaeonautica*, vol. 2 (1978), pp. 131–5; R.I. Curtis, 'Spanish trade in salted fish products in the first and second centuries AD', *International Journal of Nautical Archaeology*, vol. 17 (1988), pp. 205–10.

32 Pliny, *NH*, 31.94; J.A. Riley, 'The coarse pottery from Berenice' in J.A. Lloyd (ed.), *Excavations at Sidi Khrebish, Benghazi (Berenice)*, vol. 2 (Tripoli, 1979), pp. 157–63.

33 F. Villedieu, *Turris Libisonis* (Oxford, 1984), p. 232.

34 Pliny, *NH*, 18.66–7; Claudian, *In Eutrop.*, 1.389–409; P.J. Lacort Navarro, 'Cereales en Hispania Ulterior', *Habis*, vol. 16 (1985), pp. 363–86.

35 Cato, *Agr.*, 3.6, 11.2, 135.4; Varro, *RR*, 1.23.6; Columella, 6.12.2; Pliny, *NH*, 19.27, 19.30; Strabo, 3.4.9; *CIL*, II, 1774. Relief: R. Calza and E. Nash, *Ostia* (Firenze, 1959), fig. 106.
36 M. Díez de Bethencourt, 'Implantación de la vitis vinifera en Iberia', *V Congreso español de estudios clásicos* (Madrid, 1978), pp. 683–7; M. Walker, '5,000 años de viticultura en España', *Revista de Arqueología*, no. 53 (Sept. 1985), pp. 44–7.
37 Pliny, *NH*, 14.30, 97; Ovid, *Ars am.*, 3.645–6.
38 Pliny, *NH*, 17.249; Columella, 3.1.3–4, 3.12.6; A. Tovar, 'Columela y el vino de Jérez', *Homenaje al Profesor Carriazo*, vol. 3 (Seville, 1973), pp. 397–404.
39 Strabo, 3.2.6; Columella, 1 pr. 20; D. Colls *et al*, 'L'épave Port-Vendres II et le commerce de la Bétique à l'époque de Claude', *Archaeonautica*, vol. 1 (1977), pp. 1–145.
40 Pliny, *NH*, 14.71; Florus, *Vergilius orator an poeta*; Mart., 13.118; Sil. Ital., 3.369, 15.177; D.P.S. Peacock, 'Punic Carthage and Spain: The evidence of the amphorae', *Cahiers des Etudes Anciennes*, vol. 18 (1986), pp. 101–13; D. Colls, 'Les amphores léetaniennes de l'épave Cap-Béar III', *Revue des Etudes Anciennes*, vol. 88 (1986), pp. 201–13.
41 Mart., 1.26.9; Schol. ad Juv., 5.29; Strabo, 3.3.1; A. García y Bellido, *Esculturas romanas de España y Portugal* (Madrid, 1949), plates 212–13; F. Russell Cortez, 'As escavações arqueológicas do "castellum" da Fonte do Milho', *Anais do Instituto do Vinho do Porto*, vol. 12 (1951), pp. 17–88.
42 Beer: Strabo, 3.3.7; Oros., 5.7. Villa: J. de Navascués, 'Descubrimiento de una bodega romana en término de Funes (Navarra)', *Príncipe de Viana*, vol. 77 (1959), p. 227–9.
43 *AE*, 1955, 165; *CIL*, XIV, 397; A. Tchernia and F. Zevi, 'Amphores vinaires de Campanie et de Tarraconaise à Ostie' in P. Baldacci *et al*, *Recherches sur les amphores romaines* (Rome, 1972), pp. 35–67.
44 Strabo, 3.2.6; Petr., *Cena*, 66; *CIL* XIV, 5558.
45 Gaul: R. Lequément and B. Liou, 'Un nouveau document sur le vin de Bétique', *Archaeonautica*, vol. 2 (1978), pp. 183–4; E.M. Wightman, *Roman Trier and the Treveri* (London, 1970), p. 191. Africa: M.K. Annabi, 'Les amphores ibériques de Carthage', *Turat*, vol. 1 (1983), pp. 11–16; M. Fulford, 'Pottery and the economy of Carthage and its hinterland', *Opus*, vol. 2 (1983), pp. 5–14.
46 Pliny, *NH*, 15.1, 15.17, 17.93; Columella, 5.8.5.
47 D.J. Mattingly, 'Oil for export?' *Journal of Roman Archaeology*, vol. 1 (1988), p. 38–44; E. Thévenot, 'Una familia de negociantes en aceite establecida en la Baetica en el siglo II,' *Archivo Español de Arqueología*, vol. 25 (1952), p. 225–31.
48 E. Rodríguez Almeida, *Il Monte Testaccio: Ambiente, storia, materiali* (Rome, 1984), p. 118.
49 Gaul: P. Galliou, *L'Armorique romaine* (Braspars, 1983), fig. 50. Britain: D.F. Williams and D.P.S. Peacock, 'The importation of olive oil into Iron Age Britain' in J.M. Blázquez Martínez and J. Remesal Rodríguez (eds), *Producción y comercio del aceite en la Antigüedad*, II (Madrid, 1983), p. 263–80. Africa: Fulford, 'Pottery and the economy', p. 9.

50 N. Cambi, 'Le anfore Dressel 20 nella Jugoslavia', and E.L. Will, 'Exportation of olive oil from Baetica to the eastern Mediterranean', in *Producción y comercio del aceite en la Antigüedad*, II, 1983, II, p. 363–89 and 391–440.

51 S. Keay, 'The import of olive oil into Catalunya during the third century AD', in *Producción y comercio del aceite en la Antigüedad*, II, p. 551–68.

52 *ILS*, 1403; J. Remesal Rodríguez, *La annona militaris y la exportación de aceite bético a Germania* (Madrid, 1986), pp. 95–108.

53 S. Martin-Kilcher, *Die römischen Amphoren aus Augst und Kaiseraugst*, vol. 1 (August, 1987), p. 49.

54 *ILS*, 1340, 1342.

8 THE ROMANISATION OF BELIEFS

1 L.A. Curchin, 'Personal wealth in Roman Spain', *Historia*, vol. 32 (1983), pp. 227–44.

2 J.M. Blázquez, *Diccionario de las religiones prerromanas de Hispania* (Madrid, 1975a), pp. 44–7, 84–90.

3 J. González Echegaray, 'El Neptuno cántabro de Castro Urdiales', *Archivo Español de Arqueología*, vol. 30 (1957), pp. 253–6; cf. F. Poulsen, *Sculptures antiques de musées de provinces espagnols* (Copenhagen, 1933), pp. 70–1.

4 L. Abad Casal, *Pintura romana en España* (Cádiz, 1982), pp. 335 (Bacchus at Emerita, House of the Mithraeum), 337 (Winged Victory, *ibid.*), 353 (Fortuna or Isis at Bilbilis, possibly in a temple).

5 On all these see Blázquez, *Diccionario* (listed alphabetically).

6 A. Arévalo González, 'Las monedas de Obulco', *Revista de Arqueología*, vol. 74 (June 1987), pp. 29–35; cf. M. Mayer and I. Rodà, 'Les divinités féminines de la fertilité en Hispania pendant l'époque romaine', in J. Bonanno (ed.), *Archaeology and fertility cult in the ancient Mediterranean* (Amsterdam, 1986), p. 295.

7 Plut., *Sert.*, 11.4; J.M. Blázquez, 'La religión indígena' in R. Menéndez Pidal (ed.), *Historia de España*, 2nd edn (Madrid, 1982), vol. II/2, p. 285.

8 J. d'Encarnação, *Sociedade romana e epigrafia* (Setubal, 1979), plate 14; Blázquez, *Diccionario*, pp. 93–5.

9 Blázquez, *Diccionario*, pp. 91, 159.

10 M.L. Albertos, 'El culto a los montes entre los Galaicos, astures y berones', *Estudios de Arqueología Alavesa*, vol. 6 (1974), pp. 147–57.

11 Strabo, 3.4.16; V. Juaristi, *Las fuentes de España* (Madrid, 1944), pp. 26–7.

12 Pliny, *NH*, 31.23–4; A. García y Bellido and A. Fernández de Avilés, *Fontes tamaricas: Velilla del Río Carrion (Palencia)*, (Madrid, 1964); Blázquez in *Historia de España*, vol. II/2, pp. 297–9 and fig. 156.

13 *CIL* II, 2402, 5558.

14 *AE* 1952, 65; *CIL* II, 2405; *AE* 1974, 409; *AE* 1973, 312.

15 *ILS*, 4515.

16 R.J. Harrison, *Spain at the dawn of history* (London, 1988), ch. 9;

M. Bendala Galán, 'Die orientalischen Religionen Hispaniens in vorrömischer und römischer Zeit', *ANRW* II/18.2 (1986), pp. 348–66.

17 Strabo, 3.5.5; Sil. Ital., 3.32–44.

18 Diodorus, 5.20.2; Suet., *Jul.*, 7.1; Caes., *Bell. civ.*, 2.18.2; Dio, 78.20.4; H. Mattingly, *Coins of the Roman Empire in the British Museum* (London, 1936), vol. 3, no. 274.

19 Strabo, 3.4.16; P. Le Roux and A. Tranoy, 'Rome et les indigènes dans le nord-ouest ibérique', *Mélanges de la Casa de Velázquez*, vol. 9 (1973), pp. 218–20.

20 *CIL* II, 5612.

21 Neton: *CIL* II, 365, 5278. Acitanus: *CIL* II, 159.

22 Cic., *De natura deorum*, 1.84; P. Castañer, A. Roure and J. Tremoleda, 'Dioses Lares: El lararío de Vilauba', *Revista de Arqueología*, no. 89 (Sept. 1988), pp. 50–7.

23 *AE* 1981, 573; W. Grünhagen, 'Bemerkungen zum Minerva-Relief in der Stadtmauer von Tarragona', *Madrider Mitteilungen*, vol. 17 (1976), pp. 209–26; A.M. Vázquez y Hoys, 'La religión romana en Hispania: Análisis estadístico', *Hispania Antiqua*, vol. 7 (1977), pp. 29–35.

24 Marcianus Heracleensis, *Periplus*, 2.16–18 (in C. Müller, *Geographi Graeci minores* (Paris 1855) I, pp. 549–50); J. García Mercadal (ed.), *Viajes de extranjeros por España y Portugal* (Madrid, 1952), vol. 1, p. 221.

25 Livy, 29.2.

26 Macrobius, 3.13; cf. R. Etienne, *Le culte impérial dans la Péninsule Ibérique* (Paris, 1958), ch. 4.

27 *Inscriptiones Graecae* IV, 39.

28 Quintilian, 6.33.77; L. Villaronga, *Numismática antigua de Hispania* (Barcelona, 1979), figs. 1048, 1074.

29 *AE* 1984, 553.

30 Tac., *Ann.*, 1.78, 4.15, 4.37–8; Villaronga, *Numismática*, figs. 1050–1.

31 Etienne, *Culte impérial*, pp. 346–9; cf. *HAE*, 354–5.

32 *AE* 1966, 183; *AE* 1924, 14.

33 A. García y Bellido, *Les Religions orientales dans l'Espagne romaine* (Leiden, 1967), ch. IV.

34 Apul., *Met.*, 11.5; García y Bellido, *Religions orientales*, ch. XI.

35 García y Bellido, *Religions orientales*, ch. XII.

36 García y Bellido, *Religions orientales*, ch. III.

37 Silvanus: *AE* 1976, 331. Luna Augusta: *CIL* II, 4458. 'Iovi et Sol': J.A. Abásolo and J.C. Elorza, 'Nuevos teónimos de época romana en el país vasco-navarro', *Estudios de Arqueología Alavesa*, vol. 6 (1974), p. 247.

38 C. Castillo, J. Gómez-Pantoja and M. Dolores Mauleón, *Inscripciones romanas del Museo de Navarra* (Pamplona, 1981), nos. 19–21, 24–5, 34; J.E. Uranga, 'El culto al toro en Navarra y Aragón', *IV Symposium de prehistoria peninsular* (Pamplona, 1966), pp. 223–31.

39 J.M. Solana Sáinz, *Autrigonia romana* (Valladolid, 1978), pp. 173–201; *ILER*, 772–3, 851 (AD 399).

40 A. Beltrán and A. Tovar, *Contrebia Belaisca I: El bronce con alfabeto 'ibérico' de Botorrita* (Zaragoza, 1982); A. Tovar, 'La grande inscripción de Peñalba de Villastar en lengua celtibérica', *Ampurias*, vol. 17–18

(1955–6), pp. 159–69. Togoti: *CIL* II, 893, cf. 5861. Lugoves: *CIL* II, 2818.

41 L.A. Curchin, 'From *limes* to *Latinitas:* Roman impact on the Spanish Meseta' in C. Unz (ed.), *Studien zu den Militärgrenzen Roms III* (Stuttgart, 1986a), pp. 692–95.

42 J. d'Encarnação, *Inscriçñes romanas do Conventus Pacensis* (Coimbra, 1984), pp. 806–7.

43 E. Rodríguez Almeida, *Avila romana* (Avila, 1981), pp. 156–65; J. d'Encarnação, 'Divindades indígenas peninsulares: Problemas metodológicos do seu estudo' in J. González and J. Arce (eds), *Estudios sobre la Tabula Siarensis* (Madrid, 1988), pp. 272–3.

44 A. Tranoy, *La Galice romaine* (Paris, 1981), pp. 264–326.

45 Saguntum: G. Alföldy, 'Drei städtische Eliten im römischen Spanien', *Gerión*, vol. 2 (1984), pp. 216–17. Urso: *ILS*, 6987, chs 66–8. 'Pont. aug.': Etienne, *Culte impérial*, p. 198.

46 Pre-Roman: Strabo, 3.3.6; Sil. Ital., 3.344–5. Numantia: App., *Iber.*, 85. Urso: *ILS*, 6087, ch. 62. Townsites: Vitruv., 1.4.9.

47 G. Alföldy, *Flamines provinciae Hispaniae Citerioris* (Madrid, 1973); *Digest*, 50.4.17 pr.

48 *CIL* II, 4514; cf. R. Duthoy, 'Les *Augustales', *ANRW* II/16.2 (1978), pp. 1254–1309.

49 Curchin, 'Personal wealth', pp. 228–30.

50 Villaronga, *Numismática*, figs. 998, 1063, 1061, 1050–1; cf. D. Fishwick, 'Coins as evidence: Some phantom temples', *Classical Views*, vol. 3 (1984), pp. 263–70, expressing doubts on the Tarraco coins.

51 A. García y Bellido, 'El templo romano de Córdoba', *Oretania* (1964), pp. 157–65; T. Hauschild, 'Zur Typologie römischer Tempel auf der Iberischen Halbinsel' in J. Arce (ed.), *Homenaje a Sáenz de Buruaga* (Badajoz, 1982), pp. 145–56.

52 J. Alarcão and R. Etienne (eds), *Fouilles de Conimbriga*, vol. 1 (Paris, 1977), pp. 90–3; A. García y Bellido, 'Excavaciones en Augustobriga', *Noticiario Arqueológico Hispánico*, vol. 5 (1956–61), pp. 235–7.

53 M. Bendala Galán, 'Excavaciones en el Cerro de los Palacios' in P. León Alonso (ed.), *Italica (Santiponce, Sevilla)* (Madrid, 1982), pp. 55–6; C. Domergue *et al*, *Excavaciones de la Casa de Velázquez en Belo* (Madrid, 1974), fig. 18.

54 Symmachus, *Relationes*, 3.8.

55 Blázquez, *Diccionario*, pp. 145–6.

56 Livy, *Per.*, 49; Strabo, 3.3.6–7. Blázquez, *Diccionario*, pp. 144–5.

57 Plut., *Quaest. Rom.*, 83; Pliny, *NH*, 30.3.12; *CIL* II, 858–9.

58 Frontin., *Strat.*, 3.11.4; App., *Iber.*, 75; Cic., *Balb.*, 19.43.

59 Etienne, *Culte impérial*, p. 174 and plate II.3.

60 A. Molinero Pérez, 'Excavaciones antiguas y modernas en Duratón', *Estudios Segovianos*, vol. 1 (1949), p. 573.

61 A. Tovar, 'La inscripción del Cabeço das Fráguas y la lengua de los Lusitanos' in *Actas del III coloquio sobre lenguas y culturas paleohispánicas* (Salamanca, 1985), pp. 227–53.

62 *AE* 1973, 319.

63 M. Osuna Ruiz, *Arte romano en el museo de Cuenca* (Cuenca, 1976),

no. 12; Villaronga, *Numismática*, figs. 914, 916, 995; 1004; 1032; 940, 943; 1015.
64 G. Ulbert, *Cáceres el Viejo, ein spätrepublikanisches Legionslager in Spanish-Extramadura* (Mainz, 1984), plates 60, 76–7.
65 *Lex Irnitana*, chs 31, 92.
66 *ILS*, 6087, chs 70–1; J.L. García Aguinaga, 'Un testimonio de la celebración de las Saturnales en Calahorra' in M. Martín-Bueno (ed.), *Calahorra: Bimilenario de su fundación* (Madrid, 1984), pp. 201–5.
67 Mayer and Rodà, 'Les divinités féminines de la fertilité', pp. 293–304.
68 J.-N. Bonneville, S. Dardaine and P. Le Roux, *Belo V: L'épigraphie* (Madrid, 1988), no. 1.
69 Romans, 15:24; L. García Iglesias, *Los judíos en la España antigua* (Madrid, 1978), pp. 50–68.
70 D. Kyrtatas, *The social structure of the early Christian communities* (London and New York, 1987), p. 169.
71 R. Lane Fox, *Pagans and Christians* (New York, 1987), pp. 316–17.
72 Irenaeus, *Adversus haereses*, 1.10.2.
73 J.M. Blázquez, 'The possible African origin of Christianity in Spain', *Classical Folia*, vol. 23 (1969a), pp. 3–31; J. Marcillet-Jaubert, 'Lambaesis' in R. Stillwell *et al* (eds), *The Princeton encyclopaedia of classical sites* (Princeton, 1976), pp. 478–9.
74 B. de Gaiffier, 'S. Marcel de Tanger ou de León?', *Analecta Bollandiana*, vol. 61 (1943), pp. 116–39; Tranoy, *Galice romaine*, p. 433.
75 Cyprian, *Ep.*, 67.1.
76 Arnobius, *Adversus gentes*, 1.16.
77 Date: C.J. Hefele, *A history of the Christian councils*, vol. 1 (Edinburgh, 1894), pp. 131–7; Lane Fox, *Pagans and Christians*, pp. 664–5.
78 J. González Echegaray, *Los cántabros* (Madrid, 1966), pp. 236–8.
79 *ILS*, 4152; *Cod. Theod.*, 16.10.15; *RIT*, 998; F. Cumont, 'Les syriens en Espagne et les Adonies à Séville', *Syria*, vol. 8 (1927), pp. 330–41.
80 Conc. Toletanum III, canon 16; H. Schlunk, 'Los monumentos paleocristianos de "Gallaecia", especialmente los de la provincia de Lugo' in *Actas del coloquio internacional sobre el bimilenario de Lugo* (Lugo, 1977), pp. 199–203.
81 Cyprian, *Ep.*, 67.6.2; Athanasius, *Hist. Arian.*, 44; *Vitas sanctorum patrum Emeretensium*, 4.
82 Jerome, *Ep.*, 133.3.4.
83 Consentius, *Ep.*, 11, (in *Corpus Scriptorum Ecclesiasticorum Latinorum*, vol. 88 (1981), pp. 51–70); A.R. Birley, 'Magnus Maximus and the persecution of heresy', *Bulletin of the John Rylands University Library*, vol. 66 (1983), pp. 13–43; R. Van Dam, *Leadership and community in Late Antique Gaul* (Berkeley, Los Angeles and London, 1985), ch. 5.

9 'RESISTANCE' TO ROMANISATION

1 F.J. Haverfield, *The romanization of Roman Britain* (Oxford, 1923), p. 13.
2 Florus, 2.30.29; Tac., *Ann.*, 4.45; *HA Hadr.*, 12.3; *ILS*, 103; Strabo, 3.2.15.

3 *ILS*, 6087, ch. 103; Tac., *Ann.*, 3.44, 4.13, 4.28.

4 *ILS*, 2648; Suet., *Galba*, 10.2–3; R. Syme, 'Antistius Rusticus, a consular from Corduba', *Historia*, vol. 32 (1983), pp. 359–60.

5 *AE* 1936, 98; *HA Pius*, 7.4, *Probus*, 18.5; *ILS*, 1140.

6 Oros., 7.40.5; Hydat., 91, 171, 186; E.A. Thompson, 'The end of Roman Spain', *Nottingham Mediaeval Studies*, vol. 21 (1977), p. 14.

7 Hydat., 200; Salvian, *De gub. Dei*, 5.5, 5.23; Oros., 7.41.7; Isid., *Hist. Goth.*, 34.

8 E.A. Thompson, 'Peasant revolts in late Roman Gaul and Spain', *Past & Present*, vol. 2 (1952), pp. 11–23.

9 *ILS*, 6101; Pliny, *NH*, 3.28; T.R.S. Broughton, 'Municipal institutions in Roman Spain', *Cahiers d'Histoire Mondiale*, vol. 9 (1965), p. 139.

10 *AE* 1967, 239; Isid., *Hist. Vand.*, 72.

11 A. Barbero and M. Vigil, *Sobre los orígenes sociales de la Reconquista* (Barcelona, 1974), p. 192; J.M. Blázquez, 'Problemas en torno a las raíces de España', *Hispania*, vol. 29 (1969b), p. 246.

12 G. Fabre, M. Mayer and I. Rodà, *Inscriptions romaines de Catalogne*, Vol. 2 (Paris, 1985), no. 19; *ILS*, 3939; *CIL* II, 131.

13 M. Vigil, 'Romanización y permanencia de estructuras sociales indígenas en la España septentrional', *Boletín de la Real Academia de la Historia*, vol. 152 (1963), pp. 225–33; J. Caro Baroja, *Los pueblos del Norte de la Península Ibérica*, 2nd edn (San Sebastian, 1973), pp. 134–5.

14 A. Barbero, 'El priscilianismo: Herejía o movimiento social?' in A.M. Prieto Arciniega (ed.), *Conflictos y estructuras sociales en la Hispania antigua* (Madrid, 1977), pp. 77–114.

15 J. Dias, 'O problema da reconstituição das casas redondas castrejas', *Trabalhos de Antropologia e Etnologia*, vol. 12 (1949), pp. 126–68.

16 J. Puig y Cadafalch, *L'arquitectura romana a Catalunya* (Barcelona, 1934), pp. 373–88; C. Sánchez Albornoz, *Spain, an historical enigma*, vol. 1 (Madrid, 1975), p. 129.

17 T. Ortego, *Numancia, guía breve historico-arqueológico* (Madrid, 1980), pp. 21–9; M. Gil-Mascarell, *Yacimientos ibéricos en la región valenciana* (Valencia, 1971), p. 14.

18 J.M. Apellaniz, 'La romanización del país vasco en los yacimientos en cuevas' in *II Semana internacional de antropología vasca* (Burgos, 1973), pp. 357–63.

19 Hellenised art: M. Clavel and P. Lévêque, *Villes et structures urbaines dans l'Occident romain* (Paris, 1971), pp. 134–5. Visigothic revivals: F. de Almeida, 'Reminiscências castrejas na arte visigótica', *Trabalhos de Antropologia e Etnologia*, vol. 22 (1973), pp. 283–7.

20 F. Marco Simón, *Las estelas decoradas de los conventos caesaraugustano y cluniense* (Zaragoza, 1978), pp. 15–61.

21 A. Mócsy, *Pannonia and Upper Moesia* (London and Boston, 1974), pp. 61–3; J. Vives, *Inscripciones cristianas de la España romana y visigoda* (Barcelona, 1969), no. 1.

22 E. Frankowski, *Estelas discoideas de la Península Ibérica* (Madrid, 1920). Eyes: A. González Blanco and U. Espinosa Ruiz, 'La necrópolis del poblado celta-romano de Santa Ana', *Archivo Español de Arqueología*, vol. 49 (1976), pp. 164–70.

23 M.V. and F. Romero Carnicero, 'Cerámicas imperiales con engobe rojo y decoración pintada procedentes de Numancia', *Boletín del Seminario de Estudios en Arte y Arqueología*, vol. 44 (1978), pp. 396–402; A. García y Bellido, 'Marcas de *terra sigillata* en caracteres ibéricos: Protemus en Azaila', *Archivo Español de Arqueología*, vol 32 (1959), pp. 164–6.

24 J.M.P. *et al*, 'Neutron activation analysis of fine grey pottery from Conimbriga, Santa Olalla and Tavarade, Portugal', *Journal of Archaeological Science*, vol. 10 (1983), pp. 61–70.

25 J.M. Blázquez, 'Rechazo y asimilación de la cultura romana en Hispania' in D.M. Pippidi (ed.), *Assimilation et résistance à la culture gréco-romaine dans le monde ancien*, (Bucharest and Paris, 1976b), p. 83; M.L. Albertos *et al*, *Guía del Museo Provincial de Arqueología de Alava* (Vitoria, 1978), p. 64; J.M. Vázquez Varela and F. Acuña Castroviejo, 'Pervivencia de las formas culturales indígenas' in *La romanización de Galicia* (Sada and La Coruña, 1976), p. 81.

26 *AE* 1980, 588.

27 R. Violant y Simorra, 'Un arado y otros aperos ibéricos hallados en Valencia y su supervivencia en la cultura popular española', *Zephyrus*, vol. 4 (1953), pp. 119–30; C. Parain, 'The evolution of agricultural technique' in M.M. Postan and H.J. Habbakuk (eds) *The Cambridge economic history of Europe*, 2nd edn, vol. 1 (Cambridge, 1966), p. 153; P.J. Reynolds, *Iron age farm* (London, 1979), p. 17.

28 Mining: M.L. Sánchez León, *Economía de la Hispania meridional durante la dinastía de los Antoninos* (Salamanca, 1978), pp. 134–6. Weapons: L. Higgin, *Spanish life in town and country* (New York, 1902), p. 118; A. Bruhn de Hoffmeyer, *Arms and armour in Spain*, vol. 1 (Madrid, 1972), p. 50.

29 R. Menéndez Pidal, *Toponimia prerrománica hispana* (Madrid, 1968), pp. 31–3, 242–7.

30 Central Spain: author's calculations. Galicia: A. Tranoy, *La Galice romaine* (Paris, 1981), pp. 363–4. Tras-os-Montes: P. Le Roux and A. Tranoy, 'L'épigraphie du nord du Portugal', *Conimbriga*, vol. 23 (1984), pp. 32–3.

31 Conimbriga: R. Etienne *et al*, 'Les Dimensions sociales de la romanisation dans la Péninsule Ibérique' in Pippidi (ed.), *Assimilation et résistance*, p. 98. Amphoras: R.C. Knapp, *Aspects of the Roman experience in Iberia, 206–100 BC*, (Vitoria and Valladolid, 1977), p. 152.

32 North-west: Tranoy, *Galice romaine*, pp. 368–9. Alava: M.L. Albertos, 'Alava prerromana y romana', *Estudios de Arqueología Alavesa*, vol. 4 (1970), pp. 165–223.

33 Tac., *Ann.*, 4.45; Pliny, *NH*, 9.57, 14.30; Columella, 3.2.19; Suet., *Aug.*, 82.2.

34 *ILS*, 3259, 6891; A. Tovar, 'Las inscripciones celtibéricas de Peñalba de Villastar', *Emerita*, vol. 27 (1959), pp. 349–65; J. Maluquer de Motes, 'Dos grafitos ibéricos con nombres latinos', *Zephyrus*, vol. 14 (1963), pp. 108–10; J. Siles, 'Iberismo y latinización: Nombres latinos en epígrafos ibéricos', *Faventia*, vol. 3 (1981), pp. 97–113; *AE* 1941, 92.

35 F. Beltrán Lloris, *Epigrafía latina de Saguntum y su territorium* (Valencia, 1980), no. 78; V. Soria Sánchez, 'Nuevas aportaciones a

la arqueología extremeña' in *XIV Congreso nacional de arqueología* (Zaragoza, 1977), p. 1147; U. Espinosa Ruiz, *Estudios de bibliografía arqueológica riojana* (Logroño, 1981), p. 147.

36 A.J. Carnoy, *Le Latin d'Espagne d'après les inscriptions* (Brussels, 1906).

37 Strabo, 3.4.13, 16–17; Cic., *ad Q. fr.*, 1.1.9; Val. Max., 9.1.5.

38 D.E. Woods, 'A numismatic chapter of the romanisation of Hispania' in *Essays in memory of Karl Lehmann* (New York, 1964), pp. 383–5.

39 An earlier version of this paper was presented under the title 'Cultures in Conflict' at the conference 'Europe under Development: A Critical Millennium', held at Kalamazoo, Michigan in 1984. I thank those participants who commented on the paper at that time.

MAPS

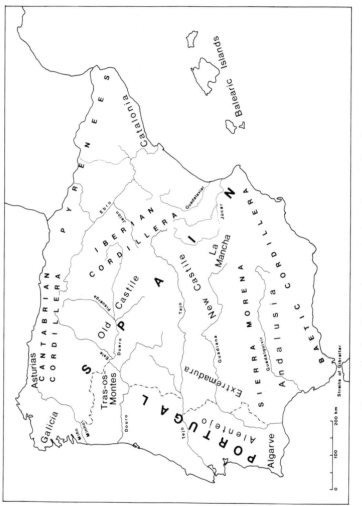

Map 1 Iberian Peninsula: mountains, rivers and regions

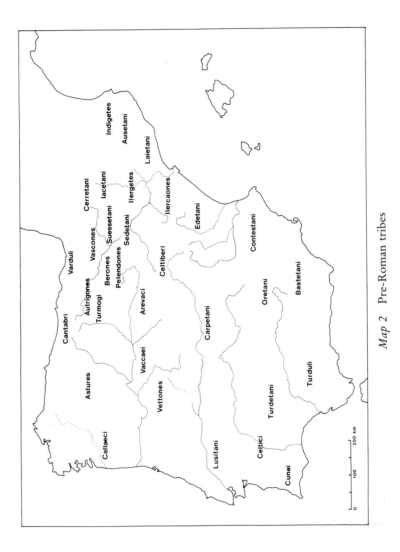

Callaeci

Astures

Cantabri

Varduli

Autrigones
Turmogi

Vascones

Cerretani

Berones
Pelendones

Suessetani
Iacetani

Sedetani

Ilergetes

Indigetes

Ausetani

Laietani

Ilercaones

Edetani

Arevaci

Celtiberi

Vaccaei

Carpetani

Contestani

Vettones

Oretani

Bastetani

Lusitani

Turdetani

Turduli

Celtici

Cunei

Map 2 Pre-Roman tribes

0   100   200 km

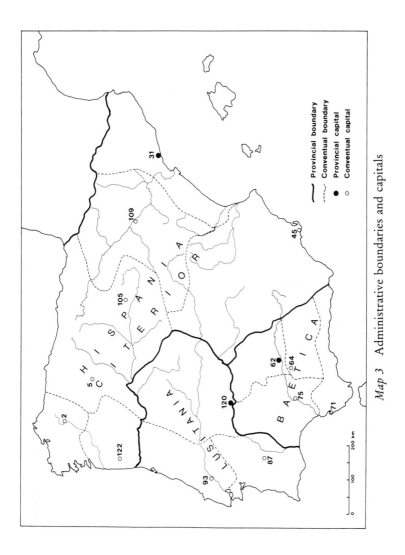

Map 3   Administrative boundaries and capitals

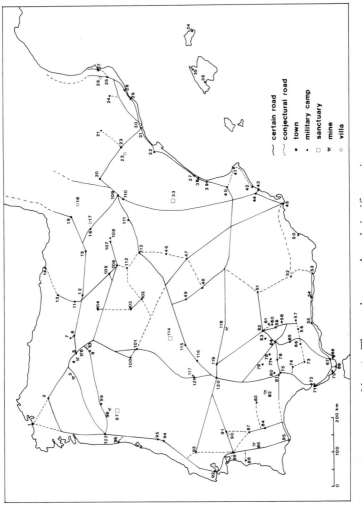

Map 4 The road network and significant sites

KEY TO MAPS

Provincial and Conventual Capitals

Astigi (Ecija) 64
Asturica Augusta (Astorga) 5
Bracara Augusta (Braga) 122
Caesaraugusta (Zaragoza) 109
Carthago Nova (Cartagena) 45
Clunia (Peñalba de Castro) 105
Corduba (Córdoba) 62
Emerita Augusta (Mérida) 120
Gades (Cádiz) 71
Hispalis (Seville) 75
Lucus Augusti (Lugo) 2
Pax Iulia (Beja) 87
Scallabis (Santarém) 93
Tarraco (Tarragona) 31

Towns

Abdera (Adra) 53
Acci (Guadix) 52
Aeminium (Coimbra) 95
Aeso (Isona) 21
Aquae Flaviae (Chaves) 99
Arucci (Aroche) 83
Arva (Alcolea del Río) 77
Ategua (Cortijo de Teba) 61
Augustobriga (Talavera la Vieja) 115
Ausa (Vic) 24
Axati (Lora del Río) 78
Baelo (Bolonia) 70
Barcino (Barcelona) 29
Baria (Villaricos) 50

Bilbilis (Calatayud) 111
Bletisama (Ledesma) 100
Brigantium (La Coruña) 1
Calagurris (Calahorra) 16
Cale (Oporto) 96
Calpe (Gibraltar) 68
Carbula (Almodóvar) 63
Carmo (Carmona) 76
Carteia (Rocadillo) 67
Castulo (Cazlona) 51
Cauca (Coca) 103
Conimbriga (Condeixa-a-Velha) 94
Consabura (Consuegra) 48
Contrebia Belaisca (Botorrita) 110
Dertosa (Tortosa) 32
Dianium (Denia) 41
Ebora (Evora) 91
Emporiae (Empúries) 27
Ercavica (Castro de Santaver) 46
Flaviobriga (Castro Urdiales) 14
Gerunda (Girona) 25
Igabrum (Cabra) 58
Ilerda (Lleida) 23
Ilici (Elx) 44
Ilipa (Alcalá del Río) 80
Iluro (Mataró) 28
Iptuci (Prado del Rey) 73
Italica (Santiponce) 81
Iulia Traducta (Tarifa) 69
Iuliobriga (Retortillo) 13
Lancia (Villasabariego) 8
Lucentum (Alicante) 42
Mago (Mahón) 34
Malaca (Málaga) 55
Metellinum (Medellín) 119

Mirobriga (Santiago do Cacém) 88
Munigua (Mulva) 79
Myrtilis (Mértola) 84
Norba (Cáceres) 121
Numantia (Garray) 107
Olisipo (Lisbon) 92
Osca (Huesca) 20
Osqua (Archidona) 57
Ossonoba (Faro) 85
Palantia (Palencia) 104
Palma (Palma de Mallorca) 36
Pisoraca (Herrera de Pisuerga) 11
Pollentia (Alcudia) 35
Pompaelo (Pamplona) 19
Portus Gaditanus (Puerto de Santa
  María) 72
Portus Ilicitanus (Santa Pola) 43
Sabora (Cañete la Real) 66
Saetabis (Xátiva) 40
Saguntum (Sagunto) 38
Salacia (Alcácer do Sal) 89
Salmantica (Salamanca) 101
Salpensa (near Utrera) 74
Segisamo (Sasamón) 12
Segobriga (Cabezo del Griego) 47
Segovia (Segovia) 102
Seguntia (Sigüenza) 113
Sexi (Almuñécar) 54
Singilia Barba (Cortijo del
  Castillón) 56
Termes (Tiermes) 112
Toletum (Toledo) 49
Tritium Magallum (Tricio) 15

Turgalium (Trujillo) 116
Ucubi (Espejo) 60
Ulia (Montilla) 59
Urso (Osuna) 65
Uxama (Osma) 106
Valentia (Valencia) 39

Other Sites

Almadén 118
Almenara 37
Cáceres el Viejo 117
Funes 17
Legio VII Gemina (León) 7
Liédena 18
Luyego 4
(Las) Médulas 3
(Els) Munts 30
Nossa Senhora da Tourega 90
Panóias 97
Peñalba de Villastar 33
Petavonium (Rosinos de
  Vidriales) 9
Quintana del Marco 10
(El) Raso de Candeleda 114
Renieblas 108
Riotinto 82
Três Minas 98
(Els) Viláns 22
Vilauba 26
Villalís 6
Vipasca (Aljustrel) 86

BIBLIOGRAPHY

The bibliography on Roman Spain is immense. For older works one may consult *Bibliografía de los estudios clásicos en España*, 2 vols (Sociedad Española de Estudios Clásicos, Madrid, 1956–68) and A. Montenegro Duque, S. Crespo Ortiz de Zárate and L. Sagredo San Eustaquio, *Bibliografía: España romana*, 3 vols (Universidad de Valladolid, Valladolid, 1972–6). For more recent publications, bibliographies appear annually in the journal *Madrider Mitteilungen* and every five years in *Revue des Etudes Anciennes*. The following bibliography is limited to works cited in the notes.

Abad Casal, L. (1982) *Pintura romana en España*, 2 vols., Universidades de Alicante y Sevilla, Cadiz.

Abascal, J.M. (1989) *La circulación monetaria del Portus Ilicitanus*, Conselleria de Cultura, Educacío i Ciència, Valencia.

Abásolo, J.A. and Elorza, J.C. (1974) 'Nuevos teónimos de época romana en el país vasco-navarro', *Estudios de Arqueología Alavesa*, vol. 6, pp. 247–58.

Alarcão, J. de (1988) *Roman Portugal*, 2 vols, Aris and Phillips, Warminster.

——and Etienne, R. (eds) (1974–9) *Fouilles de Conimbriga*, 7 vols, E. de Boccard, Paris.

Albertos, M.L. (1970) 'Alava prerromana y romana', *Estudios de Arqueología Alavesa*, vol. 4, pp. 165–223.

——(1974) 'El culto a los montes entre los galaicos, astures y berones', *Estudios de Arqueología Alavesa*, vol. 6, pp. 147–57.

——(1977) 'La mujer hispanorromana a través de la epigrafía', *Revista de la Universidad de Madrid*, no. 109, pp. 179–98.

—— et al. (1978) *Guía del Museo Provincial de Arqueología de Alava*, Diputación Foral de Alava, Vitoria.

Alföldy, G. (1969) *Fasti Hispanienses*, Franz Steiner Verlag, Wiesbaden.

——(1973) *Flamines provinciae Hispaniae Citerioris*, Consejo Superior de Investigaciones Científicas, Madrid.

——(1984) 'Drei städtische Eliten im römischen Hispanien', *Gerión*, vol. 2, pp. 193–238.

Almagro Basch, M. (1979) *Guía de Mérida*, 8th edn, Dirección General del Patrimonio Artístico y Cultural, Madrid.

Almeida, F. de (1973) 'Reminiscências castrejas na arte visigótica', *Trabalhos de Antropologia e Etnologia*, vol. 22, pp. 283–7.

Alonso Sánchez, A. (1988) *Fortificaciones romanas en Extremadura*, Universidad de Extremadura, Salamanca.

Alvarez Martínez, J.M. (1982) 'El foro de Augusta Emerita' in J. Arce (ed.), *Homenaje a Sáenz de Buruaga*, Diputación Provincial, Badajoz, pp. 53–68.

——(1985) 'Excavaciones en Augusta Emerita' in M. Martín-Bueno (ed.), *Arqueología de las ciudades modernas superpuestas a las antiguas*, Ministerio de Cultura, Madrid, pp. 35–53.

Annabi, M.K. (1983) 'Les amphores ibériques de Carthage', *Turat*, vol. 1, pp. 11–16.

Anonymous (1984) 'Herrera de Pisuerga' in *Arqueología 83*, Ministerio de Cultura, Madrid, p. 135.

Aparicio Pérez, J. (1974) 'Sobre la casa ibérica' in *Homenaje a D. Pío Beltrán*, Consejo Superior de Investigaciones Científicas, Madrid, pp. 15–20.

Apellaniz, J.M. (1973) 'La romanización del país vasco en los yacimientos en cuevas' in *II Semana internacional de antropología vasca*, La Gran Enciclopedia Vasca, Bilbao, pp. 357–63.

Arce, J. (1985) '*Spania, spanos-spane-spanon* on papyri', *Zeitschrift für Papyrologie und Epigraphik*, vol. 61, pp. 30–2.

——(1986) '*Notitia Dignitatum Occ.* XLII y el ejército de la Hispania tardorromana' in A. del Castillo (ed.), *Ejército y sociedad*, Universidad de León, León, pp. 51–61.

Arévalo González, A. (1987) 'Las monedas de Obulco', *Revista de Arqueología*, no. 74, pp. 29–35.

Arias Vilas, F., Le Roux, P. and Tranoy, A. (1979) *Inscriptions romaines de la province de Lugo*, Diffusion de Boccard, Paris.

Arribas, A. (1963) *The Iberians*, Thames and Hudson, London.

Astin, A.E. (1967) *Scipio Aemilianus*, Clarendon Press, Oxford.

Baatz, D. (1975) *Der römische Limes*, 2nd edn, Gebr. Mann Verlag, Berlin.

——(1978) 'Recent finds of ancient artillery', *Britannia*, vol. 9, pp. 1–67.

Badian, E. (1972) *Publicans and sinners*, Cornell University Press, Ithaca.

Balil, A. (1986) 'Terra sigillata hispánica: A propósito de un libro reciente', *Boletín del Seminario de Estudios de Arte y Arqueología*, vol. 52, pp. 248–62.

Bane, R.W. (1976) 'The development of Roman imperial attitudes and the Iberian wars', *Emerita*, vol. 44, pp. 409–20.

Barbero, A. (1977) 'El priscilianismo: Herejía o movimiento social?' in A.M. Prieto Arciniega (ed.), *Conflictos y estructuras sociales en la Hispania antigua*, Akal Editor, Madrid, pp. 77–114.

——and Vigil, M. (1974) *Sobre los orígenes sociales de la Reconquista*, Editorial Ariel, Barcelona.

Barceló, P. (1988) *Karthago und die Iberische Halbinsel vor den Barkiden*, Rudolf Habelt, Bonn.

Bayard, D. and Massy, J.-L. (1983) *Amiens romain*, Revue Archéologique de Picardie, Amiens.

Bell, A.F.G. (1925) 'Some Spanish flower names', *Bulletin of Spanish Studies*, vol. 3, pp. 12–15.

Beltrán Lloris, F. (1980) *Epigrafía latina de Saguntum y su territorium*, Servicio de Investigación Prehistórica, Valencia.

Beltrán Lloris, M. (1985) 'La arqueología urbana en Zaragoza' in M. Martín-Bueno (ed.), *Arqueología de las ciudades modernas superpuestas a las antiguas*, Ministerio de Cultura, Madrid, pp. 55–116.

Beltrán Martínez, A. (1976) 'Caesaraugusta' in *Symposion de ciudades augusteas*, vol. 1, Universidad de Zaragoza, Zaragoza, pp. 219–61.

——and Tovar, A. (1982) *Contrebia Belaisca, I: El bronce con alfabeto 'ibérico' de Botorrita*, Universidad de Zaragoza, Zaragoza.

Bencivenga Trillmich, C. (1985) 'Observaciones sobre la difusión de la cerámica ibérica en Italia' in *XVII Congreso nacional de arqueología*, Universidad de Zaragoza, Zaragoza, pp. 551–6.

Bendala Galán, M. (1982) 'Excavaciones en el Cerro de los Palacios' in P. León Alonso (ed.), *Italica (Santiponce, Sevilla)*, Ministerio de Cultura, Madrid, pp. 29–73.

——(1986) 'Die orientalischen Religionen Hispaniens in vorrömischer und römischer Zeit', *ANRW*, vol. II/18.2, pp. 345–408.

Bennett, W.H. (1961) 'The death of Sertorius and the coin', *Historia*, vol. 10, pp. 459–72.

Bird, D.G. (1984) 'Pliny and the gold mines of the north-west of the Iberian Peninsula' in T.F.C. Blagg, R.F.J. Jones and S.J. Keay (eds), *Papers in Iberian archaeology*, British Archaeological Reports, Oxford, pp. 341–68.

Birley, A.R. (1983) 'Magnus Maximus and the persecution of heresy', *Bulletin of the John Rylands University Library*, vol. 66, pp. 13–43.

Blanco, A. and Luzón, J.M. (1969) 'Pre-Roman silver miners at Riotinto', *Antiquity*, vol. 43, pp. 124–31.

——, ——and Ruiz, D. (1970) *Excavaciones arqueológicas en el Cerro Salomon*, Universidad de Sevilla, Seville.

Blázquez, J.M. (1963) 'El impacto de la conquista de la Hispania en Roma (154–83 a.C.)', *Klio*, vol. 41, pp. 168–86.

——(1969a) 'The possible African origin of Christianity in Spain', *Classical Folia*, vol. 23, pp. 3–31.

——(1969b) 'Problemas en torno a las raíces de España', *Hispania*, vol. 29, pp. 245–86.

——(1975a) *Diccionario de las religiones prerromanas de Hispania*, Ediciones Istmo, Madrid.

——(1975b) *La romanización*, 2 vols, Ediciones Istmo, Madrid.

——(1976a) 'Bronces de la Mérida prerromana' in A. Blanco Freijeiro (ed.), *Augusta Emerita: Actas del simposio internacional 1975*, Ministerio de Educación y Ciencia, Madrid, pp. 11–17.

——(1976b) 'Rechazo y asimilación de la cultura romana en Hispania' in D.M. Pippidi (ed.), *Assimilation et résistance à la culture gréco-romaine dans le monde ancien*, Editura Academiei/Les Belles-Lettres, Bucharest and Paris, pp. 63–94.

——(1978a) *Economía de la Hispania romana*, Ediciones Najera, Bilbao.

——(1978b) *Historia económica de la Hispania romana*, Ediciones Cristiandad, Madrid.

——(1981) *Mosaicos romanos de Córdoba, Jaén y Málaga*, Instituto 'Rodrigo Caro', Madrid.

——(1983) 'Panorama general de la presencia fenicia y púnica en España' in *Atti del I congresso internacional di studi fenici e punici*, vol. 2, Consiglio Nazionale delle Richerche, Rome, pp. 311–73.

——(1986) 'Luftbilder römischer Lager aus republikanischer Zeit in Spanien' in C. Unz (ed.), *Studien zu den Militärgrenzen Roms III*, Konrad Theiss Verlag, Stuttgart, pp. 681–8.

Bogaers, J.E. (1967) 'Die Besatzungstruppen des Legionslagers von Nijmegen im 2. Jahrhundert nach Christus' in *Studien zu den Militärgrenzen Roms*, Böhlau Verlag, Köln and Graz, pp. 54–76.

Bonneville, J.-N. (1988) 'Les patrons du municipe d'Emporiae' in F. Mayet (ed.), *Hommage à Robert Etienne*, Diffusion de Boccard, Paris, pp. 181–200.

——, Dardaine, S. and Le Roux, P. (1988) *Belo V: L'épigraphie*, Casa de Velázquez, Madrid.

Bosch Gimpera, P. (1940) 'Two Celtic waves in Spain', *Proceedings of the British Academy*, vol. 26, pp. 25–148.

Bradley, R.J. (1971) 'Economic change in the growth of early hill-forts' in M. Jesson and D. Hill (eds) *The Iron Age and its hill-forts*, University of Southampton, Southampton, pp. 71–83.

Braudel, F. (1972) *The Mediterranean and the Mediterranean world in the age of Phillip II*, 2 vols, Harper and Row, New York.

Brind'Amour, P. (1983) *Le calendrier romain*, Université d'Ottawa, Ottawa.

Broughton, T.R.S. (1950) *The magistrates of the Roman Republic*, 2 vols, American Philological Association, Cleveland.

——(1965) 'Municipal institutions in Roman Spain', *Cahiers d'Histoire Mondial*, vol. 9, pp. 126–42.

Bruhn de Hoffmeyer, A. (1972) *Arms and armour in Spain*, Instituto de Estudios sobre Armas Antiguas, Madrid.

Brunt, P.A. (1971) *Italian manpower, 225 BC–AD 14*, Clarendon Press, Oxford.

Cabral, J.M.P. *et al* (1983) 'Neutron activation analysis of fine grey pottery from Conimbriga, Santa Olalla and Tavarade, Portugal', *Journal of Archaeological Science*, vol. 10, pp. 61–70.

Caldera de Castro, M.P. and Velázquez Jiménez, A. (1983) *Augusta Emerita I*, Ministerio de Cultura, Madrid.

Calza, R. and Nash, E. (1959) *Ostia*, Sansoni, Firenze.

Cambi, N. (1983) 'Le anfore Dressel 20 nella Jugoslovia' in J.M. Blázquez Martínez and J. Remesal Rodríguez (eds), *Producción y comercio del aceite en la Antigüedad*, II, Universidad Complutense, Madrid, pp. 363–89.

Campos, J. and González, J. (1987) 'Los foros de Hispalis colonia Romula', *Archivo Español de Arqueología*, vol. 60, pp. 123–58.

Carandini, A. and Settis, S. (1979) *Schiavi e padroni nell'Etruria romana*, De Donato, Bari.

Carnoy, A.J. (1906) *Le Latin d'Espagne d'après les inscriptions*, Misch & Thron, Brussels.

Caro Baroja, J. (1973) *Los pueblos del Norte de la Península Ibérica*, 2nd edn, Editorial Txertoa, San Sebastian.

Caruz Arenas, A. (1978) 'La última campaña de César en la Bética: Munda', in J.F. Rodríguez Neila (ed.), *Actas del I Congreso de historia de Andalucía: Fuentes y metodología, Andalucía en la Antigüedad*, Monte de Piedad y Caja de Ahorros, Córdoba.

Castañer, P., Roure, A. and Tremoleda, J. (1988) 'Dioses Lares: El larario de Vilauba', *Revista de Arqueología*, no. 89, pp. 50–7.

Castillo, C. (1982) 'Los senadores béticos', *Tituli*, vol. 5, pp. 465–519.

——(1986) 'Miscelánea epigráfica hispano-romana', *Studia et Documenta Historiae et Iuris*, vol. 52, pp. 376–81.

——, Gómez-Pantoja, J. and Dolores Mauleón, M. (1981) *Inscripciones romanas del Museo de Navarra*, Diputación Foral, Pamplona.

Castro García, L. de and Blanco Ordas, R. (1975) 'El castro de Tariego de Cerrato (Palencia)', *Publicaciones de la Institución 'Tello Téllez de Meneses'*, vol. 35, pp. 55–138.

Champeaux, J. (1987) *Fortuna: Recherches sur le culte de la Fortune à Rome*, 2 vols, Ecole Française de Rome, Rome.

Chapa Brunet, T. (1986) *Influjos griegos en la escultura zoomorfa ibérica*, Consejo Superior de Investigaciones Científicas, Madrid.

Childe, V.G. (1943) 'Rotary querns on the Continent and in the Mediterranean basin', *Antiquity*, vol. 17, pp. 19–26.

Clavel, M. and Lévêque, P. (1971) *Villes et structures urbaines dans l'Occident romain*, Armand Colin, Paris.

Colls, D. (1986) 'Les amphores léetaniennes et l'épave Cap-Béar III', *Revue des Etudes Anciennes*, vol. 88, pp. 201–13.

——, Etienne, R., Lequément, R., Liou, B. and Mayet, F. (1977) 'L'épave Port-Vendres II et le commerce de la Bétique à l'époque de Claude', *Archaeonautica*, vol. 1, pp. 1–145.

Cortes, R. and Gabriel, R. (1983) 'Sobre el aforo del anfiteatro, teatro y circo de Tarragona' in *XVI Congreso nacional de arqueología*, Universidad de Zaragoza, Zaragoza, pp. 955–62.

Corzo, R. (1986) 'Die Belagerung von Ategua durch Julius Caesar (45 v. Chr.)' in C. Unz (ed.), *Studien zu den Militärgrenzen Roms III*, Konrad Theiss Verlag, Stuttgart, pp. 689–91.

Crawford, M.H. (1985) *Coinage and money under the Roman Republic*, University of California Press, Berkeley and Los Angeles.

Crinite, N. (1970) *L'epigrafe di Asculum di Gn. Pompeio Strabone*, Editrice Vita e Pensiero, Milan.

Cumont, F. (1927) 'Les syriens en Espagne et les Adonies à Séville', *Syria*, vol. 8, pp. 330–41.

Curchin, L.A. (1981) 'The creation of a romanized elite in Spain', unpublished Ph.D thesis, University of Ottawa.

——(1982a) 'Familial epithets in the epigraphy of Roman Spain', *Mélanges Etienne Gareau = Cahiers des Etudes Anciennes*, vol. 14, pp. 179–82.

——(1982b) 'Jobs in Roman Spain', *Florilegium: Carleton University Annual Papers on Classical Antiquity and the Middle Ages*, vol. 4, pp. 32–62.

——(1983) 'Personal wealth in Roman Spain', *Historia*, vol. 32, pp. 227–44.

——(1985a) 'Men of the cloth: Reflections on the Roman linen trade', *Liverpool Classical Monthly*, vol. 10, pp. 34–5.

——(1985b) '*Vici* and *pagi* in Roman Spain', *Revue des Etudes Anciennes*, vol. 87, pp. 327–43.

——(1986a) 'From *limes* to *Latinitas:* Roman impact on the Spanish Meseta' in C. Unz (ed.), *Studien zu den Militärgrenzen Roms III*, Verlag Theiss, Stuttgart, pp. 692–5.

——(1986b) 'Non-slave labour in Roman Spain', *Gerión*, vol. 4, pp. 177–87.

——(1986c) 'The romanization of Spain: An overview', *Classical Views*, vol. 30, pp. 271–85.

——(1987a) 'Demography and romanization at Tarraco', *Archivo Español de Arqueología*, vol. 60, pp. 159–71.

——(1987b) 'Social relations in central Spain: Patrons, freedmen and slaves in the life of a Roman provincial hinterland', *Ancient Society*, vol. 18, pp. 75–89.

——(1988) 'Vergil's "Messiah": A new governor of Spain?', *The Ancient History Bulletin*, vol. 2, pp. 143–4.

——(1990) *The local magistrates of Roman Spain*, University of Toronto Press, Toronto.

Curtis, R.I. (1988) 'Spanish trade in salted fish products in the first and second centuries AD', *International Journal of Nautical Archaeology*, vol. 17, pp. 205–10.

D'Arms, J. (1981) *Commerce and social standing in ancient Rome*, Harvard University Press, Cambridge (Mass.).

Delano Smith, C. (1979) *Western Mediterranean Europe*, Academic Press, London.

Dias, J. (1949) 'O problema da reconstituição das casas redondas castrejas', *Trabalhos de Antropologia e Etnologia*, vol. 12, pp. 126–68.

Dias Diogo, A.M. (1984) 'O material romano da primeira campanha de escavações na Alcáçova de Santarém', *Conimbriga*, vol. 23, pp. 111–41.

Díaz Moreno, J.L., Sierra Gómez, J., Vázquez González, A. and Zárate Martín, A. (1986) *Atlas de Castilla-La Mancha*, Junta de Comunidades de Castilla-La Mancha, Madrid.

Díez de Bethencourt, M. (1978) 'Implantación de la vitis vinifera en Iberia', *V Congreso español de estudios clásicos*, Sociedad Española de Estudios Clásicos, Madrid, pp. 683–7.

Dobson, B. (1979) 'The "Rangordnung" of the Rooman army' in D.M. Pippidi (ed.), *Actes du VII congrès international d'épigraphie grecque et latine*, Editura Academiei, Bucharest and Les Belles Lettres, Paris, pp. 191–204.

Domergue, C. (1965) 'Les Planii et leur activité industrielle en Espagne sous la République', *Mélanges de la Casa de Velázquez*, vol. 1, pp. 9–25.

——and Hérail, G. (1978) *Mines d'or romaines d'Espagne: Le district de la Valduerna* (León), Université de Toulouse-Le-Mirail, Toulouse.

——, Nicolini, G., Nony, D., Bourgeoix, A., Mayet, F. and Richard, R.C. (1974) *Excavaciones de la Casa de Velázquez en Belo*, Ministerio de Educación y Ciencia, Madrid.

Doppelfeld, O. (ed.), (1967) *Römer am Rhein*, Römisch-Germanische Museum, Köln.

Duthoy, R. (1978) 'Les *Augustales', *ANRW*, vol. II/16.2, pp. 1254–1309.

Eckstein, A.M. (1987) *Senate and general: Individual decision making and Roman foreign relations 264–194 BC*, University of California Press, Berkeley, Los Angeles and London.

Edmondson, J. (1987) *Two industries in Roman Lusitania: Mining and garum production*, British Archaeological Reports, Oxford.

——(1989) 'Mining in the later Roman Empire and beyond', *JRS*, vol. 79, pp. 84–102.

Encarnação, J. d' (1979) *Sociedade romana e epigrafia*, Museu de Arqueologia e Etnografia, Setúbal.

——(1984) *Inscrições romanas do Conventus Pacensis*, Instituto de Arqueologia, Coimbra.

——(1988) 'Divindades indígenas peninsulares: Problemas metodológicos do seu estudo' in J. González and J. Arce (eds), *Estudios sobre la Tabula Siarensis*, Consejo Superior de Investigaciones Científicas, Madrid, pp. 261–76.

Engel, A. and Paris, P. (1906) 'Une forteresse ibérique à Osuna (fouilles de 1903), *Nouvelles Archives des Missions Scientifiques et Littéraires*, vol. 13, pp. 458–66.

Espinosa Ruiz, U. (1981) *Estudios de bibliografía arqueológica riojana*, Instituto de Estudios Riojanos, Logroño.

Etienne, R. (1958) *Le culte impérial dans la Péninsule Ibérique*, Ecole Française de Rome, Paris.

——(1966) 'Les sénateurs espagnols sous Trajan et Hadrien' in *Les Empereurs romains d'Espagne*, Centre National de la Recherche Scientifique, Paris, pp. 55–82.

——(1982) 'Sénateurs originaires de la province de Lusitanie', *Tituli*, vol. 5, pp. 521–9.

——, Le Roux, P. and Tranoy, A. (1987) 'La tessera hospitalis, instrument de sociabilité et de romanisation dans la Péninsule Ibérique' in F. Thelamon (ed.), *Sociabilité, pouvoirs et société: Actes du colloque de Rouen*, Université de Rouen, Rouen, pp. 323–36.

——, Fabre, G., Le Roux, P. and Tranoy, A. (1976) 'Les Dimensions sociales de la romanisation dans la Péninsule Ibérique' in D.M. Pippidi (ed.), *Assimilation et résistance à la culture gréco-romaine dans le monde ancien*, Editura Academiei, Bucharest and Les Belles-Lettres, Paris, pp. 95–107.

Fabre, G., Mayer, M. and Rodà, I. (1984–5) *Inscriptions romaines de Catalogne*, 2 vols, Diffusion de Boccard, Paris.

Fatás, G. (1975) 'Hispania entre Catón y Graco', *Hispania Antiqua*, vol. 5, pp. 269–313.

Fernández de Avilés, A. (1961–2) 'Carrito de juguete, en terracota, procedente de Elche' in *Homenaje al profesor Cayetano de Mergelina*, Universidad de Murcia, Murcia, pp. 311–17.

Fernández Ibáñez, C. and Illarregui Gómez, E. (1985) 'Herrera de Pisuerga (Palencia): Segunda campaña de excavaciones', *Revista de Arqueología*, no. 52, p. 61.

Fierro Cubiella, J.A. (1989) 'El acueducto romano de Cádiz', *Revista de Arqueología*, no. 95, pp. 18–24.

Finley, M.I. (1973) *The ancient economy*, University of California Press, Berkeley and Los Angeles.

Fishwick, D. (1984) 'Coins as evidence: Some phantom temples', *Classical Views*, vol. 3, pp. 263–70.

Forni, G. (1953) *Il reclutamento delle legioni da Augusto a Diocleziano*, Fratelli Bocca Editori, Milan and Rome.

Frankowski, E. (1920) *Estelas discoideas de la Península Ibérica*, Museo Nacional de Ciencias Naturales, Madrid.

Fulford, M. (1983) 'Pottery and the economy of Carthage and its hinterland', *Opus*, vol. 2, pp. 5–14.

Fuller, J.F.C. (1965) *Julius Caesar: Man, soldier, tyrant*, Eyre & Spottiswoode, London.

Gaiffier, B. de (1943) 'S. Marcel de Tanger ou de León?', *Analecta Bollandiana*, vol. 61, pp. 116–39.

Galliou, P. (1983) *L'Armorique romaine*, Bibliophiles de Bretagne, Braspars.

García Aguinaga, J.L. (1984) 'Un testimonio de la celebración de las Saturnales en Calahorra' in M. Martín-Bueno (ed.), *Calahorra: Bimilenario de su fundación*, Ministerio de Cultura, Madrid, pp. 201–5.

García-Bellido, M.P. (1986) 'Nuevos documentos sobre minería y agricultura romana en Hispania', *Archivo Español de Arqueología*, vol. 59, pp. 13–46.

——(1988) 'Colonia Augusta Gaditana?', *Archivo Español de Arqueología*, vol. 61, pp. 324–35.

García del Toro, J.R. (1982) *Cartagena: Guía arqueológica*, Secretaria de Cultura, Cartagena.

García Iglesias, L. (1978) *Los judíos en la España antigua*, Ediciones Cristiandad, Madrid.

García Mercadal, J. (ed.), (1952) *Viajes de extranjeros por España y Portugal*, vol. 1, Aguilar, Madrid.

García Merino, C. (1975) 'Nueva necrópolis tardorromana en la provincia de Valladolid', *Boletín del Seminario de Estudios de Arte y Arqueología*, vol. 40–1, pp. 522–45.

García y Bellido, A. (1949) *Esculturas romanas de España y Portugal*, Consejo Superior de Investigaciones Científicas, Madrid.

——(1956–61) 'Excavaciones en Augustobriga', *Noticiario Arqueológico Hispánico*, vol. 5, pp. 235–7.

——(1959) 'Marcas de *terra sigillata* en caracteres ibéricos: Protemus en Azaila', *Archivo Español de Arqueología*, vol. 32, pp. 164–6.

——(1964) 'El templo romano de Córdoba', *Oretania*, no. 16–17, pp. 157–65.

——(1967) *Les Religions orientales dans l'Espagne romaine*, E.J. Brill, Leiden.

——(1970a) 'Estudios sobre la *legio VII Gemina* y su campamento en León' in *Legio VII Gemina*, Diputación Provincial, León, pp. 569–99.

——(1970b) *Los hallazgos cerámicos del área del templo romano de Córdoba*, Consejo Superior de Investigaciones Científicas, Madrid.

——(1974) 'Otros testimonios más de la presencia de mercenarios españoles en el Mediterráneo' in E. Ripoll Perelló (ed.), *Simposio internacional de colonizaciones*, Diputación Provincial, Barcelona, pp. 201–3.

——and Fernández de Avilés, A. (1964) *Fontes tamáricas: Velilla del Río Carrión (Palencia)*, Ministerio de Educación Nacional, Madrid.

Gil Farrés, O. (1966) *La moneda hispánica en la edad antigua*, private printing, Madrid.

Gil-Mascarell, M. (1971) *Yacimientos ibéricos en la región valenciana*, F. Domenech, Valencia.

Gómez-Moreno, M. (1927) *Catálogo monumental de España: Provincia de Zamora*, Sobrinos de la sucesora de M. Minuesa de los Ríos, Madrid.

González Blanco, A. and Espinosa Ruiz, U. (1976) 'La necrópolis del poblado celta-romano de Santa Ana', *Archivo Español de Arqueología*, vol. 49, pp. 164–70.

González Echegaray, J. (1957) 'El Neptuno cántabro de Castro Urdiales', *Archivo Español de Arqueología*, vol. 30, pp. 253–6.

——(1966) *Los cántabros*, Ediciones Guadarrama, Madrid.

González Román, C. (1981) *Imperialismo y romanización en la provincia Hispania Ulterior*, Universidad de Granada, Granada.

Gorges, J.-G. (1979) *Les Villas hispano-romaines*, Diffusion de Boccard, Paris.

——(1983) 'Remarques sur la détection de cadastres antiques en Péninsule Ibérique' in M. Clavel-Lévêque (ed.), *Cadastres et espace rural*, Centre National de la Recherche Scientifique, Paris, pp. 199–206.

Greene, K. (1979) 'Invasion and response: pottery and the Roman army' in B.C. Burnham and H.B. Johnson (eds), *Invasion and response*, British Archaeological Reports, Oxford, pp. 99–106.

——(1986) *The archaeology of the Roman economy*, Batsford, London.

Grünhagen, W. (1976) 'Bemerkungen zum Minerva-Relief in der Stadtmauer von Tarragona', *Madrider Mitteilungen*, vol. 17, pp. 209–26.

Gundel, H.G. (1970) 'Probleme der römischen Kampfführung gegen Viriatus' in *Legio VII Gemina*, Diputación Provincial, León, pp. 109–29.

Gurt Esparraguera, J.M. (1985) *Clunia III*, Ministerio de Cultura, Madrid.

Hadas, M. (1930) *Sextus Pompey*, Columbia University Press, New York.

Haley, E.W. (1988) 'Roman elite involvement in commerce', *Archivo Español de Arqueología*, vol. 61, pp. 141–56.

Hanson, W.S. (1978) 'The organisation of Roman military timber supply', *Britannia*, vol. 9, pp. 293–305.

Harmand, J. (1967) *L'Armée et le soldat à Rome de 107 à 50 avant notre ère*, A. et J. Picard, Paris.

——(1970) 'César et l'Espagne durant le second "Bellum civile"' in *Legio VII Gemina*, Diputación Provincial, León, pp. 186–94.

Harrison, R.J. (1988) *Spain at the dawn of history*, Thames and Hudson, London.

Hauschild, T. (1982) 'Zur Typologie römischer Tempel auf der Iberischen Halbinsel' in J. Arce (ed.), *Homenaje a Sáenz de Buruaga*, Diputación Provincial, Badajoz, pp. 145–56.

——(1983) *Arquitectura romana de Tarragona*, Ajuntament de Tarragona, Tarragona.

Haverfield, F.J. (1923) *The romanization of Roman Britain*, Clarendon Press, Oxford.

Hawkes, C.F.C. (1971) 'North-western castros: Excavation, archaeology and history' in *Actas do II congresso nacional de arqueologia*, Ministerio de Educação Nacional, Coimbra, pp. 283–6.

Hefele, C.J. (1894) *A history of the Christian councils*, vol. 1, T. & T. Clark, Edinburgh.

Hernández Díaz, J., Sancho Corbacho, A. and Collantes de Terán, F. (eds.) (1939–55), *Catálogo arqueológico y artístico de la provincia de Sevilla*, 4 vols, Diputación Provincial, Seville.

Hidalgo Cuñarro, J.M. (1986) 'El castro de Vigo: Nueva campaña de excavaciones', *Revista de Arqueología*, no. 64, pp. 59–61.

Higgin, L. (1902) *Spanish life in town and country*, G.P. Putnam's Sons, New York.

Hillgarth, J.N. (1976) *The Spanish kingdoms 1250–1516*, Clarendon Press, Oxford.

Hopkins, K. (1980), 'Taxes and trade in the Roman Empire', *JRS*, vol 70, pp. 101–25.

Houston, J.M. (1964) *The western Mediterranean world*, Longman, London.

Jones, A.H.M. (1960) *Studies in Roman government and law*, Blackwell, Oxford.

Jones, B. (1975) 'The north-western interface' in P.J. Fowler (ed.), *Recent work in rural archaeology*, Moonraker Press, Bradford-on-Avon, pp. 93–106.

Jones, G.D.B. (1980) 'The Roman mines at Riotinto', *JRS*, vol. 70, pp. 146–65.

Jones, R.F.J. and Bird, D.G. (1972) 'Roman gold-mining in north-west Spain, II', *JRS*, vol. 62, pp. 59–74.

Jones, R.F.J., Keay, S.J., Nolla, J.M. and Tarrús, J. (1982) 'The late Roman villa of Vilauba and its context', *Antiquaries Journal*, vol. 62, pp. 245–82.

Jorge Aragoneses, M. (ed.) (1956) *Museo arqueológico de Murcia*, Dirección General de Bellas Artes, Madrid.

Juaristi, V. (1944) *Las fuentes de España*, Espasa-Calpe, Madrid.

Kalb, P. and Hock, M. (1984) 'Moron – historisch und archäologisch', *Madrider Mitteilungen*, vol. 25, pp. 92–102.

Keay, S. (1983) 'The import of olive oil into Catalunya during the third century AD' in J.M. Blázquez Martínez and J. Remesal Rodríguez (eds), *Producción y comercio del aceite en la Antigüedad, II*, Universidad Complutense, Madrid, pp. 551–68.

Keppie, L.J.F. (1984) *The making of the Roman army*, Batsford, London.

Knapp, R.C. (1977) *Aspects of the Roman experience in Iberia, 206–100 BC*, Colegio Universitario de Alava and Universidad de Valladolid, Vitoria and Valladolid.

——(1980) 'Cato in Spain, 195/194 BC' in C. Deroux (ed.), *Studies in Latin literature and Roman history*, vol. 2, Latomus, Brussels, pp. 21–56.

——(1983) *Roman Córdoba*, University of California Press, Berkeley, Los Angeles and London.

Konrad, C.F. (1978) 'Afranius imperator', *Hispania Antiqua*, vol. 8, pp. 67–76.

Kyrtatas, D. (1987) *The social structure of the early Christian communities*, Verso, London and New York.

La Ville de Mirmont, H. de (1910–13) 'Les Déclamateurs espagnols au temps d'Auguste et de Tibère', *Bulletin Hispanique*, vol. 12, pp. 1–22; vol. 14, pp. 11–29; vol. 15, pp. 154–69.

Lacort Navarro, P.J. (1985) 'Cereales en Hispania Ulterior', *Habis*, vol. 16 (1985), pp. 363–86.

Lane Fox, R. (1987) *Pagans and Christians*, Alfred Knopf Inc., New York.

Lang, J. and Price, J. (1975) 'Iron tubes from a Late Roman glassmaking site at Mérida', *Journal of Archaeological Science*, vol. 2, pp. 289–96.

Lara Peinado, F. (1973) *Lérida romana*, Dilagro Ediciones, Lleida.

Lavedan, P. and Huguenay, J. (1966) *Histoire de l'urbanisme (antiquité)*, 2nd edn, H. Laurens, Paris.

Le Roux, P. (1977) 'Une inscription fragmentaire d'Augusta Emerita de Lusitanie à la lumière des "Histoires" de Tacite', *Chiron*, vol. 7, pp. 283–9.

——(1982) *L'Armée romaine et l'organisation des provinces ibériques*, Diffusion de Boccard, Paris.

——(1982) 'Les Sénateurs originaires de la province d'Hispania Citerior au Haut-Empire romain', *Tituli*, vol. 5, pp. 439–64.

——(1985) 'Procurateur affranchi *in Hispania:* Saturninus et l'activité minière', *Madrider Mitteilungen*, vol. 26, pp. 218–33.

——and Tranoy, A. (1973) 'Rome et les indigènes dans le nord-ouest ibérique', *Mélanges de la Casa de Velázquez*, vol. 9, pp. 177–203.

——(1984) 'L'épigraphie du nord du Portugal', *Conimbriga*, vol. 23, pp. 19–41.

Lequément, R. (1980) 'Deux inscriptions peintes sur amphores de Bétique à Alesia', *Revue Archéologique de l'Est et du Centre-Est*, vol. 31, pp. 256–9.

——and Liou, B. (1978) 'Un nouveau document sur le vin de Bétique', *Archaeonautica*, vol. 2, pp. 183–4.

Leroy, B. (1988) *L'Espagne au Moyen Age*, Albin Michel, Paris.

Lewis, P.R. and Jones, G.D.B (1970) 'Roman gold-mining in north-west Spain', *JRS*, vol. 60, pp. 169–85.

Lillo, A. and M. (1988) 'On Polybius X 10, 12 f.', *Historia*, vol. 37, pp. 477–80.

Liou, B. and Marichal, R. (1978) 'Les inscriptions peintes sur amphores de l'anse Saint-Gervais à Fos-sur-Mer', *Archaeonautica*, vol. 2, pp. 131–5.

Lloyd, J.A. (ed.) (1979) *Excavations at Sidi Khrebish, Benghazi (Berenice)*, 2 vols, Socialist People's Libyan Arab Jamahiriya, Tripoli.

Lomas, F.J. (1980) 'Origen y desarrollo de la cultura de los campos de urnas' in J.M. Blázquez, F.J. Lomas, F. Presedo and J. Fernández Nieto, *Historia de la España antigua*, vol. 1, Ediciones Cátedra, Madrid, pp. 13–28.

MacMullen, R. (1963) *Soldier and civilian in the later Roman empire*, Harvard University Press, Cambridge (Mass.).

——(1968) 'Rural romanization', *Phoenix*, vol. 22, pp. 337–41.

——(1974) *Roman social relations 50 BC to AD 284*, Yale University Press, New Haven and London.

Maluquer de Motes, J. (1963) 'Dos grafitos ibéricos con nombres latinos', *Zephyrus*, vol. 14, pp. 108–10.

Mangas, J. (1971) *Esclavos y libertos en la España romana*, Universidad de Salamanca, Salamanca.

Mann, J.C. (1983) *Legionary recruitment and veteran settlement during the Principate*, Institute of Archaeology, London.

Mañanes, T. (1983) *Astorga romana y su entorno*, Universidad de Valladolid, Valladolid and Astorga.

Mar Medina, R. and Ruiz de Arbulo Bayona, J. (1986) *La basílica de la colonia Tarraco*, Museu Nacional Arqueològic de Tarragona, Tarragona.

Marco Simón, F. (1978) *Las estelas decoradas de los conventos caesaraugustano y cluniense*, Institución 'Fernando el Católico', Zaragoza.

Mariner Bigorra, S. (1973) *Inscripciones romanas de Barcino*, Delegación de Servicios de Cultura, Barcelona.

Martin-Kilcher, S. (1987) *Die römischen Amphoren aus Augst und Kaiseraugst*, vol. 1, Römermuseum Augst, Augst.

Martín Valls, R. (1985) 'Segunda edad del hierro' in G. Delibes, J. Fernández Manzano, F. Romero Carnicero and R Martín Valls, *Historia de Castilla y León*, vol. 1, Ambito Ediciones, Madrid, pp. 105–31.

——and Delibes de Castro, G. (1975) 'El campamento de Rosinos de Vidriales', *Studia Archaeologica*, vol. 36, pp. 3–7.

——(1981) 'Hallazgos arqueológicos en la provincia de Zamora', *Boletín del Seminario de Estudios de Arte y Arqueología*, vol. 47, pp. 153–86.

Martínez Gázquez, J. (1974) *La campaña de Catón en Hispania*, Editorial Ariel, Barcelona.

Mattingly, D.J. (1988) 'Oil for export?', *Journal of Roman Archaeology*, vol. 1, pp. 33–56.

Mayer, M. and Rodà, I. (1986) 'Les divinités féminines de la fertilité en Hispania pendant l'époque romaine' in J. Bonanno (ed.), *Archaeology and fertility cult in the ancient Mediterranean*, B.R. Grüner, Amsterdam, pp. 293–304.

Mayet, F. (1975) *Les Céramiques à parois fines dans la Péninsule Ibérique*, Diffusion de Boccard, Paris.

——(1984) *Les céramiques sigillées hispaniques*, Diffusion de Boccard, Paris.

Menéndez Pidal, R. (1968) *Toponimia prerrománica hispana*, Editorial Gredos, Madrid.

——(ed.) (1982) *Historia de España*, 2nd edn, vol. II/1–2, Espasa-Calpe, Madrid.

Mezquíriz de Catalán, M.A. (1961) *Terra sigillata hispánica*, 2 vols, W.L. Bryant Foundation, Valencia.

Millán León, J. (1986) 'La batalla de Ilipa', *Habis*, vol. 17, pp. 283–303.

Mócsy, A. (1974) *Pannonia and Upper Moesia*, Routledge & Kegan Paul, London and Boston.

Molinero Pérez, A. (1949) 'Excavaciones antiguas y modernas en Duratón', *Estudios Segovianos*, vol. 1, pp. 569–84.

Morel, J.-P. (1981) *Céramique campanienne: Les formes*, Ecole Française de Rome, Rome.

Moreno Páramo, A. and Abad Casal, L. (1971) 'Aportaciones al estudio de la pesca en la Antigüedad', *Habis*, vol. 2, pp. 209–21.

Morgan, M.G. (1969) 'The Roman conquest of the Balearic Islands', *California Studies in Classical Antiquity*, vol. 2, pp. 217–31.

Munn, M.L.Z. (1983) 'Corinthian trade with the West in the classical period', unpublished Ph.D thesis, Bryn Mawr College.

Navascués, J. de (1959) 'Descubrimiento de una bodega romana en término de Funes (Navarra)', *Príncipe de Viana*, vol. 77, pp. 227–9.

Nolla, J.M. and Nieto, F.J. (1978) 'Alguns aspectes de la Romanització al nord-est de Catalunya' in M. Tarradell, M. Cura, J. Padró and J. Rovira (eds), *Els pobles pre-romans del Pirineu*, Institut d'Estudis Ceretans, Puigcerdà, pp. 235–44.

Oliver, J.H. (1957) 'A Spanish corporation and its patrons', *Eos*, vol. 48, pp. 447–54.

Ortego, T. (1980) *Numancia, guía breve historico-arqueológico*, Ministerio de Cultura, Madrid.

Osuna Ruiz, M. (1976) *Arte romano en el Museo de Cuenca*, Museo de Cuenca, Cuenca.

Palol, P. de (1969) *Guía de Clunia*, 2nd edn, Dirección General de Bellas Artes, Burgos.

Parain, C. (1966) 'The evolution of agricultural technique' in M.M. Postan and H.J. Habbakuk (eds), *The Cambridge economic history of Europe*, 2nd edn, vol. 1, Cambridge University Press, Cambridge, pp. 126–79.

Paris, P. (1914) 'Antiquités pré-romaines de Mérida', *Comptes Rendus de l'Académie des Inscriptions et Belles-Lettres*, pp. 127–31.

Parker, A.J. (1974) 'Lead ingots from a Roman ship at Ses Salinas, Majorca', *International Journal of Nautical Archaeology*, vol. 3, pp. 147–50.

Peacock, D.P.S. (1986) 'Punic Carthage and Spain: The evidence of the amphorae', *Cahiers des Etudes Anciennes*, vol. 18, pp. 101–13.

Pereira, I., Bost, J.-P. and Hiernard, J. (1974) *Fouilles de Conimbriga*, vol. 3, E. de Boccard, Paris.

Pereira Maia, M.G. (1984) 'Notas sobre a "terra sigillata" do Manuel Galo (Mértola)' in *Actas del II jornadas arqueológicas*, Associação dos Arqueólogicas Portuguêses, Lisbon, pp. 157–66.

Pérez, J.A., Funes, A. and Pumares, J. (1985) 'Minería romana en Río Tinto (Huelva)', *Revista de Arqueología*, no. 56, pp. 24–31.

Pericot, L. (1977) *Cerámica ibérica*, Ediciones Polígrafa, Barcelona

Petrikovits, H. von (1975) *Die Innenbauten römischer Legionslager während der Prinzipatszeit*, Westdeutscher Verlag, Opladen.

Pflaum, H.-G. (1960) *Les carrières procuratoriennes équestres sous le Haut-Empire romain*, Geuthner, Paris.

Piggott, S. (1958) 'Native economies and the Roman occupation of north Britain' in I.A. Richmond (ed.), *Roman and native in north Britain*, Nelson, Edinburgh, pp. 1–27.

Ponsich, M. (1974–87) *Implantation rural antique sur le Bas-Guadalquivir*, 3 vols., Casa de Velázquez, Paris and Madrid.

Poulsen, F. (1933) *Sculptures antiques de musées de provinces espagnols*, Levin & Munksgaard, Copenhagen.

Price, J. (1974) 'Some Roman glass from Spain' in *Annales du 6e congrès international d'étude historique du verre*, Edition du Secrétariat Général, Liège, pp. 65–84.

——(1987) 'Glass vessel production in southern Iberia in the first and second centuries AD', *Journal of Glass Studies*, vol. 29, pp. 30–9.

Puig y Cadafalch, J. (1934) *L'arquitectura romana a Catalunya*, Institut d'Estudis Catalans, Barcelona.

Raddatz, K. (1969) *Die Schatzfunde der Iberischen Halbinsel vom Ende des dritten bis zur Mitte des ersten Jahrhunderts vor Chr.*, De Gruyter, Berlin.

Remesal Rodríguez, J. (1986) *La annona militaris y la exportación de aceite bético a Germania*, Universidad Complutense, Madrid.

Reynolds, P.J. (1979) *Iron age farm*, British Museum Publications, London.

Richardson, J.S. (1986) *Hispaniae: Spain and the development of Roman imperialism 218–82 BC*, Cambridge University Press, Cambridge.

Richmond, I.A. (1931) 'Five town-walls in Hispania Citerior', *JRS*, vol. 21, pp. 86–100.

Risco, M. (1792) *Historia de la ciudad y corte de León y de sus reyes*, B. Roman, Madrid.

Rodríguez Almeida, E. (1981) *Avila romana*, Caja General de Ahorros y Monte de Piedad, Avila.

——(1984) *Il Monte Testaccio: Ambiente, storia, materiali*, Edizioni Quasar, Rome.

Rodríguez Colmenero, A. (1979) *Augusto e Hispania*, Universidad de Deusto, Bilbao.

Rodríguez Neila, J.F. (1981) *Sociedad y administración local en la Bética romana*, Monte de Piedad y Caja de Ahorros, Córdoba.

——(1988) *Historia de Córdoba*, vol. 1, Monte de Piedad y Caja de Ahorros, Córdoba.

Romero Carnicero, M.V. and F. (1978) 'Cerámicas imperiales con engobe rojo y decoración pintada procedentes de Numancia', *Boletín del Seminario de Estudios de Arte y Arqueología*, vol. 44, pp. 396–402.

Rostovtzeff, M.I. (1957) *Social and economic history of the Roman empire*, 2nd edn, 2 vols, Clarendon Press, Oxford.

Rothenberg, B. and Blanco Freijeiro, A. (1981) *Studies in ancient mining and metallurgy in south-west Spain*, Institute for Archaeo-metallurgical Studies, London.

Russell Cortez, F. (1951) 'As escavações arqueológicas do "castellum" da Fonte do Milho', *Anais do Instituto do Vinho do Porto*, vol. 12, pp. 17–88.

Sánchez Albornoz, C. (1975) *Spain, an historical enigma*, Fundación Universitaria Española, Madrid.

Sánchez, León, M.L. (1978) *Economía de la Hispania meridional durante la dinastía de los Antoninos*, Universidad de Salamanca, Salamanca.

Sánchez-Palencia, F.J. (1986) 'El campamento romano de Valdemeda, Manzaneda (León)', *Numantia*, vol. 1, pp. 227–34.

Santos Yanguas, N. (1979) 'La *cohors I Celtiberorum equitata civium Romanorum*', *Celtiberia*, vol. 29, pp. 239–51.

Saupis, F. (1973) *La Géologie du gisement de mercure d'Almadén*, Ecole Nationale Supérieure de Géologie Appliquée, Nancy.

Savory, H.N. (1968) *Spain and Portugal*, Thames and Hudson, London.

Schlunk, H. (1977) 'Los monumentos paleocristianos de "Gallaecia", especialmente los de la provincia de Lugo' in *Actas del coloquio internacional sobre el bimilenario de Lugo*, Patronato del Bimilenario, Lugo.

Schüle, W. (1969) *Die Meseta-Kulturen der Iberischen Halbinsel*, De Gruyter, Berlin.

Schulten, A. (1926) *Sertorius*, Dieterich'sche Verlagsbuchhandlung, Leipzig.

——(1927–33) 'Forschungen in Spanien', *Archäologischer Anzeiger*, 1927, cols 197–235 and 1933, cols 513–66.

——(1933) *Geschichte von Numantia*, Verlag Piloty und Loehle, Munich.

Scullard, H.H. (1970) *Scipio Africanus, soldier and politician*, Thames & Hudson, London.

Serrano Delgado, J.M. (1988) *Status y promoción social de los libertos en Hispania romana*, Universidad de Sevilla, Seville.

Sherwin White, A.N. (1973) *The Roman citizenship*, 2nd edn, Clarendon Press, Oxford.

Siles, J. (1981) 'Iberismo y latinización: Nombre latinos en epígrafos ibéricos', *Faventia*, vol. 3, pp. 97–113.

Simon, H. (1962) *Roms Kriege in Spanien 154–133 v. Chr.*, Vittorio Klostermann, Frankfurt.

Sivan, H.S. (1985) 'An unedited letter of the emperor Honorius to the Spanish soldiers', *Zeitschrift für Papyrologie und Epigraphik*, vol. 61, pp. 273–87.

Solana Sáinz, J.M. (1978) *Autrigonia romana*, Universidad de Valladolid, Valladolid.

Soria Sánchez, V. (1977) 'Nuevas aportaciones a la arqueología extremeña' in *XIV Congreso nacional de arqueología*, Universidad de Zaragoza, Zaragoza, pp. 1143–52.

Spann, P.O. (1981) 'Lagobriga expunged: Renaissance forgeries and the Sertorian war', *Transactions of the American Philological Association*, vol. 111, pp. 229–35.

——(1984) 'Saguntum vs. Segontia', *Historia*, vol. 33, pp. 116–19.

——(1987) *Quintus Sertorius and the legacy of Sulla*, University of Arkansas Press, Fayetteville.

Stein, A. (1927) *Der römischen Ritterstand*, C.H. Beck, Munich.

Stillwell, R., MacDonald, W.L. and McAllister (eds), (1976) *The Princeton encyclopedia of classical sites*, Princeton University Press, Princeton.

Stylow, A.U. (1986) 'Apuntes sobre epigrafía de época flavia en Hispania', *Gerión*, vol. 4, pp. 285–311.

Sumner, G.V. (1970) 'Proconsuls and *provinciae* in Spain, 218/7–196/5 BC', *Arethusa*, vol. 3, pp. 85–102.

——(1977) 'Notes on *provinciae* in Spain (197–133 BC)', *Classical Philology*, vol. 72, pp. 126–30.

Syme, R. (1964) 'Hadrian and Italica', *JRS*, vol. 54, pp. 142–9.

——(1970) 'The conquest of north-west Spain' in *Legio VII Gemina*, Diputación Provincial, León, pp. 79–107.

——(1983) 'Antistius Rusticus, a consular from Corduba', *Historia*, vol. 32, pp. 359–74.

Tarradell, M. (1978) 'Un fortí romà a Tentellatge' in M. Tarradell, M. Cura, J. Padró and J. Rovira (eds), *Els pobles pre-romans del Pirineu*, Institut d'Estudis Ceretans, Puigcerdà, pp. 245–50.

Tchernia, A. and Zevi, F. (1972) 'Amphores vinaires de Campanie et de Tarraconaise à Ostie' in P. Baldacci *et al* (eds), *Recherches sur les amphores romaines*, Ecole Française de Rome, Rome, pp. 35–67.

Thévenot, E. (1952) 'Una familia de negociantes en aceite establecida en la Baetica en el siglo II', *Archivo Español de Arqueología*, vol. 25, pp. 225–31.

Thompson, E.A. (1952) 'Peasant revolts in late Roman Gaul and Spain', *Past & Present*, vol. 2, pp. 11–23.

——(1977) 'The end of Roman Spain', *Nottingham Mediaeval Studies*, vol. 21, pp. 3–31.

Tovar, A. (1955–6) 'La grande inscripción de Peñalba de Villastar en lengua celtibérica', *Ampurias*, vol. 17–18, pp. 159–69.

——(1959) 'Las inscripciones celtibéricas de Peñalba de Villastar', *Emerita*, vol. 27, pp. 349–65.

——(1973) 'Columela y el vino de Jérez', *Homenaje al Profesor Carriazo*, vol. 3, Universidad de Sevilla, Seville, pp. 397–404.

——(1974–89) *Iberische Landeskunde: Die Völker und die Städte des antiken Hispanien*, 3 vols, Verlag Valentin Koerner, Baden-Baden.

——(1985) 'La inscripcion del Cabeço das Fráguas y la lengua de los Lusitanos' in *Actas del III cólóquio sobre lenguas y culturas paleohispánicas*, Universidad de Salamanca, Salamanca, pp. 227–53.

Tranoy, A. (1981) *La Galice romaine*, Diffusion de Boccard, Paris.

Treggiari, S. (1969) *Roman freedmen during the Late Republic*, Clarendon Press, Oxford.

Ulbert, G. (1984) *Cáceres el Viejo, ein spätrepublikanisches Legionslager in Spanisch-Extremadura*, Verlag Philipp von Zabern, Mainz am Rhein.

Uranga, J.E. (1966) 'El culto al toro en Navarra y Aragón' in J. Maluquer de Motes (ed.), *IV Symposium de prehistoria peninsular*, Institución 'Príncipe de Viana', Pamplona, pp. 223–31.

Van Dam, R. (1985) *Leadership and community in Late Antique Gaul*, University of California Press, Berkeley, Los Angeles and London.

Van Nostrand, J.J. (1937) 'Roman Spain' in Tenney Frank (ed.), *An economic survey of ancient Rome*, vol. 3, Johns Hopkins Press, Baltimore, pp. 119–224.

Vaquerizo Gil, D. (1986) 'Excavaciones en el foro romano de Córdoba', *Revista de Arqueología*, no. 64, p. 63.

——(1987) 'Serie de 39 denarios romano-republicanos, conservados en Orellana de la Sierra (Badajoz)' in *XVIII Congreso nacional de arqueología*, Universidad de Zaragoza, Zaragoza, pp. 873–93.

Vázquez Varela, J.M. and Acuña Castroviejo, F. (1976) 'Pervivencia de las formas culturales indígenas' in *La romanización de Galicia*, Ediciones del Castro, Sada and La Coruña, pp. 77–84.

Vázquez y Hoys, A.M. (1977) 'La religión romana en Hispania: Análisis estadístico', *Hispania Antiqua*, vol. 7, pp. 7–45.

Vigil, M. (1963) 'Romanización y permanencia de estructuras sociales indígenas en la España septentrional', *Boletín de la Real Academia de la Historia*, vol. 152, pp. 225–33.

Villaronga, L. (1979) *Numismática antigua de Hispania*, Ediciones Cymys, Barcelona.

Villedieu, F. (1984) *Turris Libisonis*, British Archaeological Reports, Oxford.

Violant y Simorra, R. (1953) 'Un arado y otros aperos ibéricos hallados en Valencia y su supervivencia en la cultura popular española', *Zephyrus*, vol. 4, pp. 119–30.

Vittinghoff, F. (1970) 'Die Entstehung von städtischen Gemeinwesen in der Nachbarschaft römischer Legionslager' in *Legio VII Gemina*, Diputación Provincial, León, pp. 337–52.

Vives, J. (1969) *Inscripciones cristianas de la España romana y visigoda*, Consejo Superior de Investigaciones Científicas, Barcelona.

Walker, M. (1985) '5,000 años de viticultura en España', *Revista de Arqueología*, no. 53, pp. 44–7.

Way, R. (1962) *A geography of Spain and Portugal*, Methuen, London.

Webster, G. (1979) *The Roman imperial army*, 2nd edn, A. & C. Black, London.

Weisser, M.R. (1976) *The peasants of the Montes*, University of Chicago Press, Chicago.

West, L.C. (1929) *Imperial Roman Spain: The objects of trade*, Blackwell, Oxford.

White, L. Jr. (1972) 'The expansion of technology 500–1500' in C.M. Cipolla (ed.), *The Fontana economic history of Europe*, vol. 1, Collins/Fontana, London, pp. 143–74.

Wiegels, R. (1982) 'Iliturgi und der "deductor" Ti. Sempronius Gracchus', *Madrider Mitteilungen*, vol. 23, pp. 152–211.

Wightman, E.M. (1970) *Roman Trier and the Treveri*, Hart-Davis, London.

Will, E.L. (1983) 'Exportation of olive oil from Baetica to the eastern Mediterranean' in J.M. Blázquez Martínez and J. Remesal Rodríguez (eds), *Producción y comercio del aceite en la Antigüedad, II*, Universidad Complutense, Madrid, pp. 391–440.

Williams, D.F. and Peacock, D.P.S. (1983) 'The importation of olive oil into Iron Age Britain' in J.M. Blázquez Martínez and J. Remesal Rodríguez (eds), *Producción y comercio del aceite en la Antigüedad, II*, Universidad Complutense, Madrid, pp. 263–80.

Woods, D.E. (1964) 'A numismatic chapter of the romanisation of Hispania' in *Essays in memory of Karl Lehmann*, Institute of Fine Arts, New York, pp. 383–5

241

INDEX